E. C. Cummings

Nature in Scripture

A Study of Bible Verification in the Range of Common Experience

E. C. Cummings

Nature in Scripture
A Study of Bible Verification in the Range of Common Experience

ISBN/EAN: 9783337098216

Printed in Europe, USA, Canada, Australia, Japan

Cover: Foto ©Lupo / pixelio.de

More available books at **www.hansebooks.com**

NATURE IN SCRIPTURE.

A Study of Bible Verification

IN THE RANGE OF COMMON EXPERIENCE.

BY

E. C. CUMMINGS.

—— τὸ καθ' ἡμέραν ἀνακρίνοντες τὰς γραφὰς, εἰ ἔχοι ταῦτα οὕτως.
THE ACTS, xvii. 11.

BOSTON:
CUPPLES AND HURD,
94 Boylston Street.
1887.

Copyright, 1884,
BY E. C. CUMMINGS.

University Press:
JOHN WILSON AND SON, CAMBRIDGE.

PREFACE

TO THE SECOND EDITION.

IN offering another edition of "Nature in Scripture," the author desires to acknowledge the generous recognition accorded to the first, especially the appreciative judgments of the eminent men appealed to for careful criticism. He could not, however, regard the book as having hopefully sustained its first trial, without proofs of genial interest such as have reached him from those reading it for truth's sake simply.

Important suggestions, thankfully considered, have seemed to point toward a supplementary study, rather than to essential changes within the limits of this one. An index has been added.

A very discriminating reviewer has said that "this is not a work that he who runs may read;" adding, that "it is worth the time which a thinking man may spend upon it." One does not need to go far in intellectual experience to find that a degree of temporary difficulty may be incident to the very quality on which the value of a work depends,—at least in the case of some readers. While, therefore, it is no small comfort to be assured that one's work is not unsuited to "a

Of course, the truth of the Scriptures is in what they really mean. Any theory of inspiration would contemplate that meaning of the written word which is identical with the Divine thought; but no theory of inspiration can assure us of what that meaning is. On the other hand, let the Divine thought be made clear, and it is independent of all theories of inspiration. We are satisfied with the truth, in whatever way it may have been ministered to our spirits.

The study which is to follow has reference to the meaning of the Scriptures, — not the meanings of detail, the affair of critical exegesis, but the meaning which is simple and coherent, the result of a reasoned estimate and comparison of plain popular testimony.

In the Scriptures the order of nature is the creation of God. This might suffice as the one premise on which our study should proceed. But for the sake of distinction and definiteness, it seems better to define two premises — the answers to two questions; namely, What is nature as contemplated in Scripture? and, What is Scripture in relation to nature?

1. *Nature*, as contemplated in Scripture, is the universal system of which man finds himself a part, and which he rationally refers in whole and in detail to supernatural causation.

2. *Scripture*, in relation to nature, is a complement of writings, whose distinguishing mark is not in unity of time, action, or literary form, but in unity of testimony to one self-existent Creator of all things, conceived as dealing, through material elements and spiritual messengers, with human society as a whole; especially, as advancing a chosen people to eminent service for mankind under an economy of moral control and spiritual disci-

pline, wherein the people is called to voluntary co-operation with God in his revelation, while the revelation of God is affirmed as the ruling factor in the history of mankind, till at length revelation surpasses the earlier economy, and comes to personal consummation in a Man of divine character — the Word of God, the Light of the world.

These premises are important, as indicating what the verification of Scripture involves.

There is a process of verification applicable to the Scriptures as to other writings, which is outward and incidental. Assuming the canon and the text, attentive reading is a process of verification in proportion to the reader's intelligence, whether as respects the outward representations or the inward significance of the sacred writings. Any further verification is a broader or deeper reading. It is a broader reading that is carried on in the fields of comparative philology, archæology, history, and physical science, where are sought the proofs of fidelity and exactness in the setting forth of outward aspects or objects in any region or period contemplated. The range of this reading is without assignable limits of space or time.

But the province of verification which is the most important as well as the most interesting, is inward and integral. It contemplates the quality and power of divine teaching as certified in its spiritual effects; for example, that it commands the concurrence of human reason in its own right; that it takes sovereign possession of man's higher convictions, in order to dominate his lower tendencies; that it proclaims prophetically in the human soul the overruling of man's free activity according to divine intention; that it raises the conception of God and of his government through lessons of experience and the logic of events; and so educates the human mind to an apprehension of manhood as designed to surpass the degree of physical creation, the visible image of God, and to reach spiritual consummation in the very character of the Father. This is the verification of deep reading, — on the basis of "internal evidence," but without limits of time or space.

The revelation of God set forth in the Scriptures is, therefore, co-extensive in its range with the work of God as disclosed to us in nature. But as accommodated to the spiritual apprehension and experience of mankind, this revelation is progressive and cumulative, — holding on its way according to a ruling idea and purpose. It contemplates the instruction of mankind in the knowledge of God and of eternal life, — not in the cosmical mysteries of matter and motion. Accordingly, it determines the religious consecration of language, — not its scientific development. It gives names and descriptions of material nature according to conceptions of common sense, which cover all that science can ever discover, — addressing men in their own tongue wherein they were born, not in the terminology of experts to which but few are ever trained. Hence it is logically impossible that any but constructive and transitory contradictions should ever occur between Scripture representation and scientific truth in the domain of material nature.

But in the realm of the human spirit the case is different. Here revelation makes for change, — change in the forms of conscious experience, change in the quality and quantity of being. Man is conceived as constituted in order to his being changed. It is in the progress of a personal struggle with outward nature, with his fellow-men, with himself, in fine, with the Maker of all, that man passes from what he is to what he is becoming. Hence the meaning of Scripture which concerns the divine law of personal development, the meaning of Scripture which declares itself as the oracle of life through all ages of transformation, — this is the meaning which abideth forever, the Word of the Eternal.

If, then, there is found in Scripture a convincing testimony to universal nature as the medium of a perpetual creative teaching in the human spirit for man's ultimate perfection, no wonder if it be found necessary, in each succeeding generation, to verify the vital significance of particular words, and to deal anew with questions of faith that can never be so answered as not to be asked again, till it is recognized as a rule of life, — that any one, having freely received, shall freely offer to other learners the results of such inquiry as the progress of his own mind has required him to undertake, and rewarded him for carrying through.

Under this rule the essay that follows is offered, for acceptance or correction, — not as if what is verifiable were the measure of what is true, but because the human mind is ever seeking what is verifiable in the effort to learn what is true.

PORTLAND, ME., Feb. 1, 1884.

CONTENTS.

INTRODUCTION.

                                                                            PAGE

CONCERNING SPEECH AND WORDS 3

PART FIRST.

THE WORLD TUTELAGE.

CHAPTER
- I. TUTELAGE A LAW OF NATURE 23
- II. COSMICAL TUTELAGE 27
- III. ÆONIAN TUTELAGE 31
- IV. AGES OF HUMAN DEVELOPMENT 39
- V. AGES OF DIVINE TEACHING 46

PART SECOND.

THE FALL.

- I. ORIGINAL MAN AND PRIMITIVE TRIAL 57
- II. GENESIS COSMICAL AND ÆONIAN 73
- III. MORAL DEVELOPMENT FROM DISCOVERIES OF LAW 83

PART THIRD.

THE PRINCIPLE OF JUSTIFICATION.

Chapter	Page
I. Of Faith as related to Man's Dependence and Progress	101
II. Against Transcendental Notions of Primitive Responsibility	114
III. Original Man and Historic Man	127
IV. The Perfect Faith and the Approved Man	135

PART FOURTH.

THE MANIFESTATION OF EVIL.

I. Of Speculations on Original Sin	145
II. Of Spiritual Law Overruling Physical Tendency	151
III. Of Pains and Penalties as related to Conduct	160
IV. Of Physical Death as related to Spiritual Development	175
V. Deterrent Consequences of Deliberate Unbelief	188
VI. Evil as set forth in the Christ's Teaching	193

PART FIFTH.

THE LAW OF ATONEMENT.

I. Recapitulation and Transition	213
II. The Law of Atonement in its Physical Type	220
III. The Law of Atonement in General History	228
IV. The Law of Atonement in Scripture History. Primitive and Patriarchal Sacrifice	242

Chapter		Page
V.	Sacrifice under the Law	252
VI.	Sacrifice according to the Prophets	263
VII.	The Law of Atonement Fulfilled in the Christ	271
VIII.	Immediate Sequel of the Christ's Incarnate Ministry	290

PART SIXTH.

CRISES IN THE PROCESS OF REDEMPTION.

I.	Of Justice and Judgment	299
II.	Crises under Laws of Physical Change	303
III.	Crises under Laws of Spiritual Development	309
IV.	Crises According to the Old Testament Teaching	316
V.	Crises Interpreted by the Christ	319

Conclusion 337

INTRODUCTION.

CONCERNING SPEECH AND WORDS.

"AND out of the ground the Lord God formed every beast of the field, and every fowl of the air; and brought them unto Adam to see what he would call them: and whatsoever Adam called every living creature, that was the name thereof."

GENESIS, ii. 19.

"A NATURAL action is it that man speaks;
But whether thus or thus, doth Nature leave
To your own art, as seemeth good to you."

LONGFELLOW'S DANTE, — "Paradiso," xxvi. 130.

NATURE IN SCRIPTURE.

INTRODUCTION.

CONCERNING SPEECH AND WORDS.

IT is proposed to study some parts of the Scripture teaching in the light of material objects and human experiences to which that teaching bears testimony.

To adjust one's instrument is to begin work. I know of no better introduction to the work proposed than paying some attention to speech, — that curious instrument by which all things, and all relations of things, are brought into the working of men's minds.

The fundamental teachings of Scripture are not local or temporary, — but universal. The field is the world. Accordingly, the earliest Scripture brings to our notice the universal law of human speech; and a brief consideration of this law can hardly fail to quicken and temper our judgments as to the use of some very important words in the latest Scriptures, — words by which the whole sphere of reality wherein our thought moves has been summed up.

The picture of primitive speech in the second chapter of Genesis is fresh and appreciable now, for the reason that in whatever ways the forms of speech may have changed, the inner reality is ever the same. To-day, as in the beginning, living creatures are formed out of the dust of the ground, and are brought to man. New species, or peculiar individuals, may at any time come to man's notice in the course of propagation and discovery, and still the rule holds good that whatsoever man calls every living creature, that is the name thereof. The method of naming belongs to the method of creation.

Any object brought to man's attention suggests its own name, we may imagine, by means of some striking quality or aspect. Then other objects possessed of the same quality, or presenting the same aspect, range themselves under the same name. In this way the name becomes a general or family designation; while individuals demand a further naming, according to their several attributes, to distinguish them from each other. In any case, a name once given not only stands in the mind for the object to which it belongs, but grows to be representatively the equal of the object, — puts itself into the same conditions and relations, demands connectives and auxiliaries, seeks, in fine, to become as vital and important as the existence or action it contemplates.

The name need not consist of one word only. It may be supplemented, — in fact, drawn out indefinitely. Thus there is secured to the latest comer in the world his individual right of naming. He is permitted to call the objects presented to him by names other than those already given, — names that shall correspond with his peculiar susceptibility, interest, and knowledge with regard to the objects. For example, "mountain" is a very general name. Among many mountains there is one, it may be, that attracts somebody's attention by its color or shape, and he calls it "green" or "round" mountain.

But the mountain presents itself to multitudes of observers in successive generations. Firm as it is, the mountain does not hold out unchanged. Adverse elements are at work upon it, — now fire, now frost. At one time it is denuded of trees or even of soil. Again it is overrun with various orders of vegetation, haunted by tribes of animals, explored and perused by lovers of wild scenery or analyzed and penetrated by the curious in science, to make it disclose the secrets of its formation and contents. Why would not the accurate account of all this make just so much descriptive name or repute of the mountain, exactly like one's calling it green or round? Thus there is brought before us the persistent correlation of three sorts of things, namely, outward objects, observing minds, representative names. We find the most extended descriptions depending upon a mental exertion identical with that which originated the first word-element. It is the law of existence. The world's history is the co-ordinate development of material nature, mind, and language. Mind is the luminous centre, and whatever objects are presented, the word-shadow is sure to be cast. Be the shadow one syllable or thousands of sentences, it may be called a name. There is an assumed equality of a book's title and its contents. The detail of a descriptive catalogue is only what is meant by the name that sums up the collection. The whole creation, throughout the ages of life of which man is speaking, "according to his own art, as seemeth best to him," is conceived in Scripture as the Word of God, by which he awakens thought, teaching us to give him names, — and at length a name of majesty and goodness.

Our extended sense of name implies, of course, not

simply the multiplication of words, but the organic structure of language. Words are vitally related to one another. Otherwise they could not be made to represent the intimate relations and lucid order of thought, — till they have actually grown by inflection and composition, by logical and rhetorical arrangement, to the very form and pressure of intellectual experience. The naming faculty rises to a new effort when the objects and elements of nature are studied under conditions of thought connected with accumulated results and resources of investigation, — the effort indicated in scientific nomenclature.

As speech tends to keep even pace with the intelligent appreciation of things, so a word having the beginning of its use from a certain original suggestion or starting-point of thought tends to hold on its way in the same direction. Those who use words are concerned to keep them lively and active, — equal to the vigor and variety of the objects they represent. Words in one respect are like the giant who was strong only when he touched the ground. They need to be kept in close contact with the realities which are the ground of their significance. But, if words are carried away from the real ground of their meaning, so as to acquire a fanciful or merely conventional force, then it happens, according to the saying of Bacon, "that words, as a Tartar's bow, do shoot back upon the understanding of the wisest, and mightily entangle and pervert the judgment."[1] This applies especially to words of comprehensive significance, that have their rights in part by inheritance from other words in other languages, — whose duties they are set to discharge.

[1] Works, vol. i. p. 211, — "Advancement of Learning."

The word *world*, for example, has a really inexhaustible import in the English New Testament; such, indeed, that it would be impossible to appreciate the general cast of thought to which those writings seek to introduce us, without particular attention to this word. Its fulness of meaning is due to the fact that, in our authorized version, the single word *world* has taken up into itself the force of two Greek terms, each of immeasurable import; and now it will be hard for any revision to disengage and distribute anew the values that have been treasured so long in one syllable.

It is plain that our word *world*, as a name for the sum of things, has not reached its fulness till there is a general consent as to what grand total is referred to. But when creation has disclosed the rounded system, and thought has embraced the same and confided it to this word's keeping, then, in whatever subordinate sense the word may be used, it is never wholly alienated from its supreme significance. We may have any number of worlds by reason of the world that includes them all, and by whose law they exist. Call the earth the world. It is not the world without its sun, moon, and stars. Take them away, and earth falls into chaos. Speak of the world of mind in distinction from the world of matter. But it is mind in relation with matter that we mean. The two worlds are one. Refer to the world of art or science, — the religious, the political, the social world. But these are not worlds apart from the grand total which is the world. Say there is a world of law in a drop of water. Yes: because the same law "preserves the stars from wrong." Any kind or order of world implies the world-total. Each variety of the idea requires the unity to constitute it. The ultimate reach of thought which a word registers is inseparable from the minor phases of its meaning; because throughout its gradations the word is animated by a common soul.

Let us take now the Greek word *cosmos*, to whose properties and functions our word *world* has fallen heir in the New Testament, and see how the same law is illustrated.

Cosmos seems to set out from a fundamental idea of orderly relation and harmony of parts, and to rise through humbler uses to its high significance. An ornament making an impression of harmony and beauty on the observer, the fine arrangement and keeping of dress, a well-ordered army animated by a single mind and will, — these are examples to indicate the kind of objects to which, by reason of a certain common quality, the word *cosmos* was applicable at first. But when all visible order is apprehended as the reign of invisible law, when the heavens and the earth with all their hosts are seen to exhibit a harmony so pervading as to awaken the belief that the order of nature is unbroken, — then there is not only this or that thing which may be called a *cosmos;* there is *the cosmos*, the totality of order and beauty, the revelation of transcendent Intelligence and Power. Let this ultimate idea be once in the mind, and it takes possession of the word also. Throughout the range of its minor uses the word carries henceforth the grand cosmical conception, and refers the least example of real order to universal law. Indeed, the word has a tendency to give up its primitive applications, as too little in keeping with its great calling as a name for the material universe.

It is natural that the words "world" and "cosmos," though starting from different original suggestions, in different portions of the human family, at different times, should come to be the equivalents of each other, since both reach a unity of significance in the sum of things. Of course this unity overrules all distinctions; and, moreover, in the intellectual process of comparison and translation, either word would easily appropriate to itself any power of suggestion that might once have been peculiar to the other.

Having before shown that the word *world* is not degraded from its high service by lending itself to limited conceptions, it is hardly necessary to remark how naturally it comes down to well-known and well-inhabited regions, — for example, in the New Testament, the realms ruled by Caesar Augustus, — or to remind ourselves that we have an "old world" according to the measure of former knowledge, and a "new world," the glory of modern discovery. It is perhaps more needful to mention that several places in the Greek Testament give *oikoumene*, — very properly rendered "world," and pointing particularly to the earth's inhabitants, — the household world of a period contemplated as vitally interested in events described.

But our word *world* is more than a name for the material universe; it is a name for universal history also. The world is not a consummation of harmony and beauty, that admits of no change. It is an enduring world, and still a world of life, growth, and vicissitude. The world exists for a purpose, and that purpose implies the reason for its continuance. While we have been here and there, going through with various forms of personal experience, all things have moved with us in so steady a round as to afford us exact measures for different parts of common duration, — signs, seasons, days, and years.

Now, in Greek, there is not only a word to represent the world as existing in space (*cosmos*), — the nursery and theatre of life, — there is also a word (αἰών, — "æon") to sum up the invisible progress of life itself, and stand for the inner world of conscious being and collective history. Times measured mechanically and registered punctually, by means of regular movements of bodies in space, give an outward and abstract notion of continuance; but life has a chronology of its own, that cannot be tabulated, and the *æons* are measured only in themselves. Therefore, those who, in giving us the English New Testament, merged *cosmos* and *æon* in one word *world*, failed to mark adequately those ages on ages, somewhat distinguishable yet really dateless, that ensue by historic development upon the original creation.

The Greek word *aion* represents, commonly, a thing of life, having the law of its duration in itself, not independently, but subject to universal elements and laws of being. It denotes not time in the abstract, but a lifetime — as of a man, a family, a nation, a race. Let the term be applied to particular things, and there may be as many æons as there are objects, having each a vital constitution, upon which, under general conditions of life, the measure of its existence depends. Every æon may be signalized by outward phenomena of life whose times and changes may be noted. But the interior process of life, the very essence of the æon, is too subtile for chronometers; and it suggests rather than defines its own limits. It is in virtue of this vital quality that the word rises above the applications of detail, and reaches a comprehensive and even supernatural significance. Thus, using instead of *æon* the familiar word *age*, we may speak of the age of plants or animals, individuals or species; we may contemplate the age of governments, systems of thought, modes of worship; but we reach the unity of finite duration in the sum of things. Every living creature has its own period, and all creatures combine to constitute the living age in general, — that reality of unmeasured existence which is the world of far-reaching history. The scientist has to do chiefly with the world as *cosmos;* the historian has to do chiefly with the world as *æon.* The *cosmos* is attributed to God as Creator; the *æon* is oftener referred to God as Providence, Ruler, or Redeemer. When the world is spoken of as one whole, without reference to the varying phases of its physical and moral order, it is *cosmos.* When the world is distinguished from itself, so to speak, — when it is contemplated as many worlds in as many successive periods, as the world that now is or the world that is to come, as the world beginning or the world ending, — then it is *æon.*

"Through faith we understand that the worlds were framed;"[1] but it is important to understand also that the writer of the Epistle to the Hebrews is referring to *æonian* worlds, — not to the cosmos merely. There is the conception of a sin incompatible with forgiveness, whether in this world or in that which is to come.[2] And both worlds are æons, periods of moral government. "The harvest is the end of the world;"[3] "so shall it be in the end of this world;"[4] "what shall be the sign of thy coming, and of the end of the world?"[5] In these instances, not to mention others,[6] it is the consummation

---

[1] Heb. xi. 3.   [2] Matt. xii. 32.   [3] Matt. xiii. 39.
[4] Matt. xiii. 40.   [5] Matt. xxiv. 3.
[6] Mark x. 30; Luke xviii. 30; xx. 34, 35; 1 Cor. x. 11; Gal. i. 4; Eph. i. 21; 1 Tim. vi. 17; 2 Tim. iv. 10; Titus ii. 12; Heb. i. 2; vi. 5; ix. 26.

of the æon, or world-age, which is referred to, — a consummation by no means of necessity final in such a sense that another world-age may not be expected to emerge from the one that is ready to pass away.

Thus far we have reached no æon whose nature does not admit the possibility of limits, albeit to forecast or definitely to mark these limits is not given to finite minds. Ages arrive and pass in a movement of incomprehensible reality. The ages of ages, surpassing all reach of imagination, do not carry the mark of absolute duration. The metaphysical eternity is that which the ages of ages are not, and to which they can bear no rational proportion. It is the antithesis, not the synthesis, of limited periods. The wheeling of planets is as irrelevant to the abstract idea of eternity as the ticking of the clock.

Moreover, if it be true that *æon* signifies properly not abstract duration, but an enduring life, then the law of thought demands absolute Being, or else it admits of no absolute *æon*. Plato, in the Timaeus, affords an example of what was the law of his thinking. There the Creator is the Eternal, let us say the Eternity. The created universe is after an eternal pattern. But "time," he says, "was generated with the universe, in order that, being produced together, they might together be dissolved, if their dissolution should ever happen." Time, according to Plato, is an image of eternity, — *aionos eikon*. But both eternity and time are conceived as realized in beings. The image of self-existence is in the ever-present now of conscious life, of which we do not say that it begins or ends; and so all ages of life, past or to come, afford a shadowy suggestion of measureless existence. In this way of thinking, all passing times and numbered eras have their life and law from the Eternal. True, the supreme Æon, transcending all finite thought, has been thought of differently by different minds. Some, given to speculation, taking their notions as the higher sphere of their knowledge, have ventured far, and even thought to find proceeding from the depth of unbegotten Being a whole hierarchy of spiritual æons on the way down to worlds and ages here below. But the pretence of knowledge in what is beyond experience is sure to encounter the reaction of minds predominated by an opposite tendency, — minds slow in trusting themselves to a speculative drift, for fear of being borne away from solid reality. Each of the tendencies referred to, however, is essential to human nature. The two are developed together in every mature person, though not always in stable equilibrium. Only by the action of both, exciting and restraining each other, is the full-orbed revelation of history possible. Yet, while the too presuming and the too sceptical, the gnostics and the agnostics, may be alike losers for a time in something of sober truth which a rational comprehension may possess, neither the one class nor the other can avoid the logic of words. To both *æon* stands for existence, having a law of enduring life within, — implying a duration not to be mathematically demonstrated, no matter whether the existence be wholly of ideal stuff, or of the palpable material by which the senses are addressed. But the æons of revelation are not æons of philosophic fancy. They are genuine world-ages, whose secret is life, organic law, holding on its way beneath and beyond the shows of things, binding different elements and existences in unity, and so opening a broad avenue of thought to one supreme Being, the Source of life, — in all, through all, over all.

The study of the New Testament *æon* cannot come to a satisfactory end, however, without bringing in the adjective formed from the noun. As we find æons within æons, æons before æons, and æons succeeding æons; as every æon may be looked upon as an age of ages, and all æons are conceived in the New Testament as conditioned with respect to other æons, according to the eternal purpose and operation of God; it is hard to imagine that the adjective *æonian* could be alienated from the objective variety and fluxional nature of what it grows from. What belongs to unseen life, universal causation, organic law, we should naturally think, might be called emphatically *æonian*. So, at any rate, St. Paul seems to think, when, speaking of the hidden and surviving man in distinction from transitory forms of organization, he declares that "the things which are seen are temporal, but the things which are not seen are *æonian*."[1]

As *æonian* does not recognize beginning or ending in terms of time, so it does not deny beginning or ending in so far as either may be implied in the proper conception of elements described as æonian. In classic Greek the life of a man is referred to as an æon. A man's life is also an age of ages. St. Paul speaks of what was the character of his life at different periods. All the elements of his being were childish during the child-age. And, although he does not note the moment when childhood ended, it is plain that it did end; for, when he became a man, his life took on the characteristics of another age. Now this presents a perfect likeness to the manner of speaking in the New Testament about the æon of mankind, — that is, the world-ages.

[1] 2 Cor. iv. 18.

In the second chapter of the Epistle to the Ephesians there is set forth an inner reality and progress of human existence that was expressly "according to the course (æon) of this world (cosmos)" as governed by invisible principles and agencies working in the souls of men; and this æonian experience was so alien and insensible to the highest revelation of divine life as to be described under the figure of death. The immortal life, the perfect law of being, the Ephesians had not received by tradition from their fathers, but were relatively "dead in trespasses and sins." This æonian death, however, was to be limited and annulled by new life communicated through the revelation of Jesus Christ; and, the impartation of the divine life to that æon was to avail for the ages (æons) to come, that God might show them "the exceeding riches of his grace" through the same revelation of Jesus Christ. Thus the æonian life, that is such by way of eminence as being imparted to men by the eternal Spirit, struggles with and overcomes the æonian principles that are negative to itself, superseding the æons of ignorance and error due to man's immaturity and proneness to low appetites, with other æons that declare man's resurrection and joint heirship with the Son of God.

As certainly as the Creator desires to correct the mistakes and perversities of his offspring, and thus to take away their sins, so certainly he desires that punishment may give place to those moral results which punishment contemplates. Accordingly the twenty-fifth chapter of Matthew sets before us the coming of the Son of Man in the glory of his revelation as involving not only a life-giving energy but a judicial process. The æonian life evinced in love and service, to whomsoever done, meets approval and reward in the larger fellowship of æonian life to come; while those who recognized no divine call in the sufferings of their fellow-men are sent away into an æonian punishment. We know at once that this is not a punishment to be summed up in a sentence, which is to be mechanically executed within punctual limits of time. What is æonian is revealed under relations of cause and effect known as organic law; and, herein is the common quality of æonian punishment and æonian life. Neither is a thing of arbitrary prescription. Manifested in individual experience, — not, it may be, without distinction of times, — both are conditioned and determined in the nature of things, which is another name for the reign of God. Having recognized, therefore, the common relation of both life and punishment to the divine energy and authority, we are bound also not to overlook the distinction between the two. The life of love is divine and eternal as having its source in God, — its perfection in harmony with the divine character. The endurance of punishment (*kolasis*), on the contrary, is the mark of an immature nature, or of a perverse will, needing to be changed and superseded. It belongs to an economy of teaching and correction. The suffering experienced enforces a just demand for reformation of conduct, and so declares the discipline of creative Goodness with reference to a moral end. The end achieved, the experience of punishment has passed into the development of character.

If æonian life may annul the death of sin, so may the law of love do away with the discipline of chastisement that has gained its moral end. The adjective quite overdoes its function when, instead of qualifying its substantive, it contradicts the very element of truth which the substantive represents. But suppose punishment should aggravate the moral distemper: what then? May not punishment, which is negative to the perfection of existence, be negative also to the perpetuity of existence that cannot be reconciled with love? Failing of its moral end, may not positive punishment reach a natural limit in the cancelling of an abnormal being, just as sickness ends in death? At least, there is nothing in the conception of punishment as æonian to force upon us the conclusion that the Creator is determined to communicate his immortality of being to those who will only outrage the law of well-being. The experience of punishment may be conceived as reaching either a moral or a physical limit according to divine law, without the least sacrifice of its æonian character. The only remaining hypothesis, that of incorrigible character and endless being, needs no discussion. But, as we are dealing now, not with doctrine, but with the use of a word, I will call attention to a text having no direct bearing upon any disputed tenet. It is the three last verses of the Epistle to the Romans, — the concluding ascription to Him who is able to establish believers in the gospel, "according to the revelation of the mystery which hath been kept in silence through times *eternal* (æonian), but now is manifested, and by the scriptures of the prophets, according to the commandment of the *eternal* (æonian) God." The æonian times expressly limited by revelation, and exactly noted in the phrase "since the world began," — what proportion have they to the eternity of the æonian God?

Having in our language a name for the sum of things, and endeavoring to verify the use and range of the name in the New Testament, we have found our world to be cosmical and æonian. From the masses that make up the world of space we have passed to the living realities that make up the world of history, and have recognized the tendency of human minds to rise above dependent existences to the thought of one absolute Being. The conception of God transfigures our worlds. They pass into the universe. The ages are inspired with boundless meaning. The name that properly marks the periods of world-life connotes the ever-existent Originator and Governor of all things. The most ephemeral organism has life from the Eternal, and is an æon by itself. But the word *æon* receives a consecration which withdraws it from common associations. Taking lower forms of being into silent partnership with higher, and marking all life-periods with the æonian stamp as "times and seasons which the Father hath put in his own power," *æon* becomes a comprehensive name, and is set apart to high service in connection with those cycles of being that are God's revelation in the human race.

In fine, that man should conceive of outward nature as the building and temple of God by reason of responses in his soul from the inner sanctuary, which responses he utters in hallowed names and sacred writings, is an auspicious token of man's place and calling in the universe. It indicates his birthright, — to "dwell in the house of the Lord all the days of his life, to behold the beauty of the Lord, and to inquire in his temple." All truth is man's province; his vocation is discipleship. His earlier conceptions may be crude and mistaken. But if he knows but little of the cosmical world, he himself is part and parcel of the æonian creation; and when the fulness of times has developed the motive and tendency of the divine working, then assurance begins to take the place of doubt. The movement of humanity according to a ruling Reason becomes more prophetic than the prophets. The dispensation which culminates in the divine Man gives the Word of perfection for the future of mankind. It introduces us to the sphere of the Father's spiritual creation, — to the reign of God, which is within us.

Without assuming man's destiny as bound in a necessary immortality, — since it seems to be the implication both of Nature and Scripture that an existence given by the Creator can be cancelled by the same Power, — we may say at least that every intelligent agent is naturally bound, and morally free, to make trial of life, that life may the more effectually make proof of him. Pupils of nature, yet represented in Scripture as heirs of God, each of us is called to study in his own way the natural elements and the inspirations from above which go into the growth of character and the maturing of destiny. Taking Nature and Scripture to be witnesses for each other, we can examine them as to the situation and experience of the race to which we belong. We can interrogate them; namely, —

I. As to our common subjection under the constraints of cosmical conditions and social governance, — THE WORLD TUTELAGE.

II. As to the presumably peculiar inability of primitive man to cope at once with the problems confronting him, and the special danger of his yielding, from unwise choice, to physical tendencies against the higher law of his being,— THE FALL.

III. As to that faith and loyalty in man through which he is open to suggestions from above, and can move in a manner to be held approved, reasonable, and acceptable in a provisional way,—in default of advanced knowledge, faultless obedience, or ideal devotion,—THE PRINCIPLE OF JUSTIFICATION.

IV. As to the development of man's apprehension and experience of the not-good as necessarily correlative to his progressive knowledge of the good; together with his possibly wilful violation of faith with respect even to obligations on which his physical welfare depends,—THE MANIFESTATION OF EVIL.

V. As to the motive and method of man's reconciliation with God in the revelation of his character and will, and of his deliverance from the errors and corruptions of a comparatively irresponsible and childish career,—THE LAW OF ATONEMENT.

VI. As to the judgments in which faith is appealed to, knowledge increased, and law enforced, till the consummation of the world-history,—CRISES IN THE PROCESS OF REDEMPTION.

These are indissoluble parts of the Creator's teaching. They indicate the orbit of divine revelation as conceived in Scripture, and they mark the high road of human experience. They combine all ruling conceptions proper to human nature, irrespective of any limits, whether in time or space.

PART FIRST.

THE WORLD TUTELAGE.

"Now I say that the heir, as long as he is a child, differeth nothing from a servant, though he be lord of all, but is under tutors and governors until the time appointed of the father. Even so we, when we were children, were in bondage under the elements of the world."

GALATIANS iv. 1, 2.

"Quid enim sibi volunt multimodæ formidines, quæ cohibendis parvulorum vanitatibus adhibentur? Quid pædagogi, quid magistri, quid ferulæ, quid lora, quid virgæ, quid disciplina illa qua Scriptura sancta dicit dilecti filii latera tundenda, ne crescat indomitus, domarique jam durus aut vix possit, aut fortasse nec possit?"

ST. AUGUSTINE: De Civitate Dei, lib. xxii. c. 22.

PART FIRST.

THE WORLD TUTELAGE.

CHAPTER I.

TUTELAGE A LAW OF NATURE.

THE common schooling of life in the world is the basis of man's study and teaching since the world began. As the world grows in age the schooling of the world gains in scope and effectiveness by the subordination of special achievements to the common instruction. The beginner in life, content if not wearied at first with the most rudimentary exercises, is by and by full of excitement at finding that even these are his introduction to a limitless learning. And, as if to meet his growing need of guidance, the enlightened souls and choice writings of the race are peculiar by reason of their unlimited range of thought. They salute the eternal Wisdom in the progress of ages, and find, contiguous to our earthly domain, an invisible realm of spiritual activity, whither every generation of mankind migrates in its turn. Thus, from teachings and efforts that have made life what it is at any time or place, there results the discipline of life into which at birth every human being is entered.

But the distinction between teachers and taught, governors and governed, in human society is not absolute. The power exemplified in parental influence and control finds public expression in various forms of government, civil or ecclesiastical, that stand for social order and moral regulation. Yet this general exercise of power is always checked. Nature is made to outgrow institutions. All government struggles with the reactions of advancing life, till the advancing life prevails, only to give way in its turn. The sovereign cannot govern his people without being governed by them; as the parent cannot justly guide and restrain the child, without learning how much the child is commissioned to guide and restrain the parent. All teaching involves the effort and resistance by which the teacher also is taught. Thus it is that under organic law, which is the expression of creative wisdom, all the life of man defines itself as tutelage. The conscious subjection and docility of the moment is typical of a continuous experience of life, wherein the destiny of mankind is never to escape entirely from the earlier physical limitations, and never to carry out to completeness the later spiritual intentions. The ideals of perfection are for a higher order of development than is accorded to mankind on earth.

The experience of life puts personal faculties and character to such constant proof, that a man's whole career in the world is often looked upon as a probation; and, as holding a necessary and just relation to his whole career in a world to come. But probation is not an arbitrary enactment, but something in the course of nature. Therefore it needs to be guarded at the outset from conventional constructions; and, especially, with reference to what Bishop Butler has set forth as "the general doctrine of religion, that our present life is a state of probation for a future one."[1] This general doctrine does not justly involve anything artificial or arbitrary. But it has been systematically construed as ascribing the limits

[1] Analogy, part i. ch. iv.

of physical life to a spiritual trial, whose limits cannot be experimentally ascertained, and are not definitely revealed.

Our personal probation, as a verifiable reality determined by our spiritual constitution and the law of the universe, is not measured by our physical life. On the contrary, it is reasonably apprehended as fulfilling itself according to a progress of the spirit into whatever conditions the spirit may pass. That which begins and ends with physical life is the physical trial, — the struggle for life which man exhibits in common with the animal creation. In this trial success or survival is seen to have no paramount relation to spiritual character. Life often ends before spiritual probation can have begun, as well as at all stages of moral trial, without reference to its fulfilment. Therefore, to call "our present life," meaning our life in the body, "a state of probation for a future one," which by implied antithesis is a state of retribution without probation, is a partial use of the analogy contemplated. For, if we are to reason of unending life from the analogy of our earthly existence, we can do no less than take the whole testimony. Conduct in the present life is found to develop retributive consequences. Hence retributive consequences may not unreasonably be expected to disclose themselves in the future life. But in the present life retributive consequences are an essential element of probation. Then, by analogy, retributive consequences must be a mark of probation equally in the future life.

Or, to put the thought so as to recognize the general relation of the present life to the future life, without denying any spiritual facts which may possibly be common to both, let us ask: If the whole life, after death, is conceived as retributive in relation to the whole life in the body, while the whole life in the body is conceived as probationary in relation to the whole life after death, is there anything in this general relation which should or can contradict either the retributive experience of the present life, or the probationary character of the future life, considered by itself? What valid objection to inferring that the future life is probationary in being retributive, since the present life is confessedly retributive in being probationary? But an administration conceived as judicially cancelling all liberty or power of personal reformation on the part of offenders, whose personal reformation is demanded by eternal law and prompted by corrective experience, involves an absolute contradiction, — the contradiction of the supreme Lawgiver by the supreme Judge.

Therefore, whatever modifications in the elements and conditions of moral experience may ensue upon the crisis of death, we are naturally forbidden to assume *à priori* that character will crystallize into immovable destiny at the moment of our deliverance from the constraints of mortality. The nature of man indicates the contrasts of character which his trial may determine; not any point in a personal career at which character is no longer capable of change. Hence we rationally look at the nature of our probation for a theory of its limits, not at assumed limits of probation for our theory of its nature.

CHAPTER II.

COSMICAL TUTELAGE.

HAVING premised what would be misplaced argument, were it not for the importance of clearing our range of thought from obstructions, we have no more to do with the abstract idea of probation. That idea at once pervades the whole reality of the world-tutelage. It belongs to the constitution of moral government. Any statute of limitations is an incidental matter, that must present its own credentials, and keep its own place. Our preliminary considerations pass at once into a general statement, which contains in sum the truth we desire further to unfold.

Man's normal development as a moral being starts from the least degree of self-control with the greatest degree of outward constraint, and moves on toward the least degree of outward constraint and the greatest degree of self-control.

This direction of development, if it can be verified, infers the ruling purpose of man's training; namely, that deliberate choice may more and more adjust itself to the requirements of law, until personal aims shall coalesce with universal truth in final maturity of character and general harmony of being.

Material nature is bound fast in its own law, that the

free activity of man may learn by trial what support and what resistance to expect. As material nature is subjected to the imperfect treatment of man by the creative will, so also by the same will is man in subjection under the tutelage of material nature.

If we look at man with respect to his cosmical environment simply, deferring for the present any consideration of his growth, we find him even in the fulness of his powers not a little dwarfed in comparison with the elements he is required to deal with. The magnificence of the home with the profusion of its treasures is certainly a testimony to the quality of the occupant; but should not the occupant be master of his possessions? Yet man is a pupil — never done with learning to call things presented to him by their right names. Face to face with all the world contains, his possessions are too grand and vital for his faculties. "What is it?" is the riddle which nature is proposing in every object; and the answer is at no little peril of life. To find out what a thing is, and to name it well, much as it concerns man's destiny, is far from being an instinctive action of powers that unerringly fulfil their own law. It is an effort demanding good-will and patient attention, while after the best endeavors the secrets to be known are infinitely beyond the most penetrating intelligence. The more our answers seem to be allowed, the deeper the mysteries into which nature's questioning withdraws. We have no sooner proved the reality of our powers than we have become aware of their deficiency. Fresh discoveries are required to correct previous mistakes; and other mistakes are incident to fresh discoveries. In the midst of over-curious researches we are under correction as to the simplest problems of life.

Moreover, that primacy of intellect, whose privilege it is to look deep into the nature of things, is for very few. The multitudes have their faculties chiefly occupied in seeking the satisfaction of animal craving. "What shall we eat?" "What shall we drink?" "Wherewithal shall we be clothed?" These are the preoccupations that absorb the energies of mankind, and hold them back from higher aims. Nature holds out her gifts for man to appreciate. With other orders of living things man is invited to take what is suited to him. Only, his choice is that of a superior being. The hungry rapacity from hand to mouth must learn to wait upon diligent and judicious selection. What the offered thing is, even as to its commonest use, it is not for momentary sensation or the accompanying suggestion of thought fully to tell; and its final significance may be infinitely far to seek. Let man try to know any bulk or any atom, and the more he knows the more is he baffled by the universe of which his inquiry takes hold. Thor thought to drain the drinking-horn of Utgard-Loki at the first pull, not being aware that it was connected with the sea: a symbol this of what the stoutest personal energy amounts to as against the magnitude and coherency of material nature.

What is it? The question is, first of all, practical. What is to be done with it? To what account can it be turned? The vision that came to the entranced Peter for his spiritual direction was not unconnected with his physical wants, — was indeed substantially the every-day vision of mankind in general: "All manner of four-footed beasts of the earth, and wild beasts, and creeping things, and fowls of the air." To arise, to kill and eat, to taste the tree's fruit, to use things according to their nature, is on the way to higher knowledge. Though the cuckoo name itself in its note, still naturalists and poets listen long to know what the name may mean. And no matter how many things may be said or sung about it, the bird-note remains untranslated, — a voice that wanders through all years to call forth a response from all singers.

So, in general, while most men find their poetry of life in the practical arts of life, a few take the hint of nature in a higher sense. They give us masterpieces in architecture, sculpture, painting, literature. But nature is mistress of all the masters. Their works have a peculiar finish, but a minor dignity. Nature's works are of their own kind, — things of life, of original design. Man's monuments decay, and fall into neglect. Then, it may be, nature adopts them as her own. But in majesty of building, in breathing forms, in glory of color, in mystical voices, nature is ever fresh and productive. The cosmical teaching grows more mysterious as it proceeds. It bears witness to its source. The most divinely gifted of men are the most apt to recognize a supernatural in the natural. Man in his minority, in the primitive trial of his powers, while giving proof of his pupilage in every experiment he makes, is still quickened, inspired, instructed by the infinite Wisdom speaking through the things that are made, whether they be things in earth or things in the infinitude of the sky.

CHAPTER III.

ÆONIAN TUTELAGE.

BUT we must think of man as growing, — as exhibiting a personal and collective development, to which no limits of time can be assigned. Here at once cosmical conditions become subsidiary to social environment. The house is made for the family, not the family for the house. Man may make trial of some powers, as an inhabitant of the planet; but even this trial, and especially the formation of character connected with it, belongs to us as members of the human family. We take conscious intellectual and moral training from those with whom we come into intellectual and moral relations.

Every child of our race is brought into the world at the lowest degree of its capabilities. In this extreme of minority man is under a reign of social law. Spontaneous self-assertion yields of necessity to pressures from without. There is no force in infancy to sustain a practical conflict with adult powers. The child is set to forming habits under the sway of ideals which it knows nothing about, in order that those ideals, when they shall have taken possession of the child's nature, may have the advantage of trained and obedient service from subordinate faculties. Not any formal correctness is sought at first; but a discipline of powers that may result in approved modes of action by and by. Yet there are no perfect masters even of this primary discipline. The chiefs of households and leaders of society address themselves to various problems of conduct; but the solution is in no case a thing of outward demonstration. Last, as well as first, the demand is for docility. One man's well-doing may furnish suggestion and motive to another man, but not a formula of righteousness. The child, whose praise is that it does not rebel against natural control, rebukes the adult, who resists the spiritual admonition given him for warning or direction. The moral of life, to those experienced in their own imperfections and the errors of mankind, is that they should be born anew and become little children through a spiritual inspiration from the Father, to whom they owe their being. Our spiritual development demands a discipline superior to that of natural guardians. Man realizes at length a certain personal function, in which he goes not only beyond the cosmos, but beyond the authorities and influences that make up the age in which he lives, and is drawn into the presence of the eternal Power,— Source and End of all beginning and ending things.

As the thought of God comes to man in his contemplation of outward nature, so there is a communication and growth of the same thought in connection with social discipline. The thought seems to arrive by natural and universal suggestion, to be subsequently shaped by outward images or quickened by inward teaching. But whatever may be said of the origin of man's religious conceptions, we are sure that the idea of God asserts a power both in the thinker and over thought. It becomes a common element of spiritual trial, a law in the interpretation of things, an assurance, not to be slighted, of supernatural Reason ruling in all destinies.

We are obliged, therefore, to contemplate the growth and experience of mankind, not only with respect to material elements and the physical economy, not only with respect to society in the different phases through which it may pass, but above all with reference to that law of the rational spirit according to which an invisible and unlimited Power is recognized, under whatever names, as affirmed in creation and history. Such are the grand aspects of our schooling in the world. It is not for man to throw off the physical, social, or religious regimen. To live by suitable nourishment and protection of the body, to live as belonging to our kind, to live as the creatures of our Creator, — this is simply to live.

But life has successive phases of development, whether in the individual or in society. Though all principles of life may be present in germ from the beginning, still their growth is such as to exhibit varied proportions of knowledge and successive types of activity. The great motives of action come to their practical predominance in a regular order of time. If duties have a transcendent range, and are liable to come into mutual conflict, they may well wait a little upon one another. The primary and most pressing demands receive the earliest attention, that the more important obligations may employ the more developed power and mature judgment in their discharge.

The different functions of society are not sharply discriminated at first. The religious practice may be mingled with industrial and social habits under a patriarchal authority, that commands the children and the household after it in all the round of service. The tribe compelled to maintain its own existence in more or less hostile competition with other tribes will not furnish its offspring with the protection of stable institutions. The patriarchal authority is a primitive tutelage. In the progress of civilization this tutelage is not superseded, but supplemented. Families and tribes are reduced to harmony under a common administration of authority. Yet the kingdom, bringing order and comity out of confusion and contention, affords no perfect law; though it may justly claim to be better than the anarchy which it supersedes. The king may do what the patriarch cannot do. He may not only organize a more comprehensive regulation of common affairs, but he may encourage and secure the special institution of religious functions. Civil order, however, tends to become universal. States incorporate other states, as tribes reduce to subjection other tribes. The imperial ruler takes his turn; and, with a genius for conquest and government, controls powers that had been foreign and hostile, extending to customs and worships before estranged a common recognition. But, though empires may accomplish what other forms of government cannot undertake, has any empire exhibited the consummate type of society? Can more be expected of the empire than that it shall surpass in justice and magnanimity the powers which it holds in check? Is it anything but a larger school, in which the pupils may be brought on towards that inward and universal revelation of law, which will have perfect individuals as the constituents of perfect society, and regards personal duty to God, the supreme Ruler, as including all duties to one's self or to one's kind?

It is evident, therefore, not only that human nature is constituted to develop religious institutions in connection with industrial or political organization but also that religion, being first in rank as regards the realities and aims contemplated, is for that very reason last to reach its full power and expression in the order of successive developments. Religious institutions come to maturity in history as an endeavor to fill out the human ideal and destiny to its ultimate possibility, — the possibility of communion with the divine Source of being.

Is it true, then, that in religious institutions man has found a perfect guidance and restraint? Nay; if we identify religion with its institutions, we are compelled to ask, from what evils has religion been able wholly to deliver man, and to what evils has it not been able at times to persuade him? In the sphere of religion the world-tutelage has shown itself most disastrously unequal to its aim. It has ever, in seizing upon the highest authority, furnished the most flagrant examples of what is not the law of perfection. It has compelled the divinest personal illumination to confirm its testimony with the most ignominious sufferings. Nor has it been able to guard the sanctuary of conscience in undeveloped natures from formality and hypocrisy. An institution or discipline accommodated to the habits and capacities of imperfect creatures is of necessity below the standard of ideal wisdom; nor can it do absolute justice to the claims of even the humblest learners. What is it that outward law has made perfect? In the administration of outward law, wisdom is shown in not being wise overmuch, — in not transgressing the narrow limits of provisional jurisdiction.

We have to confess, moreover, that far from reaching anything like perfection in our earthly training, the very conditions and gradations of our progress, such as it is, are the occasion of ever-fresh ebullitions of passionate egotism and partisan desire. Taking his chance with his kind, man appears in space and in time according to a natural movement of creation. If he belongs to the whole school of life, he belongs immediately to his own class. But the whole school being not wise, the different classes compare themselves among themselves, and measure themselves by themselves, to some useful purpose certainly, but with much injustice. The less advanced have little appreciation of their superiors; the more advanced are wanting in respect for those below them. Peoples full of prejudices about gods of the hills and of the valleys, gods of rivers or of the sea, divinities of woods, caves, fields, and dwellings, have a training, it may be of many generations, before them, if they are to reach the grand and simple conception of one God, from whom all things have their being and law. But in the elevation and zeal of faith in one God, believers are apt to feel that idolatrous nations are enemies to be destroyed or subjugated. The faithful, as they think themselves, with God upon their side, are infinitely in the majority of strength; how should they not conceive themselves as having an equal preponderance of rights? It is the fault of faith to interpret the government of the world according to its own views; till, in due time, the schooling of life corrects this natural assumption, and shows that all degrees of service are needed, — that no unkind pretensions are tolerated. Those reckoned low in the scale of being are taught to look upward. The elevated are set to learn condescension. To all are the lessons of righteousness.

The child of nature, whose strength is from touching

the ground, is naturally driven to disgust and desperation by the cunning arts of a selfishness more disciplined, if not more aggressive, than his own, which he makes proof of in his civilized fellow-man. The adventurous pioneer of civilization, on the contrary, finds the simple savage no fellow of his; but practically assigns him a middle rank between the wild beast and the foul fiend. Up to a certain point the mutual acquaintance of the two is apt to force the growth of mutual distrust and hostility, dooming the sentiments of humanity and religion on either side to a corresponding depression or distortion.

Let the religious power come in to compose the quarrel. Let that spiritual conviction and organization which represents divine law and human fellowship — the best motives and rules for living together — mediate between imperial enterprise and barbaric obstruction. Cannot those in chartered communion with the infinite Father mete out approximate justice to contending children? But here the religious power is an interested party, not an impartial mediator; and, though it should claim to sit in judgment or to make reconciliation, it would inevitably open the way to other divisions and conflicts. Not peace but division is the outward mark of human progress. It takes only a little too much assertion of spiritual authority to provoke either violent reaction on the one hand, or prudent and ambitious co-operation on the other. Religion itself is ever on its trial among men with respect to its sincerity and sobriety. If hypocrisy and scepticism invade the domain of faith, shall not contemptuous neglect or active rebellion rule in the ranks of unbelief? Church and State are likely to be most deeply at variance when most they affect to be one; and the spiritual power is most distrusted and cheated by individuals, when most it appeals to the secular arm for the enforcement of its dictates. Progress is through patience. It is for the wise to teach; not to gain an easy victory over the illusions and abuses of unthinking people. The sufferings of the prophets are less to be pitied than the crime and misery of those who ignorantly reject or destroy their prophets. Men cannot but value the things whereto they have already attained. Has a thing no worth because we cannot take it with us on the march? It is a costly thing to move onward.

CHAPTER IV.

AGES OF HUMAN DEVELOPMENT.

IMPERFECT as the world's discipline may appear at any time, when we consider long periods we find that despite the downward and backward tendencies of nature there is an upward and onward movement of mankind. We mark the current of history from far away. Man was once the child of nature. He worshipped her powers and learned her ways. He found companionship and wealth in flocks and herds, hunted wild beasts, and fought strange tribes, — exhibiting only the simplest household habits. Again he appears in highly organized society, possessed of multifarious and refined arts, which it required much time to develop; while his progress is celebrated in national memorials, attested in ancient institutions, asserted in military and naval powers, commercial activity, and far-reaching supremacy of law.

And still the movement is onward. History is not left to grow sluggish and dead in common achievements; but takes a new impulse and inspiration, aspires to a higher law, apprehends a reign of divine benevolence and boundless hope, — an inheritance of glory and virtue to be enjoyed, though all material elements should be dissolved. Nothing is more impressive than the lights and shadows that come upon the world's face from the unseen life of its inhabitants.

Man's advancement is not seen alone by looking into the dim background out of which he has emerged. It is shown in the warning and awakening contrast of retributive effects, that marks opposing motives and differing degrees of human endeavor. It seems both a physical and moral necessity that humanity should be appealed to, not only from the examples of conspicuous progress, but also from its aboriginal and degraded types. Those who do not march with the column must be known as lingering in the rear; and when in the natural distribution of life it is found that the lot of some human beings is cast in languid air and spontaneous abundance, an invading force is called for to break up an animal repose not corrected by any recurring compulsions of earth and sky. Is it thought that some men "builded better than they knew," and others worse? Then at least their works are not looked upon with indifference by their successors. Men will fall below the standards of the past, if they do not learn to judge and surpass them. The ripest civilization will sink into decadence if it cannot bring up reserves of native vigor and simplicity to aid in reorganizing the elements of old renown. As both empire and church trace their lineage from the same primeval manhood, so both must have men of a primitive sort to save their glory from becoming a fading flower. Æsthetic and religious luxury, the repose of wealth and civil order, combine to produce an enervating moral climate; and the too happy possessors are liable to forget what is due to a common brotherhood, unless aroused by the challenge and threats of lawless claimants. The schooling of life measures progress by service. To do kindness to the fallen and disinherited, to raise untutored peoples to civilization and baptism,—

this is the way of salvation not for the degraded alone. It is the highest proof of a divine calling which the most disciplined and privileged of mankind can give.

Meanwhile, the progress of liberty keeps even pace with the reign of law. It is the rule of law that a call to high service is a mark of special confidence. The civil ruler is, in idea, the servant of God, with ample powers and large discretion for the purpose of guiding the efforts, and controlling the excesses, of persons too little trained in their duties, and naturally overbearing in the assertion of their own claims. The office of the ruler may be tentatively and tyrannically administered; but it may not be dispensed with. Gradually the experiment of government works its way toward a common judgment and practical consent, which, written or unwritten, has the force of law. Legislation learns to take hints of those for whom the laws are made. Executive administration becomes the practical trial of what has been deliberatively enacted. Law reigns over rulers and subjects. Personal rights, liberties, prerogatives, are practically defined, moderately asserted, and peacefully accepted. All this goes on independently of theory or form, through a conflict of forces not in stable equilibrium, but under a necessity of composing themselves as they can in a career of general order.

Nor can it be denied that it is under the banner of religion, in spite of all abuses of the name, that law and liberty move on together. There must be a tribunal of last appeal. We take guarantees and hostages of every power but the Power who gave us to ourselves that we might fulfil his intention in our being. Religion appeals to man as free, as possessed of conscience, reason, faith, the elements of a sacred and inviolable personality, which to profane were worse than death. Over and above the religious principle and sentiment in men of authority and power, there is the voluntary and permanent organization of popular religious conviction, — public teaching and practice, which contemplate the divine authority, and man's final accountability to God alone. It is impossible to measure the moulding, restraining, and inspiring influence of religion as a factor in the common experience of mankind.

This ever-mounting conception of duty, — this ever-enlarging discipline of obligation, by which liberty is defined as well as promoted, throws a backward light upon the new-born, untrained creature of appetite and impulse, which shows even infancy as not without the image of God. That ignorant outreaching of the child, which unconsciously opens a breach between itself and its governors, which by and by, perhaps, seems at odds with society, at odds with institutions, at odds with the overruling Power, is equally at odds with the child's own higher and better possibilities. Through that opening breach comes the hint of a principle of freedom in human nature, in which man's birthright is so involved, and his destiny so wrapped up, that all outward authority needs to stand in awe before the sovereign man that is to be; while through the same breach of harmony comes to the insubordinate learner of life his calling to rule in a sphere of his own, — to compose the factions of his nature, to harmonize body, soul, and spirit, to reconcile the claims of self, society, God.

Experience determines also the progress and play of ideas. The pupil of nature thinks himself almost her master by and by, so much has he learned by obedience to her laws. Just so man comes to look upon himself as not by any means the creature of political institutions and social customs, but rather as the source whence customs and institutions originate and the standard by which they are to be judged. Rebellions and revolutions come to be regarded as more lawful than the power they bring into judgment. History has its turn of being written and read from the point of view of undistinguished people. The oracles of man's spiritual nature give responses from the life that now is as to the life that may be hereafter. Departed souls are conceived as treasuring up and carrying on the moral achievements of incarnate humanity. The dead are not of necessity held to inhabit an under-world, but rise in thought to the brightness of a spiritual heaven. Unable to limit that career of invisible manhood, whose tendencies and issues are typified in our earthly training, the prophets of the future avail themselves of the imagery and colorings of transitory existence to depict their anticipations of eternal life. In view of such anticipations, the perfection of our whole provisional discipline, like that of our individual infancy, seems to be, not in any prescriptive and faultless outward action, but in the development of inward principles and motives, such as shall by and by dispose and enable their possessor to originate just conduct independently of outward constraints. Accordingly, the final proof of creative goodness depends upon the mature results of our disciplinary experience, and cannot reasonably be looked for in the happiness immediately accruing from our present conditions. And, as the faith demanded of us in the conditions of our nonage goes on towards its justification in the evidence of a consummation to come, so the anxiety incident to partial views undergoes a necessary transformation into the confidence of maturer knowledge.

We may now recur to the opening of our discussion, and briefly go over the general movement of thought thus far. Man's point of departure in life was set forth as "from the least degree of self-control with the greatest degree of outward constraint." The instinct of liberty does not fail to appear in the earliest life. It appears, however, in the law of spontaneous and unreflective self-assertion. This early motive and manifestation of liberty demands checks and regulations, and demands them more peremptorily the more unguarded and dangerous the natural self-assertion appears. But checks and regulations from without, necessary and useful as they may be, are not growth, and cannot secure a perfect development. It is the inward law that determines the fulfilment of being.

Again, it was said that the normal movement of life is "toward the greatest degree of self-control with the least degree of outward constraint." The instinct of liberty is gradually transformed, and passes into the rational law of liberty. The type of freedom changes from that of spontaneous self-assertion toward outward objects to that of conscientious obedience to the inward revelation of truth. The inward revelation is at last sovereign. When the reign of God announces itself with assurance in man's spirit, he is commissioned to judge what he owes to tutors and governors. It is the mark of a spirit inspired of God to master the world in refusing to be mastered by it, though the world should summon all machineries of coercion to its aid. There is a sphere of personal liberty in which a man is alone with God, and in this liberty is the consecration of all great service to mankind. To be saved from the evils of excessive self-assertion, man must submit to provisional restraints; and in winning his way to ultimate freedom he must not decline the struggles and sacrifices that are the price of redemption from usurping ordinances.

Under the laws of physical life, however, our emancipation cannot be fully realized. Were the full development of spiritual being possible under earthly conditions, which is not conceivable, such a development is practically denied to mankind in the fact of death. What is of the earth returns to the earth. What is spirit must reach its higher destiny under the trial of new disclosures and new responsibilities, or else the whole life of man is "a vapor, that appeareth for a little time, and then vanisheth away." The hard service of mortal existence, the bondage through fear of death, the bondage of corruption, — all this is but the antithesis and prelude of perfection, if we are sons of God. Tutelage is ministerial and transitory. The reign of the Father is eternal.

CHAPTER V.

AGES OF DIVINE TEACHING.

IF human beings, as they enter the world, are actually entered into a discipline of life, if the reality of tutelage is universal, and essentially one under all varieties of form, then this tutelage belongs to the constitution of nature. In other words, it is in the intention and working of the Author of nature. Hence for men to recognize a genuine leader is in effect to salute the creative Leadership. It is the grand distinction of the Scriptures that they give us an interpretation of the world's history through a long succession of men who regarded themselves and regarded mankind as under the guidance and discipline of one God.

No doubt, every note in the scale of human possibilities finds some sort of utterance among all men; but the historic harmony involves distinction of parts. Any group of human beings may have leaders, individuals brought to the front by force of nature, by force of circumstances, — chieftains in the struggle of life, hereditary heroes, imperial masters; and even a polytheistic faith will recognize a nameless *numen* in the chief of the state. But the great demand is for one divine leading, for a religious primacy, for the man who shall best mediate to the world a guidance coming down from the

Father of lights. The Scriptures are alive with the belief that not only the being, but also the well-being, of mankind, depends finally upon God. Men are not sufficient for themselves. Hence leaders are conceived as servants of God for the welfare, not of a peculiar people only, but of all mankind; while nations, like men, are given precedence or rebuke according to the service they are rendering in the direction of interests that are universal. The movement of thought in the sacred writers is according to a method of revelation which contemplates the coming of the divine Man, the perfect Leader, and so the Saviour of mankind.

The men chosen to prepare the way for this ultimate leadership were selected spiritually by a law of faith in one God, the knowledge of whom was to fill the earth. The whole action, through every scene, belongs to a theocratic drama shadowing forth the eternal reign. Noah's family is not represented as having escaped the deluge by a natural struggle; it was saved by divine interposition on moral grounds. Abraham's calling of faith had reference to no immediate worldly pre-eminence; it was in the assurance that he would not only command his children and his household after him, but that in him and his seed all the families of the earth should be blessed. Moses was the lawgiver of Israel, not by the natural claim of Egyptian learning, but as a man taught of God. It required much more than an able military leader to settle the twelve tribes in the land of promise. It was no natural gift of divination that made a prophet, but the word of Jehovah becoming the burden of a human spirit. There was a priestly family; but no law of physical descent could make a priest, unless he were called of God, as was Aaron.

And royalty, — was it natural inheritance, anointing oil, state, power? No. It was truth, justice, piety. Nothing was real, nothing answered to its name, without the divine inspiration, the seal of the supreme Sovereign. No prophecy was of private interpretation. The anointed man was consecrated to service on behalf of his kind. Prophet, priest, or king was forbidden to transgress the proper limits of his calling. "I am not the Christ" was the tacit if not express confession of all forerunners of the Christ.

But when the Christ is come, there is in him an independence of traditions, a mysterious infinitude of spirit, importing the fulfilment of Nature's original design. He is conceived as the mystery of communion with the Father, that he may be the revelation of love to the children; the Son of God, that he may be the perfect Son of Man. He came into the course of nature from above, that he might show the true meaning of what was from beneath. He was King by the truth and grace of God, or he could not have taken the form and ministries of a servant with absolute fidelity to man. He was the impersonation of the Father's reign, or he could not have been the example and inspiration of loyalty to his brethren, who had failed to recognize their birthright under the solicitations of appetite and worldly desire. On the other hand, if Christ had not done full justice to what was true in the schooling of the world, he could not have carried out that rudimentary teaching to the fulness of its eternal meaning. If he had not honored with meek heart and due obedience those sitting in Moses' seat, he could not have reproved their works in the name of divine justice. If he had not rendered to Cæsar the things that were Cæsar's, he could not have rendered to God the things that are God's. It was for him to divide the light from the darkness, to reveal the reign of God and the law of perfection in the weakness of the body and under all temptations of the world. He was to rebuke the world's routine methods of self-aggrandizement and success in the wilderness. He was to vanquish the world's tyranny, that had the power of death, upon the cross. He was to rise to the life immortal, and be recognized as the successful Initiator of the era of redemption. He was to reign in the glory of the Father, till he should witness the consummation of the divine purpose, — the deliverance not of man only, but of the whole creation, from its primitive bondage into the glorious liberty of the children of God.

Such is the Biblical conception. In the Christ incarnate the Scriptures represent to us absolute spiritual superiority to outward constraints; though the Son appears in the house of bondage, is called out of Egypt in a deeper than the literal sense, through a Red Sea more terrible than that in which Israel of old was baptized unto Moses. In the conception of Christ risen from the dead the Scriptures give us the idea of man's sonship and majority, in communion with the Father without the obstructions incident to the natural life.

Who but the Christ should sum up for us the Scriptural interpretation of the world? What has he told us in word or action of the world-tutelage? Did he call it a dead failure? In demonstrating its errors did he deny its usefulness? In denouncing its sins did he refuse any longer to employ it in working out righteousness? In suffering its oppressions was there no joy of it set before him in his hopes? Surely, he did not come to abolish the imperfect government by which the natural man is kept in some kind of order and training for better things. Harsh Roman masters had done much in bringing mankind to the fulness of the time when the Christ should come; and would do still more in extending the protection of imperial law over the progress of his gospel among the nations. Moses was faithful in all his house as a servant. The mastership of Moses was not to be repudiated, but fulfilled in its full intention. More wonderful still, the will of the Father, that forbade an unconditional subjection to hierarchical or imperial demands, was not supernaturally to hinder the governing powers from having their way in the infliction of suffering to be sacrificially endured. In this infliction the proper function of earthly government was recognized, its perversion by the powers of evil was judged, and the Son of Man was glorified. Nor in the resurrection is he represented as counting his sacrifice too great. His word to two sad disciples is:— "O foolish men, and slow of heart to believe in all that the prophets have spoken. Behooved it not the Christ to suffer these things, and to enter into his glory?" Then, from Moses, and from all the prophets, and in all the Scriptures, he interpreted the things concerning himself.

To whom, according to the New Testament, is the revelation of the Christ to appeal? Who are personally interested in its effects? Who are to share in its influence and success? The men of all ages. Abraham, who rejoiced to see the day of the Lord; Moses and Elijah, whose presence with him in the holy Mount shows them as awaiting the universal transfiguration; the men of faith, from Abel down, mentioned in the eleventh chapter of Hebrews, who were not to reach their perfection but in fellowship with their brethren of the Christian era. In the third chapter of the First Epistle of St. Peter the Christ is represented, having first suffered for sins, as hastening in spirit with his proclamation to the once disobedient antediluvians. The remotest residents of hades are conceived as not beyond his reach. For, if the men of faith need to know their Leader in order to reach perfection, certainly, according to the New Testament, the men of unbelief must come to the truth, which is to put their conduct and destiny also in the proper light. But in the fourth chapter of the same Epistle, sixth verse, a broader statement is made. We are told that the gospel was preached "also to the dead," for this purpose, that they might not only "be judged according to men in the flesh" (as they had been), "but live according to God in the spirit." In fine, the scope and unity of God's revelation, according to the wisdom given to St. Paul, may be read in the third chapter of Ephesians: "Unto me, who am less than the least of all saints, was this grace given, to preach unto the Gentiles the unsearchable riches of Christ; and to make all men see what is the dispensation of the mystery which from all ages hath been hid in God, who created all things; to the intent that now unto the principalities and the powers in the heavenly places might be made known through the church the manifold wisdom of God, according to the eternal purpose which he purposed in Christ Jesus our Lord."

We may add, then, that, whether we inquire of Nature or Scripture, we gain a reasonable assurance on three points: First, bodily life is made to serve in the propagation and training of spiritual men. Secondly, while disunion and servitude mark the world's history, the divine revelation indicates the creative purpose as one of reconciliation and freedom; namely, "to gather together in one all things in Christ." Thirdly, if this purpose, ruling in spite of obstructions in our earthly history, is to reach perfect fulfilment, it must be in history transcending our present experience; that is, in history conceived as the eternal reign of the Father in the life of the resurrection.

The process of spiritual training permits something to appear which is to disappear. In the world's experience the moral trial is not a thing of spiritual instinct and speculation alone, but a reality of practical moment, the effort of overcoming the worse with the better. The wheat and the tares grow together. The church of the Redeemer carries along with her, through all phases of her earthly history, the antichrist from which she is to be redeemed. The visible Christianity of the modern age, like the old Jerusalem and the old Rome, exhibits not only the vices to which its virtues are opposed, but faults which spring from virtues that have not reached their fulness. The reign of God moulds and moves to its own purpose that governance which the nature and needs of imperfect men will not dispense with. Divine efficiency is working through human deficiency. Without the reactions of the world to come, the Christian calling could not have its distinctive character in the world that now is. Without the trials of the world that now is, the earthly generations of men could not effectively conceive or actually win the triumphs and joys of the world to come. The consummation of man as partaker of the divine nature revealed in the Christ does not disown connection with the physical laboratory of life. The bruising of the serpent's head, and the deliverance of the spiritual man, not without suffering, dates from that far receding period of the garden and the living creatures, — when above the beasts, yet like them of the earth, the first human pair is conceived as erring in a primitive choice between the seductions of animal appetite, or intellectual ambition, and the divine voice of benevolent restraint and authority. The principles and tendencies that have asserted themselves in historic human nature hitherto are set forth in Scripture as belonging to original man.

PART SECOND.

THE FALL.

"THE first man is of the earth, earthy."
                                            1 COR. xv. 47.

"NEMO ergo quærat efficientem causam malæ voluntatis; quia nec illa effectio est, sed defectio. Deficere namque ab eo quod summe est ad id quod minus est, hoc est incipere habere voluntatem malam."
                    ST. AUGUSTINE: De Civitate Dei, lib. xii. c. 7.

"Now, son of mine, the tasting of the tree
    Not in itself was cause of so great exile,
    But solely the o'erstepping of the bounds."
            LONGFELLOW'S DANTE: Paradiso, xxvi. 115-117.

"WHAT fear I then? rather, what know to fear
    Under this ignorance of good or evil,
    Of God or death, of law or penalty?"
                    MILTON: Paradise Lost, ix. 773-775.

"SOME falls are means the happier to arise."
                    SHAKSPEARE: Cymbeline, Act iv. Scene 2.

PART SECOND.

THE FALL.

CHAPTER I.

ORIGINAL MAN AND PRIMITIVE TRIAL.

IT is seen that man, though started in life as the feeblest factor in his own destiny, exists in such organic relation with universal nature as not only to be subject to a necessary tutelage, but also to co-operate voluntarily with the spiritual purpose revealing itself from age to age in the progress of human society.

If, therefore, the progress of every human being opens a growing contrast between the inappreciably small beginning of life and the immeasurably great objects and efforts to which life is addressed, what are we to think of the ever-growing contrast between the opening trial of original human nature and the teachings of experience in the vast career of mankind as a whole? Would the earliest human mistake or misdoing be naturally looked upon as a peculiar mystery and scandal? Or, would it not rather be regarded as something quite within the range of personal liabilities; something to be reasonably expected from the spontaneous development of inward principles, that require the discipline of experience for their proper ordering and lawful restraint?

At any rate, we cannot study the Scripture conception of man's primitive moral error without giving some heed to the obvious teaching of nature as to its source and character.

The drama of Eden does not come down to us as the thought of primeval man. It is part of the literature of a people, peculiar by reason of their advanced theological conceptions, whose calling was in a world no longer young. The experience of ages had taught the mortality of man's physical nature. To die was to be judged "according to men in the flesh;" while the administration of this judgment was recognized as having a persistent reference to a moral discipline, by which mankind might learn to live "according to God in the spirit." But since no man of the by-gone generations had survived, as an example of what it is to fulfil the divine law of life, of course the common transgression of law, by which death was found to invade the human body, was carried back to the beginning of human experience. From the first, the race of man was one to be instructed, to be held responsible, and to be judged. Such was the organic law of life. The discipline which all succeeding generations have inherited is presumably the discipline into which the original family of mankind must have been initiated.

This moral initiation is set forth in Scripture according to the very elements and image of Nature. But it has also been enveloped in a transcendental halo by theological speculation and dogmatic systems, in such a way as very much to obscure its verifiable features.

We are now concerned with what is in the order of nature, — and so, verifiable. We take the words of St. Paul, "howbeit that is not first which is spiritual, but that which is natural; then that which is spiritual,"[1]

[1] 1 Cor. xv. 46.

for a verifiable statement as to the common order of human development. Life in its beginning is preoccupied with material objects and physical necessities, while spiritual revelations are reserved for a later day.

That a creature of God is entered into such an order of development is shown by what he begins to do, not by how he began to be. Science may penetrate the method of creation, if it can. It may try to determine whether the different species of living things were brought into reproductive being at an instant word, or the creative fiat be more reasonably conceived as the working out of various organic forms and functions through secret processes and inscrutable generations of life. The postulate of Scripture with regard to man is, that such and so much as he originally appeared in the order of nature, such and so much he was created and made by the Author of nature. Here, at this stage of intelligence, we are told in effect, is the beginning of the human movement in the history of things. Here is represented a creature of physical organization, to be developed more and more as a rational and moral power; a creature instinct with natural motives that imply a career of spontaneous activity, yet limited in faculty, checked in thought, sensibility, and effort; a being conscious of a free initiative, yet held to a constant reckoning with outward objects, that react upon him according to no choice of his.

In nature also are the limits of any instruction to be communicated. Teaching must be according to the learner's powers and conceptions. Creative tuition may, nay, must have reference to conditions and laws, of which man is not only ignorant at first, but of which he cannot be taught by mere intellectual suggestion.

Hence the mark of divine teaching is its condescension and accommodation to finite capacity. The material envelopment is made to mitigate the uncreated light, and adjust it to human vision. The same material nature is man's defence against malignant spirits, if such be supposed to act against him. In whatever guise they may be fancied to appear, man cannot be an intentional accomplice in their spiritual aim. He is not taken into the secret of it. The human trial is in the universe, to be sure; but it is meted out in the measure of human nature, in order that the universe may be gradually and safely apprehended in experience and thought. The plain story of human conduct at any particular moment is not verified, but is rather made unverifiable, by being complicated with what is foreign to itself. It is postulate enough that man, as part of creation, lives and moves, and has his being in the Creator.

That the moral trial of humanity was social in the beginning cannot be held as otherwise than favorable to its success. What is essential to the development of our race is represented in Scripture as conducive also to personal welfare. So far as man and woman are distinguished from each other, this is equivalent to the larger range of their united powers, and to more ample security against individual weakness. But since man and woman are two in one, the unit of the race, their conduct is set forth as pertaining to one nature, — a nature conceived as originally without taint of moral depravation, without bias of foregoing example. Man's career is, in Genesis, the central reality of a physical creation which is of God, and very good. Nature was in the beginning, is now, and ever shall be, perfect in principle, wise in organic law, — yet having reference not only to an immediate personal discipline, but to a vast spiritual design requiring unknown ages for its fulfilment.

The danger of life is the danger of transgressing the law of life. So far as we have evidence that man was, or is naturally liable to transgress the law of his being, the evidence connects this liability with two phases of our individual and collective history: namely, first, the peculiar proneness of unschooled nature to practical errors of ignorance; and, secondly, the discipline of physical and moral law for the better regulation of conduct. Each of these phases of our history can be discussed with the certitude that goes with conscious experience.

From the nettle danger to pluck the flower safety is the natural allotment of all living creatures upon earth. Man's dangers are to be estimated by the vast range of interests that are at stake upon his conduct. The experienced chemist does not handle the elements and apparatus of his own laboratory without a care which signifies danger. How, then, shall the novice of a race make his way in the laboratory of creation and the chemistry of life without risk, wisely as all things are arranged for his guidance and warning? However exalted in faculty the original man may be conceived to have been, he was constituted to be schooled, at least physically and intellectually, by his own mistakes; not to move on tentatively in experiments of life, and come to no practical error. Indeed, man comes upon occasions of stumbling and falling so various and recurring that he cannot afford to be preoccupied with shunning mishaps, for fear that such a preoccupation might be the greatest mishap of all. He will gaze at the stars in spite of the danger of stumbling at the stone in his path. He is even diverted and stimulated by the risks to which his spontaneous movements expose him, and wins familiarity with outward things through a somewhat heroic disregard of hurts and pains.

The original man has it before him to learn and practise the arts of life. He is to make trial of the difference between thought and bodily organs, as well as of the difference between bodily organs and the more inert material through which the mind's intention must be carried out. The muscular movement does not obey with inevitable precision the inward mandate. The organ is untrained, and the instrument is rude. The stroke slips away from the mark, and the manufacture falls below the idea. What was not too well conceived is but too ill done. Only by degrees can mechanical execution rise above its early failures towards those better patterns which the mind is gradually working out. To hold the thing done as at once equal to the idea, — this were the most disastrous fall, the fall of the idea itself to the level of the manufactured article, the fall from the birthright of progress, wherein all future achievements are stored. Instead of this, the thing done becomes an object to be judged, a proof of how the effort fell below the design, a pungent suggestion of failure on the one hand and of possible improvement on the other. Thus the artistic judgment and sensibility, the artistic conscience, becomes active through a sense of practical deficiency, and moves on to better efforts and worthier results. If it were needful to account for primitive failure in manual exertions, how could the truth be better summed up, on reflection, than by saying that the work, not having been done according to the perfect conception of what was required, could be recognized, not as free from forbidden elements and unqualifiedly good, but only as containing elements of good and evil. The highest law, of course, demands good only, and is against the knowledge of good mixed with evil. Must we not suppose that in the first man especially there was a practical deficiency, due to inexperience and the consistency of his clay, the recognition of which would prick him on towards what might be due to the nobility of his spirit?

But if in the simplest beginnings of art there is a natural law of practical failure; if the law of the mind is intellectual and æsthetic, while the law in the members is physical and cosmic, so that at first it seems good luck rather than good effort when the mark is hit,— how is it in the sphere of science? Did flesh and blood ever so inherit the inscrutable laws of physical life as to be under no liability of transgressing their bounds? On the contrary, is not this liability the portion peculiarly of initial existence? That there are things contrary to the law of life may soon appear; but what, and how many, are the forbidden things, or the forbidden relations of things, not even the largest experience can fully tell. Only we know that the things forbidden by organic law or by artistic judgment are by and by forbidden by the moral sense as well. The physical and industrial habits are gradually taken up into the moral training, in order that the body itself, and all temporary forms of activity, may be brought for their day under spiritual control. Here, too, in the sphere of rational faith and righteousness, the man of primitive nature left us no perfect example.

But who is to cast the first stone at the first man? Certainly not we, who share his moral infirmity after ages of instruction and experience. Is man a creature to originate perfect moral conduct from partial and prohibitory hints of moral obligation? No. He is constituted to originate conduct freely, that in the judgment of that conduct, as the particulars of it complete themselves, he may learn to distinguish the good from the not good. As in art, so in morals, judgment and sensibility are combined in the consciousness of what is done in a way to rebuke the mixture of good and evil in motive or action, that the spirit, inspired with faith and hope, may be spurred on toward what is good only.

Primitive moral trial — what is it? Is it not a self-government, constitutional but untutored, in which the personal power is necessarily moved to action, but under limits of knowledge and liabilities of inexperience such that, if the danger of practical error be great, the danger of contracting moral guilt is correspondingly mitigated? Witness the pointed teaching of the New Testament, that the gravest spiritual perils are associated with the final word, not with the first lessons, of revelation.

The primitive liability to failure is connected indeed with animal appetites, together with a certain awkwardness of muscular effort and resistance of matter; but it reaches also to the complex and comprehensive moral calling that gradually opens to the mind. Duty discloses itself in the sphere of art, in the sphere of physical law; but it goes beyond these spheres, and contemplates the effort of all powers toward their rational ends. All personal relations, all service and loyalty, are leading on to the apprehension of infinite righteousness; while at the same time the uninformed and inexperienced soul is open to only partial hints, shut up within the narrowest bounds of knowledge, and occupied about details of immediate and pressing requirement, that make up the rudimentary lessons for a far-off perfection of being. Is there a discrepancy between our ideal and our actual, which all the discipline of life cannot cause to disappear? — which the discipline of life may for a time make more and more apparent? And is there no necessary difference between creative thought in universal nature and the rude essays of unschooled faculties? Is man held to have been highly endowed at first, a spiritual nature far above the common range, in the invisible likeness of ideal Divinity? How, then, should not his gifts be quite out of proportion to his earthly calling, and he, the apprentice in practical methods, be perpetually humbled and irked by lowly and tedious trials on the very threshold of existence? Or, suppose the spiritual gifts and calling to be reserved for a later period of personal development, and the habit of being to take shape for a time in quiet harmony with earthward relations and efforts, how should not these natural preoccupations absorb energy and limit development, so that by and by the spiritual calling would appeal to the awakened consciousness with incitements and reproofs in view of sensual and sluggish days? Grant the divinest tempering and harmony of powers, organs, and exercises; there is at least the liability to fatigue, the natural limit of every exertion, and of every indulgence. There is in idea the line of perfection, the boundary at every point between not too little and not too much, in which all opposing claims are reconciled. But can we suppose that the true orbit of a combined physical and spiritual movement, which has never been intellectually demonstrated, is, in the very first trial, to be spontaneously described? Only the fulness of the creative Godhead in man is equal to such a result, — not man, as a stranger in the earth, set to labor, to listen, to learn, and to obey. A healthy desire to do the right thing degenerating into an anxious scrupulosity has already missed the mark; and so has the quiet assurance of having done as well as it was possible to do. No sooner does the inward purpose formulate itself in outward conduct, than there appears an action to be reviewed and judged. Was it perfect? If so, the actor has hit the mark of his calling at one point only. Was it well meant, but worse done? Then there takes place at once a corresponding distinction and judgment with regard to it. The act is not simply good, but good and evil. Thus, a phase of completed moral action becomes the practical prelude to the revelation of a higher law of conduct, — a law which finds fault with what went before, and beckons onward to nobler exertion. The higher law enters by reason of what is seen to have involved, however unintentionally, an element of transgression; and the expression for moral advancement is that of the Psalmist: "I have seen an end of all perfection, but thy commandment is exceeding broad."

Now, if it be urged that the unavoidable distinction between inward suggestion and outward performance is accounted for and justified by the organic law of our existence, and that a man is to be blamed only so far as he has acted from a faulty intention, there is no occasion to object. What appears is that our organic law does involve a necessary missing of the ideal mark, a necessary falling below the ideal standard, especially in the momentary efforts of initial experiment. In other words, man was originally set to win his way and to win his prize by voluntary discipline and self-sacrificing obedience.

But there are tendencies in human nature that make against discipline and obedience. It follows that a faulty intention, or a disloyal passion, or a disobedient purpose, is an evil into which an untried virtue might fall for a time, through inappreciable processes of temptation. Here we come to that freedom of moral agency in which man learns to know himself as a prince, and possibly to think of himself as like his Maker. He is under a necessity of legislating for himself in detail, and he judges himself in detail; but he can only spell out in part, and never fully know, the divine law; which is over him as well as in him, and by which he is, however mysteriously, brought to judgment. If the new man, being both prince and apprentice, has adjudged various doings of his own to be what he would not have the same kind of doings to be in future, would it be the way of a generous and upright spirit to say, "There is no fault of mine here; I disavow all responsibility for what is done amiss; it is all due to the law of my creation"? On the contrary, shall not the reverent and conscientious susceptibility be prompt to suspect some personal delinquency, and even to accept a responsibility not literally forced upon it, — assured that the supreme Judge can do no wrong? Conviction of error is one element in the conviction of sin, and for a time the chief, possibly the sole, element; but the other element, the feeling of blame-worthiness, is not far off. It is ever ready to come in with the after judgment of any regrettable act, whose character was not distinctly known or duly weighed beforehand.

This would hold true in a special sense of a first disobedience. Disobedience, while man is little aware of the significance of law, may be determined upon, not as wrong, but as probably advantageous, or at any rate as not likely to be very injurious. How can the disobedience be realized as wrong before it has fulfilled itself so as to prove its own character, and thus enable the conscience quickened by experience to pass judgment upon it; or, what is the same thing, to feel the force of a higher judgment saying, "That was wrong"? At this later stage, the least foregoing suspicion or doubt is transfigured into a clear warning, that condemns the error and precipitation of the disobedient act. If the man refuse to own his responsibility; if he set himself to prevaricate, to escape the mortification ensuing upon his conduct,— what is this but to aggravate the fault and difficulty into which he has fallen, to prepare the way for a more painful recoil from what is done, and for a severer discipline in what is still to do? As there is a demonstration of error inseparable from a slow and difficult progress in truth, so there is a development of practical wrong in acts that grow imperceptibly to their fulfilment, through infinitesimal increments of motive and energy; and the wrong is appreciated only when the act is fulfilled. It is when something is produced out of harmony with the law of the mind, that one becomes aware that in the members there is a bondage of sin, a rule not to live by, but to be delivered from. So it comes to pass that, on the side of provisional experiments and unsatisfactory results, man finds himself lapsing, failing, and his works perishing; but on the other side, the side of a noble purpose and a beneficent teaching, he finds himself going on and up, enlarging his range, disciplining his powers, and producing works, not immortal indeed, but not so soon or so willingly allowed to perish.

It is not in the primitive action alone that the question is put, What motive shall be honored, and what master shall be served? That action is the opening of a trial, that continues open. More and more pressingly with every new experience does the great alternative recur: law and life, or disobedience and death. It is a princely probation. Law may seem severe for the moment; yet law is vital and progressive, an austere but beautiful queen. Lawlessness may seem real and vital in a way, and pleasantly indulgent to the senses; but lawlessness is a treacherous mistress with forbidden fruit, rejecting the higher only to fall under the lower requirement — the law of death. Life discloses no full justification in what a man has done, no matter how well. Nothing that man can finish, or formulate in act, is man's whole duty or perfect obedience. He must go on and up. This is his law, and his blessedness. He is not to talk of being tantalized with an unapproachable perfection. He is to move towards the excellence he apprehends; or else fall into the beggarly listlessness that seeks no higher good — and lives no more.

Contemplate the accumulation and continuity of failure through which the best discipline of life has realized its measures of good; and so appreciate the life itself — the spirit begotten and nourished from above for so arduous a progress. If man is not constituted to originate conduct of ideal perfection at first, how significant the fact that he never fails to develop the polarities of thought and sensibility known as conscience; and that, when conscience affirms something of evil even in what was meant only for good, not even the good mixed with evil can save the whole from that active resentment which demands a new trial and a better result. Thus man's natural liability to fall into evil becomes the ground of a high calling: "Be not overcome of evil, but overcome evil with good." And while we may well believe, with St. Paul, that sin is not imputed as intentional transgression while as yet no positive law has been announced, still we must recognize the fact that unintentional transgression needs to be corrected; and so, it may well be by reason of such transgression that the divine law enters, bringing with it the knowledge of sin.

The distinction of what is done according to opposite poles of thought, — good and evil, right and wrong, — originating, as we have seen, from the centre of personal judgment through the teachings of experience, does not confine itself to its own sphere, but goes out into a dualism that conceives the universe, whether of space or time, as exhibiting a like polarization of energy. Man reconstructs all things according to this original antithesis. He makes new heavens and a new earth with elements of good and evil. Æonian powers before the world was are at odds, — Ormuzd and Ahriman, Odin and Loki, powers of good and powers of evil. The same antithesis rules in the conception of the limitless future. The carnal mind and the spiritual mind are represented respectively in actions and powers that signify a truceless warfare. The moral discord seizes upon all natural contrasts and incompatibilities, as its symbols. It becomes the interpreter of the world, transfiguring things and names, that it may assign them to service in the spiritual realm. Day and night, summer and winter, earth and air, fire and water, health and sickness, growth and decay, life and death, become expressions for inward struggle and vicissitude. Of course, the inward struggle comes to conscious vigor according to the development of races and individuals; but it takes all literature to record it, and all life to utter its voice. The Brahmin looking upon limited experience as ambiguous and illusive, longing to be absorbed through knowledge in the universe of being; the Buddhist trying by meditative discipline to shorten a tedious metempsychosis and reach that mysterious Nirvana, good at least as the negation of evil; the Christian finding no adequate repose here, but sighing for a sabbath-rest that remaineth for the people of God; the whole creation groaning and travailing in pain, waiting for redemption or reconciliation, that shall rule out the irrational elements of finite destiny, — these are some of the notes in a universal chorus of testimony to man's deficiency and failure in realizing the good, to the discord and mortal agony of his experience in the knowledge of good and evil.

But if man is impelled to look beyond himself for deliverance from evil, he is obliged to find the source of his defection from good in his own nature. The momenta of personal conduct are in the person. It may seem little to know; but when we inquire into the natural history of man's defection, we justly conceive it to be a falling from the harmony of an original constitution attributable to the Creator alone, of whose work no evil can be predicated, into an immaturity and uncertainty of action, at necessary odds both with creative wisdom and with the growing ideas of creaturely perfection. The fall appears as a childish proneness, for a time, to trial of things not known to be good, or even presumed to be evil; whose rashness or precipitancy may be accounted for, if not excused, by the natural limits of apprehension, the predominance of physical nature pending the gradual development of spiritual powers, the conceivable lack of dutiful attention to the better and worse aspects of proposed conduct through ignorance or preoccupation, and finally, by the tendency, in view of things already done, to a sluggish or self-willed complicity with what needs to be corrected. Thus, the smallest deviation from the perfect law of being is just so far a partaking of forbidden elements, a turning of experience from the knowledge of good simply, to the knowledge of good and evil, an opening of life to inroads of decay and death. It is with reference to this gradual process of defection, too unconscious and obscure to be seized upon and defined, till it is summed up in some deed, that St. Augustine conceives our first parents to have moved in secret disloyalty to their act of outward disobedience.[1]

[1] In occulto autem mali esse cœperunt, ut in apertam inobedientiam laberentur. — *De Civitate Dei,* lib. xiv. c. 13.

CHAPTER II.

GENESIS COSMICAL AND ÆONIAN.

IT is a mark of Scripture that not only its general representations, but even its particular figures or phrases, come promptly to our aid, when we are trying to reach the truth of nature. The living Word is that which sets forth what the Creator declares in the very realities referred to. In the things that are made is the divine thought, — whether the things are presented immediately to the senses, or represented to the mind in words. Scripture is of its own kind, but in the common order of thought. It is not the possession of specialists; but has to do with universal religious faith, and with nature as depending upon God, and known in the common consciousness. It sets forth the words which the Creator spoke in things that were made, words which man is to hear, according to St. Augustine, not with his bodily ears; for God "speaks in the truth itself, if any one is ready to hear with the mind, not with the body."[1] If, therefore, we desire to hear God speak in the truth itself, as the author of Genesis heard him speak, we shall avoid the anachronism of trying to find the discoveries of modern science in that ancient form of knowledge and faith. We shall bear in mind that the relation of the Creator

---

[1] De Civitate Dei, lib. xi. c. 2.

to his works is the truth itself, no matter how little or how much those works may have disclosed their secrets to human inquiry. God made the world, in whatever way man may conceive or represent the world. The fresh witness of the morning is not to be contradicted or corrected by the dry brilliancy of midday. The world that was made, in whole and in detail, is the world that continues to be made, that always presents itself in some phase of its well-ordered harmony to common sense and universal intelligence.

In studying the Scripture testimony to man's moral beginning, however, we have to do with two accounts in Genesis, often treated as in part at least varying narrations of the same facts, with no very serious effort to ascertain the essential difference between them. We have nothing to do here with critical inquiries about different documents. Our concern is only with the sense of what is written. Any distinction in the sense must be unavoidable, obvious to the most uncritical reader, when once pointed out, or the distinction may be held not to exist. But, on the other hand, if the distinction be easily marked, and its application brings out clearly the unity and coherency of the parts, then the distinction is presumably real and necessary.

What, then, is the distinction which assigns its own sphere to each narration? Simply this: that the first account, including the first chapter of Genesis and three verses of the second, contemplates universal nature as the completed *Cosmos*, and sets forth the creative work in relations of space; while the account that follows, beginning with the fourth verse of the second chapter, and going on in the story of Eden, regards nature as involving development in relations of time, and sets forth creation with respect chiefly to the *æon*, or world-history. In the first account we have fiats of consummation, the work of *Elohim*, who spake and it was done, whose thought and will are realized and reflected upon in distinctions and groups of things conceived as complete and very good. The second account brings before us the work of *Jehovah Elohim*, of God ever existent and ever active, whose thought and will are revealed, not only in natural processes, but in spiritual and historic creations as well, wherein things naturally good may fall into temporary evil.

Go through the two accounts with this distinction in mind, and see if it be not essential. What is the sphere of the first narration? Light, as distinguished from darkness upon the boundless abyss; earth, as distinguished from atmosphere and sky; earth with its vegetation, as distinguished from seas; sun, moon, and stars, as dispensing light and marking time; distribution of animal life in water and air; distribution of animal life upon the earth, ending in man: these are determinations of nature in space. Spoken from the depths of eternity, they are represented in the light of common days. The cosmical artist does not give us the perspective of time. His compositions are peremptorily foreshortened to the measure of, "He spake, and it was done." As presented in nature, and as represented in Scripture, the groups of created things strike the sense and govern the common intelligence, though having no more to tell directly of interior development and natural duration than have Michael Angelo's pictures in the Sistine Chapel. The original aurora flashes upon the background of chaos at the word. The celestial clock-work is set in order with omnipotent abruptness. All the prolific parts of creation are produced in full career. The creation is punctual, simultaneous, complete, — universal harmony and happy correlation. The different sections contemplate no verifiable order of time. Hence, they may be divided conventionally by common days before the sun is said to have been set in heaven. "For what man possessed of reason," asks Origen, "would deem that a first and second and third day, evening and morning, came to pass without sun, moon, and stars?"[1] The infinite conceptions of divine achievement and divine repose are commended to the feeble memory of mankind by association with the week of ordinary work, rounded by a day of rest, — according to the plain understanding of St. Augustine, that though we cannot have evening but from the setting of the sun, nor morning but from his rising, the period of six days was still made use of in the narrative, not as if God required time or could not create all things at once, but because by this number the perfection of his works was signified.[2]

Try the second account. We have come to generations, — a genesis of things in a different order of thought. It is the order of thought contemplated by our Lord when he said, "My Father worketh hitherto." Withdrawn from the luminous outlines and objective coloring of space, we have passed into the indistinguishable depths of time. We have to do with physical change and organic development moving mysteriously on to world-history. There is a chaotic period of crude material and creative energy before any plant or herb of the field had grown in the earth, — a chaos of negations, no rain, no man to till the ground. Creation is not the completed work, but the continuing

[1] Quoted in Hagenbach's History of Doctrines, vol. i. p. 135.
[2] De Civitate Dei, lib. xi. c. 7, and 30.

process. The day when the Lord God made the earth and the heavens is an æonian day. There is a striking absence of chronological exactness, whether as respects the origin of things or the progress of man towards his recognized place and character in history. The human race is represented, not as developed and mature in function, chief of the works of God, but as inchoate and progressive, coming forth from earthly elements into vital being. The organic perfectness of humanity, created male and female, honored and blessed with an endowment of fruitfulness and a commission to rule over the works of God, gives place to individual experience and effort in a certain subjection and serviceableness to surrounding nature. A garden becomes the narrow scene of a drama without assignable limits of duration, just as the conventional week afforded a convenient method for marking off the different parts of a visible universe without assignable limits of extension. Man is set to fill up actual days in the garden, to dress and keep it. He acquires instruction about his manner of living, — what to eat and what not to eat. He touches the border-land of science, — observation, nomenclature. He comes to the consciousness of social needs. Animal or intellectual isolation is not good. "Male and female" become "man and woman" in a social and spiritual correspondence, "husband and wife," in a conjugal destiny and marriage institution. Man's genesis as a creature of God's moral government ensues in process of time upon his genesis in the order of the physical creation. There is indicated an awakening out of the deep sleep of animal existence — through observation, comparison, reflection — to love and worship, to law and discipline, to the hope of a spiritual career.

Here is a progress, as I have said, in time, — not time measured, not time told off in days, weeks or years, but time as belonging to conscious being — life-time. In awakening life there is ever new trial. The senses are quickened. Curiosity refuses to sleep. There is an instinct of freedom and self-possession, a growing confidence of being able to take care of one's self, a tendency to experimental knowledge at all risks, possibly even a pride in refusing to be governed by reasonable restrictions and warnings. In fine, there is a fall at length from an earlier simplicity of faith and obedience. Generic humanity is pictured under conditions of temptation which every child can apprehend, and as acting with an immaturity of judgment and character which every child in some way illustrates. But with transgression there is announced a change. Life becomes moral discipline, in distinction from native innocency. There is no going back to the simple constitutional goodness to which transgression cannot be imputed. The whole history of good and evil in the world comes in this way to its original epitome and rehearsal.

If the distinction set forth be one grounded in the nature of things, if it be self-evident that the days which it requires the completed orbs of space to make are not days which can denote the duration of the process by which those orbs were made, then the days in question are at once resolved into elements of literary representation. The *quasi* day's-works are a mode of summing up and distinguishing the vast effects exhibited to common observation in the ordering of nature, which effects are summarily referred to the word of the Creator. They also furnish an ideal type of legitimate human effort and rest. But, especially as marking a modest range of verification really open to us, the distinction is important. A writing is properly verified in the order of thought in which it is conceived, and to which it is addressed. The scripture of common observation is not verified in terms of transcendental physics, nor the scripture of common inward 'experience in terms of transcendental metaphysics. There may be conceptions in science, or even in mythology, which we accept as ideally true, without the power to test their objective reality; and these may help to explain other conceptions which we accept as true simply because we can and do appreciate their fidelity to nature. But in comparing the plain language of Genesis with the common sense of things, we have apparently as little concern with geological periods for construing the six day's-works as we have with St. Augustine's mythological theory that "let there be light" refers to the creation of angels, in construing the fall. For, supposing that "let there be light" does refer in some secondary way to the creation of angels, and that, as St. Augustine further sets forth,[1] part of the angels fell into the darkness from which the light was divided, thus determining two hostile states, which were to make the new creation of God the theatre of their strife; still, as this setting-forth is beyond the whole range of reality with which we are acquainted, we pass it by, as belonging to an order of unverifiable conceptions.

Let us therefore take the cosmical genesis as simply scenery and prelude, with reference to an æonian revelation of God in human history.

A garden which man is set to keep and dress is no strange thing. A tree allegorically named is likely to

[1] De Civitate Dei, lib. xi. c. 9.

be not of an extinct species. All life has its proper nourishment, its authorized enjoyment, the law of its best and longest career. This law transgressed by any forbidden indulgence, evil begins to be known in contrast with good; and death, no longer marking the necessary goal of existence, shadows the progress and obstructs the achieving energy of life. Fruit which is a desire to the eyes, animal appetite, precipitate curiosity, and rash ambition of new knowledge, whether of good or evil, — this tempting solicitation from below creeping darkly up to the height of an intellectual argument, as it was the original, so is it the universal, temptation of man. Here is no violent assault, nothing but quiet and plausible suggestion, wholly within the range of natural motives, yet without the due apprehension of natural consequences, — the easy and unawed movement of a moral nature in need of prohibitory injunctions, but prone to unreflecting determinations, and liable, with no excited consciousness of wrong intent, yet with a certain deliberate purpose of self-gratification, to disregard the rational persuasions of duty ministered from above. It is the ancient and universal error. It imports natural infirmity. It discredits spiritual dignity. It is of a piece with the latest yielding to temptation; only, being conceived as at the beginning of moral agency, when the human mind was open to the voice of God in nature, but not to the same voice articulated in the parental and social guardianship that watches over the actions of ordinary childhood, the fall of the first pair is referred directly to the judgment of God, and so the highest sanction is given to the subsequent verdicts of the human conscience.

But if in the fall man was stung with the knowledge

of evil, the knowledge of good was not to be denied him. He did not fall from the guardianship of God. He did not fall from the calling of faith and obedience. The good still beckoned to him. The voice of duty still pursued him. Hope still went before him. But life and history assume at once a dualistic character. A bad suggestion fulfilled in a disloyal act opens the door to discord, prevarication, contradiction. The man and the beast are contradistinguished in the same body and soul. Divine service is alloyed with self-seeking. The loss of inward peace brings on a conflict with outward nature. The processes of life are mysteriously flavored with the sentence of death; and death itself is armed with a moral sting, a new and punitive terror. The serpent of temptation has entered upon his typical function as both beast and false prophet. Wherever peace on earth is violated, or there is war in heaven, there is the "dragon of the prime," to be bound, cast out, killed, but again to live and act whenever that first falsehood is repeated — that man by himself, man in virtue of appetite, intellect, or ambition, shall be as God. Against such a suggestion there is the girding of man for his moral struggle. Man did not stumble that he might fall; but rather through his fall there came the prompting to more wary and virtuous endeavor, to a conscious and principled reaction against wrong, the promise and potency of the Creator's redeeming work.

In the Scripture genesis, nature sums up the things that are made; and there is one supernatural Maker — God. Whether the works be conceived as complete in space, or the divine operation be represented as going on in time, the Creator and Mover is one and the same. This exhaustive distinction implies that man, as a creature, had his original motives and laws of conduct from his Creator, under outward conditions which the Creator had arranged. If, then, human nature was constituted not to realize spontaneously an ultimate and perfect form of action, but to be taught by its own failures and deficiencies to depend upon continual help from above; if human nature was peculiarly liable to transgress the law of life, when there was everything to learn as to what the law of life is; it becomes a fact of the utmost significance that man was constituted to hear the voice of his Creator from within and from without. By the nature of man's powers, as well as by the nature of things with which man had to deal, the Creator shaped experience, fashioned thought, inspired conviction, and so led on to the very language in which the divine teaching should be afterwards rendered. Man was encompassed by natural law, which was the effective vehicle of instruction, of warning, of judgment, perfectly adapted to convert the rational soul from delusive aims and lead it on toward its proper perfection.

CHAPTER III.

MORAL DEVELOPMENT FROM DISCOVERIES OF LAW.

THE Scripture conception of primitive man as passing from original innocence to positive moral discipline by disobedience to a divine command, was interpreted by St. Augustine as involving the certainty, not only that all mankind would fall in the same way, but also that this voluntary defection would become a permanent habit of existence and a final bond of social organization for a very large proportion of the human race.[1]

This interpretation assumed that the divine administration of law, seen to be universally corrective in its moral intention, was to be not universally remedial in its personal effects. Hence the kingdom of darkness, the profane state, would naturally be developed and strengthened in constant struggle with divine law as exemplified in the holy state or kingdom of God. The gloomy support which this theory of human destiny has in the conflicting moral tendencies of mankind is only too apparent. But, as Augustine himself intimates, the

[1] In hoc primo homine, qui primitus factus est, nondum quidem secundum evidentiam, jam tamen secundum Dei præscientiam, exortes fuisse existimemus in genere humano societates tauquam civitates duas. — *De Civitate Dei*, lib. xii. c. 27.

ultimate issues of the divine government of the world are not in evidence with us. They are subjects for religious faith and rational anticipation. What we are now concerned to verify is the practical efficiency and spiritual aim of law with reference to transgression, as taught in the Scripture of the fall. Are the penal consequences of wrong-doing as much in favor of man's final rectitude as they are against his primitive errors?

It speaks well for the nature of things, that man in his immaturity should not go on in error and misdoing without being arrested and instructed by the consequences that wait upon his actions. Outward nature is so adjusted to interior consciousness as with it to constitute an unfolding and progressive law of conduct, involving the conditions of well-being, and even of being at all so far as our bodily organization is concerned.

A law of life is such in contradistinction to everything negative or injurious to life in whatever degree. The law of life is a law to which nothing is indifferent. Whatever is not for life is for not-life, — that is, for death. No measure of anything is indifferent to the law of life; though what is conducive to life, may be far from ensuring immortality, and what makes for death need not reach the ultimate effect in a minor degree of its application.

The elements, earth, air, fire and water, are related to life; and this relation is regulated by law. Pass the limit within which either of these elements is conducive to life, and instantly you are in the realm of death. Earth is good. It affords us a theatre of action, productive fields and gardens for the nourishment of life; but do not let yourself be thrown upon the earth in any rash or accidental way, lest you fall under the law of death. Water is an element of life; but disregard the law and measure of its use, and at once it shows itself the minister of death. The floods can exact a heavy tribute of us, can even dismiss our breath to the common air, whose law we must also obey for our lives. And fire? How genial and vital in serviceable relations! But how sharply it warns us of its fatal power, if we so much as touch it in an unlawful way! In its large intention it is good as the beneficent sun. Transgress that intention — it becomes deadly as Moloch or Gehenna. Only, here as elsewhere, the creative intention reaches beyond the incidental suffering and loss incurred by transgression, and contemplates the paramount and permanent good of obedience.

Relatively to conscious well-being at any moment, therefore, we find in our world-elements a limit of good and a possible beginning of evil. Nor do we look to find any product of these elements that shall not exhibit the same distinction. To everything that can nourish or protect life there is the measure of its wholesome use; while too much or too little is a divergence from the perfect law. There is no fruit which is not forbidden fruit, when one transgresses the proper mode and degree of its use; no tree of life whose fruit does not hold out the possible knowledge of good and evil. Life itself is at stake, not only upon our having the things provided for its nourishment, but upon our treating them according to the kindly intention which has adapted them to our service. There may be that which to us is wholly forbidden. Good for something, it is not good for us. It is on this account that life is developed under strict guardianship. Obedience to parents is first a law of existence, that it may be afterwards a commandment with promise.

Beset with dangers, humanity knows good, and remains in happy ignorance of evil by checking the motions of a meddlesome or ambitious curiosity, and cheerfully consenting not to judge for itself as to what is advantageous or otherwise in advance of trustworthy information. The law of truth is laid up in the things that are made. It is a law that can be marked and learned, so that the hidden wisdom shall more and more disclose itself. But our law of learning is, to think divine thoughts under divine guidance, not of ourselves to be as gods, knowing good and evil. It is the beginning of death to pluck and eat presumptuously; for so we overstep the boundary of good in order to acquire a disastrous knowlof good and evil. To know all things in their true relation to the satisfaction of right desires, — this is indeed the wisdom by which the earth is founded, and the understanding by which the heavens are established. This wisdom "is a tree of life to them that lay hold upon her."[1] But this wisdom is laid hold of by docile obedience. It lays hold of the self-confident and disobedient through disappointment and correction. Nature brings home to us the consequences of disregarding her law; and so the spiritual judgment is developed and fortified by motives of action and means of discipline drawn from the distinction of good and evil in what pertains to the physical life.

He by whose wisdom the earth is founded, and by whose understanding the heavens are established, knows the best way of bringing his wisdom and understanding to bear upon finite faculties; what can be done by warning, what can be done by correction. But he to whom anything is forbidden upon pain of death, by necessary

[1] Prov. iii. 18.

implication is both mortal and ignorant. He is a creature liable to prove his mortality by the mistake of a moment; a creature of moral judgment, however, on whom the thought of dying, as a consequence of transgression, is designed to operate in favor of obedience. Instruction avails little without experience. But if the most inexperienced person not only does what is prejudicial to physical life, but what is contrary to spiritual duty at the same time, the physical injury is complicated with the moral defection. It is the worst kind of fall, if it be the least degree of it. The fault of the free agent is judged in the fatality of physical law. Something is lost that cannot be regained. The tree of life, conceived as the largest possibility of well-being in the nature of things is interdicted; and probation falls by a wise arrangement to worse physical conditions for the sake of better spiritual training.

So far, at least, the Scripture drama of the fall is the drama of universal experience. All men have occasion to verify the representation in themselves and in others. All men make their appearance in the world not having sinned after the similitude of Adam's transgression; all are occupied about natural things before coming to the consciousness of spiritual relations; all have, by and by, broken a command in partaking of what they were naturally, and it may be formally, forbidden to touch; all fall into worse conditions, whether as respects what they do or what they suffer, than might have been theirs under the good providence of the Father; all know what it means to hear the voice of God within saying, "Where art thou?" "What is this that thou hast done?" All are warned that there is no return to original innocency, as by the sword of the cherubim flashing upon an awakened moral vision. To all there is the lot of mortality; but to those who have knowingly sinned death is armed with a peculiar sting, so that physical death has a darker significance as the wages of sin, and life is no longer the fulness of life when the law of life has been broken. To all there is hope in that Seed of promise, whose is the victory over temptation; and for all there is conceivably the possibility of a new access to the tree of life, in the spiritual paradise of God.

But is this simple truth of nature really what is contemplated in the Scripture narrative? The question is not insignificant, for the reason, among others, that this truth of nature has been allowed to fall very much into the background, that men might picture to themselves unearthly and preternatural things: a tree of knowledge and a tree of life, — not in an allegorical, but in a literal sense; a personal enemy of great power and cunning speaking in a serpent; and the Creator himself holding sensible intercourse with man, notwithstanding the uniform representation of Scripture to the effect that God cannot be recognized by the senses, but is to be known and worshipped in the spirit. If a Scripture contain truth for all ages, then the cast and coloring of its own date should not contradict the revelation of later times. Accordingly, while the Pentateuch is marked with the early tendency of mankind to interpret the inward voice as proceeding from outward things, and to think of the divine power as so enshrined in sensible objects as to point out some objects for special manifestations of the divine Presence, this tendency is not left to utter itself without restraint, but is carefully guarded, that it may not interfere with a purely spiritual conception of the Supreme Being. No image — no likeness of anything in heaven above or in the earth beneath — could so much as symbolize to the worshipper the infinite One, whose attributes the created universe could but inadequately shadow forth. This transcendent and inscrutable Godhead was guarded by special legislation in the Decalogue itself, besides being vindicated by the rebuke of all gratuitous attempts on the part of prophetic souls to penetrate the secret things of the Eternal. Any but the most simply spiritual rendering of the Mosaic Genesis will have the effect of conforming the story to the type of ordinary mythology. Why not, then, allow ourselves to see in the story at once, if not a history, then at least a conception of something possible in history? Let us therefore inquire what elements of thought, if any, inspiration can be supposed to have given us in the original discipline of law, that are not identical with those given us in common experience. What is there in the ancient way of thinking that is essentially different from the modern wisdom? And what hinders the truth of old time from being recognized and fulfilled in the truth of the latest days? Doubtful constructions of Scripture cannot appropriate the authority of inspiration. Hence it is well that sacred words should mark for us, if they will, a certain measure of distinct reality.

In what words, then, do we find the law of life before the fall summed up? "And the Lord God commanded the man, saying, 'Of every tree of the garden thou mayest freely eat [eating thou shalt eat]: But of the tree of the knowledge of good and evil, thou shalt not eat of it: for in the day that thou eatest thereof thou shalt surely die [dying thou shalt die].'" Here is certainly the common law of physical life raised to the dignity of a moral requirement by being conceived as the command of the

Creator himself for man's preservation and welfare. It says to man, in effect: You are of a mortal nature; your life, such as it is, has its proper nourishment, and you may freely partake of it; but there are limits within which good things are good for you, and beyond which you are liable to know them not simply as good, but as evil also. Be content with knowing things as good; and do not push your indulgence to that forbidden degree where the knowledge of good passes into the knowledge of evil; for that is the beginning and the way of death. A law this, indisputably divine, adapted to a nature that is of the earth earthy, sweet and wholesome, but very liable to be transgressed through the serpent-like movings of sense, appetite, and curiosity; yet to be faithfully administered withal, that man may lay up the treasure of moral teaching even at the cost of physical suffering and decay.

The common law of mortality, recognized in the divine command as in the universal experience, is incompatible with the idea that "the tree of the life," so called, implied any assurance or possibility that there was originally open to man a way of escape from physical death in the simple eating of its fruit. "Lest he reach forth his hand, and take also of the tree of life, and eat and live forever," is, to be sure, in our version, the reason assigned for man's expulsion from the garden. But the expression rendered "forever" has the law of its meaning in a Hebrew word corresponding to the Greek *aion;* and this word, according to Gesenius, does not stand for duration without limits, but for duration whose limit in the future "is to be determined by the nature of the subject." We are thus referred to reality for the meaning of a phrase; and certainly the phrase in question, referred to reality, cannot justify the idea that man's original æon of physical life was "forever," or might have been "forever," in the absolute sense. "Forever," according to the measure of a man, is not forever in the absolute sense; and our English Bible, however it may suggest, certainly refuses to corroborate, such a sense in its customary use of the expression. We have "forever" used again and again where the duration referring to no assignable limits is nevertheless limited in the nature of the enduring thing. Thus, "a servant forever"[1] means simply that the servant is not to be set free during his life-time; and that "the earth abideth forever,"[2] is nothing against the teaching that the earth may at some period be dissolved. A man's "forever" of earthly existence is the unknown but not infinite period of physical life; and if that "forever" is to be lived to the utmost of its natural possibility, it is plain that the relation of life to the elements that support and nourish it should be wholly in accordance with the organic law of being. Disturb this relation, and a man will not live out all the days of his "forever," limited as the number of those days may be. When the life itself is deteriorated, the life-period is prejudiced. The negation of life — that is, death — enters at the point where the law of life is transgressed; and the crisis of death will not fail to sum up all transgressions of life's law.

By the same compulsion of reality we have a natural interpretation of what is said about the trees of the garden. When St. Paul would make use of persons understood to be historical in a representative and mystical way, he takes occasion to say: "Which things are an allegory." But there are things which are marked as

---

[1] Deut. xv. 17. [2] Eccl. i. 4.

allegorical by their very names, of which things it would be superfluous to say either that they are allegorical or that they are not realistic. Thus the distinction between the natural and the metaphorical trees of Eden is boldly indicated, — the realistic detail including all the natural resources of life contemplated, namely, "every tree that is pleasant to the sight and good for food." It would appear, then, that the metaphorical detail could not be reckoned as an addition to the realistic inventory; for, if one has included every object of a given kind, no more objects of that kind are in the account. Hence the metaphorical detail may sum up all the resources of life in their relation to man's duty and destiny as a rational creature, conscious of being under law. As in the paradise of the Apocalypse the tree of life stands for the various resources of life in their unity, — though there are twelve manner of fruits, the yield of every month, with leaves of healing virtue, — so in the earthly paradise "the tree of the life" may stand for all the natural resources of the garden, in their unity of relation to the healthy nourishment of man in the world. Similarly, "the tree of the knowledge of good and evil" may stand for the same resources of life, however various, in one relation — the relation to their possible misuse. Transgress that measure of use within which they bring the knowledge of good, and you pass into that abuse of good which brings the knowledge of evil in addition to the knowledge of good, — good *and* evil.

And this construction does not appear foreign to the Hebrew manner of speaking. For, as we may grant that we should not be grammatically forbidden to regard the two spiritually named trees as real objects, coming in for special mention by means of the conjunction rendered "also," so it may be urged that the same conjunction is used to connect words strictly in apposition, or to connect clauses when the latter expression resumes the former by way of explanation.[1] Thus we might read: "And out of the ground made the Lord God to grow every tree that is pleasant to the sight and good for food; *even* the tree of the life, and the tree of the knowledge of good and evil;" all the trees being taken concretely as one tree in their relation to the support of life, all being taken as one, also, in their common liability to pass into the service of death.

But the truth is always too true, too essential and deeply interfused, to be very dependent upon literary form or verbal criticism. Conceive "the tree of life" and "the tree of the knowledge of good and evil" to be nominal, or conceive them to be real, they are equally allegorical. They are signs of a reality that does not belong to the signs alone. They symbolize potencies that inhere in whatever can properly minister to the nourishment of human life. As man's trial cannot be confined to one act, so neither can it be limited to one object, but is co-extensive with the vast environment and diversified productions that describe the range of his actual experience. If Adam and Eve transgressed a special command about a special object, that typical transaction is blended with common experience, the veil of universal nature is thrown over it, and it becomes the figure of man's natural history from age to age. A particular tree forbidden to man's touch, by an audible voice, upon pain of death, — this could imply no higher authority than that

---

[1] See the examples of this use referred to by Gesenius: 1 Sam. xxviii. 3, "in Ramah, *even* in his own city;" Dan. iv. 13, "a watcher, *even* a holy one;" Is. lvii. 11, "have I not held my peace, *even* of old?"

of the Creator. The gradually maturing conviction of a forbidden use of anything in nature, working upward from instinct through observation and experience, till it reaches the moral sense and becomes a law in conscience, — this can imply no lower authority than that of the Creator. The signal and exemplary thing shows what is inherent in all things. Of all real elements and objects it may be said, "which things are an allegory." Our Lord took the allegories by which he illustrated the realities of the spiritual realm from every realm of nature. He himself is the bread, water, wine, — all the nourishment which the spirit needs. Yet he is the source of knowledge to men, — not of good simply, but of good and evil possibly; since he puts men on trial with respect to the spiritual life, as nature puts men on trial with respect to the physical life. Hence St. Paul's anxiety about the Corinthian Church. For, he says, "I fear lest by any means, as the serpent beguiled Eve through his subtilty, so your minds should be corrupted from the simplicity that is in Christ." The higher the revelation of righteousness, the lower the fall of men, if they are seduced into disobedience. From the revelation of physical life and common mortality in primitive man to the revelation of spiritual life and immortality in the man Christ Jesus, the principle of trial is one. It is inseparable from man's constitutional freedom and responsibility, as related to the divine revelation at every conceivable stage of its progress.

But in the Scripture relating to man's earliest error, we have not only the law which he transgressed, with the penalty annexed, but the judicial construction and application of the same. God's law is the truth. In the Eden administration the truth contemplated is the organic law, — the law which reaches its fulfilment in the subjects of it by the ordinance of universal nature, within no definite limits of time, and with no need of ministerial interference. It is a divine judgment and a divine execution, when the deterioration of life and the deterioration of outward things are made to ensue by a process of inscrutable change, as a testimony against the transgression of law. Man was warned of the natural liability of unsuspecting innocency and inexperience to go astray, was advised of the penalty to ensue upon disregarding the dictates of a wisdom above his own, a wisdom available only on condition of docility and obedience; what, then, in effect, was the judgment and the penalty meted out to the self-excusing, but disenchanted pair? It was that disturbance of natural harmony, that painful exercise of life's functions, by which we mark the change from the unconsciousness of infancy to the struggle of life, — a change which imports nothing less than that the struggle will inevitably end in physical death. Man having misused the elements of life, the elements of life are at odds with man. Outward nature is divided, according as it takes the side of the spirit or of the flesh in human nature. "Cursed above all cattle" is the serpent, as the type of that animal seduction which, in the complex constitution of man, can move stealthily to the violation of spiritual order. Now natural processes are become punitive in a degree. The labor of woman, and the toil of man, the social mastership of the strong, the social subjection of the weak, the common compulsion of natural conditions, all are more stringent and coercive than a free and deliberate dutifulness would require them to be. The products of the ground are distributed into symbols of a beneficent Providence, and symbols of a corrective discipline. The hope of mankind is in offspring, in the progress of the race toward a manhood that can tread temptation under foot; yet this higher humanity will be developed by the suffering and death of the lower, whose destiny is to return to the dust whence it was taken, — the natural process of decay becoming obtrusive, and possibly abrupt, as a consequence of wrong-doing. In fine, the Eden life, the tree of life conceived as bringing the knowledge of good simply, is wholly withdrawn; while the tree of a dualistic experience, the tree of the knowledge of good *and* evil, may be found in any wilderness of the world to which man's character may conduct him.

Forbidden as we are to affect a final judgment as to personal character by outward semblances, would it not become us especially to heed the silence of Scripture as respects man in that mysterious remoteness, when no prophet of his own race has uttered a word for his direction? Is it not significant that a certain construction of the fall, which has been conspicuous by its presence in speculative divinity, is equally conspicuous by its absence in the original story? Here is no "covenant of life," but life itself; no promise of impeccability to ensue upon a temporary or particular obedience; no hint of how much the character of posterity might be involved in a single error of the first parents; no invasion of a mighty spiritual foe, or war of wiles to compass the ruin of an unsuspecting race in its "federal head;" no denunciation of death, except as the law of death is inseparable from the law of life; no infliction of death but in the order of nature, and as a means of saving man from that other death, which takes place, according to St. Augustine, when God abandons the soul, as natural death takes place when the soul leaves the body.[1] We cannot conceive that God is deserting the souls of his offspring, when to moral discipline he adds a provident tenderness for their bodily welfare. What, then, is the natural and Scriptural conception of the fall? Is it a spiritual catastrophe, or a moral espisode? Is it the total negation of man's communion with his Maker, or a practical warning that an undeveloped potency of holy character is not incompatible with a natural liability to sin? Is it the prelude of a human society without hope, or of a divine revelation wherein reproof and correction are the infallible sign both of the children's birthright and of the Father's faithfulness? Does it involve the condemnation and casting away of human nature, or does it mean that man was originally constituted to realize spiritual righteousness, not as punctual attention to specific injunctions, important as such attention must be held to be, but rather as personal integrity and habitual loyalty, depending upon faith in the guidance from above?

[1] Mors igitur animæ fit, cum eam deserit Deus; sicut corporis, cum id deserit anima. — *De Civitate Dei*, lib. xiii. c. 2.

PART THIRD.

THE PRINCIPLE OF JUSTIFICATION.

"Is the law then against the promises of God? God forbid: for if there had been a law given which could make alive, verily righteousness should have been by the law. . . . So that the law hath been our tutor unto Christ, that we might be justified by faith."

GALATIANS iii. 21-24.

"Cum vero Apostolus dicit justificari hominem per fidem, et gratis; ea verba in eo sensu intelligenda sunt, quem perpetuus Ecclesiæ Catholicæ consensus tenuit, et expressit; ut scilicet per fidem ideo justificari dicamur, quia fides est humanæ salutis initium, fundamentum, et radix omnis justificationis, sine quâ impossibile est placere Deo, et ad filiorum ejus consortium pervenire."

COUNCIL OF TRENT: Decretum de Justificatione, caput viii.

"FIDES in Christum est pars et species, quæ continetur sub notione generali fidei."

FRANCISCO TURRETINO: Institutio Theologiæ Elencticæ, vol. i. p. 516.

"CERTAINLY I have always considered that obedience, even to an erring conscience, was the way to gain light, and that it mattered not where a man began, so that he began on what came to hand and in faith; and that anything might become a divine method of truth; that to the pure all things are pure, and have a self-correcting virtue and a power of germinating."

JOHN HENRY NEWMAN: Apologia pro Vitâ Suâ, p. 206.

PART THIRD.

THE PRINCIPLE OF JUSTIFICATION.

CHAPTER I.

OF FAITH AS RELATED TO MAN'S DEPENDENCE AND PROGRESS.

WHAT we are taught in Scripture of man's first disobedience, as a spiritual fact in the order of nature, may be included within two negative statements: namely, first, man's original righteousness did not preclude his original sin; and, secondly, man's original sin did not preclude a future progress in righteousness.

Between these two negative terms we conceive the movement of living and progressive humanity, — whatever may have been the nature of the primitive error.

Exactly at this point there opens upon us the question of man's possible justification: what palliations of his fault; what law of righteousness applicable to him, things being as they are; what hope in the discipline of divine judgments; what redeeming quality in his own being? The act of disobedience cannot be justified. Can the man from whom that act came be made just, and be recognized as righteous, — not according to some legal fiction, but because he is really acceptable to God, approved of men, and not without testimony to his inward harmony with the universe in the peace of his own spirit?

There is an error, as we have already seen, which the fall logically disposes of, and puts aside forever. Man is not to be as God in knowing good and evil. He is to know good and evil relatively, not absolutely. The absolute law of his perfection is in his Creator, not in himself. He cannot act independently. Therefore it is for him to be loyally dependent, to be persuaded of the care and guidance of his Maker, to be persuaded of the divine wisdom and authority ruling in his life, in order that this persuasion, or faith, may make him attentive and obedient to the communications of truth, and be evermore the vital principle of right conduct.

But faith is a spiritual energy, that comes by listening to truth, and grows with experience of life. Faith is imparted to the human spirit from above, and comes with the spiritual revelation of God, and with the spiritual growth of man. The physical constitution may enclose the spiritual germ, it cannot at first exhibit the full strength of spiritual character. The principle of righteousness grows, or ought to grow, with the practical demands of righteousness. "Touch not, taste not," may be a divine command, a very salutary physical regulation, to be observed by the law of faith disposing to all right observance; but faith would be the spiritual element of righteousness in the case, and without faith it would be impossible to please the Lawgiver, though the command were outwardly obeyed. But to fail in the specific act of faith is not of necessity to lose faith; while "touch not, taste not, handle not," is possibly a very partial expression even of outward requirement. Taking man for what he is, a creature to be developed according to his organic law, we can trust the divine Father to bring him up to righteousness in his own way and time; and if so, we cannot believe that man becomes wholly alien to righteousness through the first unfaithful act.

For, grant what we may as to possible deterioration or improvement of nature, we know that either the one or the other must go on according to the law of existence. No instant's action can take place or be judged alone. It belongs to a series. Only in the judgment of all that went before and all that shall come after in the individual life, can the instant's action have the record of its true character. In the larger sphere of humanity as a whole, the same continuity and solidarity of development is observable through all the conflicts of history. The unripened fruit is not satisfying to the taste. But it is changing both in quantity and quality by the law of its creation; and, if the fruit be good at last, there was no point in its progress when it was not good. So spiritual and moral manhood is ever passing through a transformation; while the vital flavor of any period in personal or collective human existence carries with it the divine judgment in the creative law, which determines its relation to both the qualities that shall be revealed and the qualities that shall disappear. The Creator says: This is not your rest, as it is not your perfection. What has not reached its consummation has not reached the full demonstration of what it is.

It is thus we conclude the æon or life-time to be essential to the life-quality; exactly as the revelation of truth, natural or supernatural, by which experience is conditioned and character ripened, is essential to it. The details of outward conduct are by no means unimportant. Requirements and regulations that concern outward conduct have their proper season and necessary use. But they do not give life. Justification is of life; and life is of faith, — the spiritual source and energy of real virtue, the principle of genuine obedience to the law of truth.

Hence, faith appropriates, as the ground of assurance in action and of hope as to the results of action, not only the powers of the universe, but the persistency and duration of those powers. A man's faith associates him not merely with the known, but with the unknown; and so he prosecutes the trial of existence in a docile way, loyal not only to all that is known, but to all that is.

The personal life is a profound mystery. One cannot know the difference between himself in this instant and himself in the next instant. We are in the process of creation. The mysterious differential element of quantity and quality does not define and measure itself in consciousness. Suppose a whole foregoing life to be summed up in a single practical expression; the vital process does not pause. Other critical actions and other judgments are to come. And the judgments, so far as they are divine, will have in evidence not only the previous trial, motive, and stress of circumstances, under which an action came to birth, but also the actor's reaction with regard to it. If the act be blameworthy, does it signify anything that the doer of the act looks back upon it with remorse and self-accusation? If the offence be condemned, and the punitive woe overtake the offender, is it in his favor that he by and by recognizes and honors the unfolding law of Goodness under which he suffers? Moral discrimination may be slow, through the infirmity of our nature; and may for that reason be quickened by terrifying examples of things permitted to take place only that they may be the more effectually and permanently disallowed. But to take the side of demonstrated evil is a self-destructive experiment, and man arrives at mature and suicidal wickedness, if at all, only through long and stern conflict with benevolent admonition and just authority. In history as we know it, this obdurate and malignant quality of disobedience is never, and in reason never can be, the sudden catastrophe of an unschooled nature. As little, on the other hand, can a spiritual and final justification be realized on the ground of obedience in a single particular of lawful requirement, — or in all particulars of lawful requirement during a period of discipline shorter than the actual maturing of personal character into its ultimate moral relation with the highest Authority may require.

The law of faith cannot contemplate duty as capable of being adequately expressed by literal requirements, or duly guarded by literal prohibitions. When all the things that must be done, and all the things that must not be done, have been officially defined and enacted, this law is only a shadow of life. Life itself is the reality and revelation of law. The outward economy and discipline of government, in state or church, makes use of signs and sacraments wisely accommodated to the actions and relations of time, because these actions and relations furnish both the exercise and assurance of eternal life. All temporary judgment refers to the tribunal of last appeal. We may look upon actions as well-intentioned, or otherwise. We may insist that some things were worse done than we were entitled to demand, that other things were better done than anybody was entitled to expect; though, whether we blame, justify, or applaud, we are sure that it is not in us to judge perfectly, either the actor or the act. Thus the faith which receives law from the Creator in the revelations of life is one with the faith which judges nothing before the time. Forbidden to set ourselves up as judges of our fellow-men, we are equally incompetent to judge ourselves. St. Paul, referring to faithfulness in his stewardship, not only counts it a small thing that he should be brought to any day or to any decision of men, but also declines to assume his justification on the ground that he is not conscious of wrong-doing. He is not his own final judge, but must await with others the coming Lord and Master of life; at whose appearing the mature manifestation of personal character shall bring to each man his proper sentence from God.[1]

This is in accord with all the teaching about justification in human experience. It is not only of faith as regards the reign of God, to whom all homage and obedience are due; it is also of faith, as distinguished from demonstration, in respect to the actions and efforts in which the signs of obedience and homage are made. The rule of what to do or what not to do outwardly cannot be a perfect test of man's inward life. The law that undertakes to regulate conduct enters because of transgression, and brings with it the knowledge of sin, both as a matter of positive experience and of recognized human liability. But the justification of life passes by the evidence of formal obedience or formal transgression, in order to reach its true basis in the loyal mind and will, — faith working by love. Faith appeals in humility and penitence from all finite judgments to the All-judging; faith accepts presently and by anticipation all divine testimonies, however adverse to details of personal conduct, and so affirms and maintains the spirit, though not the absolute expression, of perfect obedience. Hence, he is the just man who confides himself to God as the universal Justice; not he who only says, "I have not knowingly broken the divine commands." To avoid the forbidden thing

---

[1] 1 Cor. iv. 3-5.

shall make for your welfare, possibly save you from sudden or premature death. To believe in God shall make for your righteousness, though it be the righteousness which condemns your past doings and acquiesces in death as their just due. The man called perfect and upright, fearing God and eschewing evil, must not flatter himself that he is free from sin. The malefactor confessing his crimes and enduring their punishment must not despair of justification. For justification under the reign of God goes beyond the present range of human relations and actions, is administered by the Judge of all, and is available to each one through the faith in God which is the denial of self. In fine, the justification of man implies on the part of God not only the acts of pardon and grace by which human confidence is awakened and sustained, but also the eternal administration of law in the spiritual creation from which all such acts proceed; while, as regards man, the process of his renewal in righteousness contemplates all the elements of life, — the natural conditions of being, the æon of development, the Almighty and Eternal as Source of nature and Object of faith. He alone who causes his mind and will to be faintly apprehended in a growing human consciousness, who knows all his works, whose ordinance it is that the communication of Heaven's gift must condescend to earth's necessity, and the pursuit of glory, honor, and immortality, be complicated with the struggle for physical life, — He alone can conduct life to its final harmony and complete justification.

The general history of man's spiritual development will, of course, be a history of faith, in the different phases of its manifestation. Faith, taking hold of the parts of the Creator's ways, brings to conception and action the rational creature's calling. Faith is the taproot of our whole spiritual growth. If faith decays, manhood decays. If faith grows, manhood grows. Faith sees no perfection in past efforts, but accuses or excuses them as a medley of evil and good. Faith does not place personal perfection in the order of nature, but presses toward the mark for the prize of a high calling made known in the revelation of God. God, as conceived by faith, is the germ of truth springing up out of the earth. God, as the Word of revelation, is the Sun of Righteousness looking down from heaven. Men must feel after God in the things that are made, if haply they may find him. But God is not far from every one of us, since in him we live and move and have our being. The blind groping of the past is ignorance, unbelief, sin, death. The docile pressing on toward the future is knowledge, faith, righteousness, life. Sensuous forms of worship have to be condemned as idolatries at length, that the image of the invisible God may be revealed in the human spirit. The righteousness of faith is loyalty to the revelation of truth.

Of course, faith is not an affair of formal logic, any more than of formal ethics. Faith has its conflicts of argument, and often the argument is pressed with a heat akin to the vital character of the question in debate. But faith combines the opposing forces of thought in a line of movement, which is the ruling persuasion of life. The limits of finite intelligence cannot defeat the evidence of an infinite Spirit. Would all the manifestations of energy through boundless space and absolute duration be only equal to the demonstration of the infinite Power? How, then, shall Power, which is forever proving itself, be said ever to have been proved? But the argument which excludes the quantitative demonstration is essential to the qualitative demonstration; and between the two faith finds the idea of Divinity. So in all the feeling after God, as indicated in objects and processes wherein men are persuaded that haply they have found him, there are contrarieties of thought, thesis and antithesis; while the reconciliation of contrarieties, the synthesis of different movements, marks the progress of revelation.

What is, in short, the natural history of religion among men? "I have found my God," says the credulous fetich-worshipper. "No," says the advanced thinker, "you are worshipping what is infinitely less divine than yourself. You are the image of your Maker." But by the law of nature each is moving in the way of divine revelation; for is there not a sign of the Creator in the rudest lump of matter, in order that the Creator may be unfailingly signified in the lowest order of mind? There is also the idol of the tribe, and nations find their own gods; but the better inspiration grasps the unity of things, and declares that God is one. Yet is there not a teaching and symbol of God in the parts of his ways, in order that man may at length adore the undivided Power he cannot comprehend?

If, then, God be one, where is he? In what heaven does he reside? On what mountain does he hold his earthly court? "Here!" exclaims one. "There!" points out another. But revelation satisfies both in denying both. The reign of God does not disclose itself to geographical research, or even to celestial observation, but to the spirit in man: it is within, and it is everywhere. What is the character of God's reign? "Good!" chants one part, "He has loaded us with benefits."

"Evil," wails another part, "He has overwhelmed us with distresses." But both notes are harmonized in the revelation of righteousness as the aim of all divine judgments. Thus, while knowledge is increasing in opposite directions of thought, faith is the abiding loyalty to universal Truth, the growing persuasion of absolute Goodness. Yet, notwithstanding the continuous proofs of divine guidance in history, of eternal Power and Godhead in things made, the fullest light of revealed truth, like the rising sun, shows ever a retreating world in such shadow and darkness, that it is described as relatively "without God and without hope." For God is light, and in Him is no darkness at all.

No age is without its own feeling after God. No age is without its own trial of faith. As in the world of matter, so in the spiritual world, not only does day utter speech unto day, but night unto night showeth knowledge. There are those who sleep in the day-time for the purpose of consulting the stars. There are those who shut their eyes upon the light of theological systems that they may make investigations in the twilight of nature. Especially, when the professed representatives of spiritual reality become conventional, theatrical, dogmatic, then the devotees of physical science have their innings in the struggle for truth, and appear fresh, earnest, and aggressive. They may even insist that speculation and faith have no business outside the limits of induction, and that the organ of mental vision, like the bodily eye, has no vocation to inspect itself. The latest philosophy, however materialistic, does not, indeed, worship rude images, nor dote on refined ritualism, nor stand in awe of official parade. What Bacon calls idols,— "idols of the cave, of the tribe, of the palace, of the theatre,"—

scientific philosophy looks down upon. It is feeling after the genuine force, the ruling law of the world-movement, in a word, God. What it shall find, however, it will call by a name of its own. One philosophic seer finds that the setting forth of world-phenomena, as summed up in the experience of life, implies a persistent energy, to be called "Will." But it is will of such wily malignity that all attractions of life are merely the ruse by which the living are lured to suffering and death. The "Will" of Schopenhauer is an idol of hideous features, to be superseded in less time than it took to set it up. It may be likened to King Stork. Its antithesis in the same line of thought is King Log, "the Unconscious" by name. The order of succession is an improvement upon the fable of the frogs. The features of the new idol can be seen in different lights, somewhat in accordance with the will of the observer. One does not quite despair by reason of "the Unconscious." But cannot criticism combine the arrangements of nature that indicate thought, and the vital energy of nature that affirms will, in a higher conception that shall declare a moral purpose? Yes. There is "the not ourselves that makes for righteousness." If this is not the true Divinity, it is something well found in the search for him. Indeed, the ablest and best-instructed criticism coming from the party of reputed opposition is destined to quicken the sense of reality in the party of a ruling faith, by the contribution it makes to the knowledge of the things that are made, and thus to the conception of the invisible Maker. On the other hand, a strong flavor of reality must rule in any system of religious doctrine, or else the altars of worship will seem to have been built to "the unknown" and "the unknowable." Still, the known is of a piece with the unknown. The Revealed is also the Incommunicable. Whom men ignorantly worship, he is evermore to be declared.

But are there proofs of man's spiritual progress? Is there hope of his reaching the goal? What most deeply concerns our faith is the fact that the swing of human nature, this way and that way, in the struggle of thought and action, is not for its own sake. It is for the sake of the progress of humanity. It belongs to an onward movement, and develops in process of time the antithesis, not of this momentary tendency. and that, but of the natural man and the spiritual man, the first man and the final man, the ages of darkness and the ages of light, times of ignorance and times of consummation. It is a mark of the Scriptures in their unity that they regard and interpret history with equal fidelity to the struggle of the hour and the consummation of the age. They place the hope of man's justification and acceptance with his Maker, not in outward acts, but in the living spirit; not in what a man is doing or going to do, but in what he is becoming or going on to be. It is this which constitutes them the classic and canon of man's moral development. The fifteenth chapter of First Corinthians depicts the spiritual glory of the second Adam on the dark background of mortal manhood as represented by Adam the first. It is in the relation of these two men that history through all ages is summed up in the Scriptures. If it had been distinctly revealed that the first-man had personally reappeared on earth to be justified and glorified as the spiritually first-begotten of God, and Saviour of his race, it would have afforded no clearer assurance than we possess of the creative intention. For Christ's gospel is the gospel that was given to Adam as well as to Abraham, — the gospel of promised blessing in the development of a promised Seed. As the elect man, the divine man, the First-begotten of the Father, is connected by natural descent with man as originally created by God; so the man of the earliest creation and making of the race is bound by the law of faith to that course of spiritual development in his offspring which brought the spiritual man into the world to enthrone him as Head of the human brotherhood. The drama of justification opens with the drama of transgression. In the experience of the race, as of the individual, the outward man is perishing that the inward man may be renewed day by day.

Having studied somewhat carefully the Scripture teaching as to man's natural insufficiency, as indicated in his first disobedience, together with the discipline of law for his reproof and correction, we have now, at the risk of some repetition, to study the same testimony in its bearing upon the inward law and discipline of faith for man's ultimate righteousness. For the first man made, no more than the last man born, can know what he is in himself, except by knowing what he is in relation to the history of his race.

CHAPTER II.

AGAINST TRANSCENDENTAL NOTIONS OF PRIMITIVE RESPONSIBILITY.

LET me remind my reader again, by way of apology for what may seem a needless discussion, that we are concerned with human nature as exhibited in Scripture; not with the same as depicted by speculatists or as formulated in dogma. We want to understand what the story of the primitive pair as given in Genesis would naturally teach us, not only as to the real measure of their fault, but as to the hope of their recovery to rectitude and favor. If their error required that they should be kept in hand by a tutor, by the constraints and corrections of law, was there an appeal at the same time addressed to their faith, looking to the inward revelation of paternal goodness in a spiritual sonship, which should honor the legal schooling by evincing its serviceableness to the eternal life?

In the training of immature natures a systematic exaggeration of childish errors and faults is found to make against the development of a perfect character. The perfecting of mankind, as involving a divine governance of physical law and spiritual inspiration, would necessarily demand that candor of practical procedure on the part of the Creator which would naturally foster a sense of justice, and fortify the assurance of receiving just treatment on the part of the moral creature. On the other hand, the finite apprehension of illimitable authority and immeasurable power is naturally timid; the reaction of wrong-doing often quickens this moral timidity into a servile prostration, which needs to be patiently and condescendingly corrected; while systematic theologians, setting up for augurs and prophets of human nature in its relations with Divinity, have been prone to take the auspices from their fears or ambitions rather than their faith, and even to make a virtue of regarding universal humanity as justly doomed to endless perdition by its first offence — for the greater glory of God in the redemption of the elect.

Hence the inestimable value of our right of appeal. We can appeal from ourselves to our Maker; from inferential and overwrought opinions and forebodings, whether of disinterested or designing judges, to the simple conceptions and hopeful predictions which are commended to us as bearing the marks of divine teaching and primitive procedure. We may interrogate the Scripture record with a pointedness and particularity comporting with the importance of the facts recorded, and so possibly learn something of how we are defended by our Advocate in the heavenly court.

We seek a response from a recognized oracle of truth, on a question fundamental, long disputed, and still in debate. Did man fall "from the estate wherein he was created" by the first disobedience; or, was "the estate wherein he was created" one involving the natural liability to mistakes and sins, and placing the hope of coming to spiritual wisdom and goodness in the lessons of experience and the development of life? More particularly, was the first disobedience a catastrophe of the human race, — an act of so fatal an importance as to change radically the whole plan for the discipline of mankind, — or was it an immature act, the mark of undeveloped character under conditions of necessary trial, with simply that bearing upon human destiny, for evil or good, which is involved in the organic law of life and liberty asserted in every moral act? Was the original sin of a character unique and transcendent, or was it personal, typical, the constitutional liability of the last earth-born man as of the first, and of the first in the same sense as of any other?

Our inquiry is not one of personal curiosity, but one which has appealed to the Source of light in the devout worship and anxious sacrifices of unnumbered generations. If, then, the oracle is reticent or ambiguous, it is not for us to break through its reserve or to make its responses more clear. But if the oracle be charged with a judicial sentence of transcendent terror, then unmistakable explicitness in the terms of the sentence becomes an indispensable element of justice. If the Scripture record lends itself reluctantly to an extreme construction, — especially if such a construction can be referred to a change in mental parallax, or in the prevailing medium of thought, — we cannot throw the burden of later philosophies and figures of speech upon first statements; nor can we support unnatural conceptions by an appeal to supernatural authority. If there be that in the revelation of Jesus Christ of which Tertullian could say: "It is credible, because it is foolish; it is certain, because it is impossible," we are to remember that not everything foolish is credible, and the impossible is not commonly the true.

As a matter of fact, however, our primitive Scripture

meets us upon the ground of common sense and common faith. Read the third chapter of Genesis for the sake of what is plainly said, though not without a parable. The sacred writer speaks to us as the prophet of God only by being "Nature's priest," rendering the realities of life in the name of the Author of life. The nature shown us is that nature of which we are a part; the experience represented is the experience in which we all share, — the struggle of life and the certainty of death, the kindly fruits and the stinging thorns, the discipline of sorrow, the rewards of effort, the encouragement of hope. The harmony conceived as belonging to the constitution of things has given place to the disciplinary working of undeveloped powers, and the heaven that lies about infancy has faded into the light of common day. The trial which has evinced the capacity to receive instruction has proved, also, the proneness to error which needs instruction. Especially the law given for the control of piquant and dangerous physical solicitation, — the calm, remote, authoritative command, exacting faith, watchfulness, loyalty, — has not found due reverence. As respects the qualities born not of the will of the flesh nor of the will of man, but of God, man has proved himself in the spiritual nonage of flesh and blood, unprepared to exemplify the reign of God as overruling sensual and social instincts. His rank in the order of nature corresponds with his place in the order of time; he is the first, the natural, the earthly man, falling into the first, natural, earthly error; the type of a universal spiritual nonage.

What is the act recorded which determines this conception of original humanity? Here it is: "And when the woman saw that the tree was good for food, and that it was pleasant to the eyes, and a tree to be desired to make one wise, she took of the fruit thereof and did eat; and gave also unto her husband with her, and he did eat. And the eyes of them both were opened, and they knew that they were naked: and they sewed fig-leaves together, and made themselves aprons."[1]

Considered in itself, and as literally taking place, this act has no peculiar mystery or conclusiveness. It is exactly what the sensual appetite is always prompting the children of nature to do, before they are disciplined to higher considerations. As a parable, its application is as broad as the truth that natural temptation leading to moral disobedience opens the eyes to consequences which disclose themselves according to an unknown law, — consequences totally distinct from the gratification sought, whether the gratification sought be conceived as sensual or intellectual.

But a moral act cannot be so trivial in itself as not to be magnificent in its relations. Each moral act takes its place in an organic series, and thus marks a point of view from which the mind may look over æonian reaches of life before and after. Ages of the divine providence presiding over human destiny in favor of reasonable and loyal living, are continually imparting their gracious movement to the mind of well-instructed childhood in its earliest moral actions. The physical law which makes something seem desirable, but does not prescribe the season and measure in which it may be safely enjoyed, is ever under the premonitions and reproofs of benevolent wisdom, seeking to adjust ignorance and inexperience to the laws of life, and appealing to faith and obedience against danger and death. To see tempting

[1] Gen. iii. 6, 7.

fruit and be forbidden to touch it is the characteristic trial of well-protected childhood. That the child may not know evil, nor incur death, is the characteristic motive of parental restraints. "Lest ye die," "that thy days may be long," — here is the appeal for docility and subjection; but to suffer for disobedience, not to live out all one's days, and finally to die, yet withal to say, "Good is the word of the Lord," — this is a triumph of faith and a mark of righteousness.

There is laid down for us, in our mental and moral constitution, a law of correlative proportions, of maxima and minima, to regulate our judgments. For example, the lowest degree of knowledge and experience in any human being goes with the highest degree of necessary dependence upon outward support and control. Again, the highest degree of necessary dependence upon outward support and control is the lowest degree of moral responsibility. Again, the lowest degree of moral responsibility, grounded upon knowledge and experience, implies the highest degree of natural liability that grave physical evils may ensue upon immature acts of disobedience. The same law is applicable to two parties in their relations with each other: the greatest weakness of the child not only implies the greatest dependence upon its guardians, but tolerates the least neglect or exaction on their part; while the smallest spiritual capacity in the erring creature furnishes the largest excuse for his errors in the estimation of his judge. In short, as is the actor, so is the act in its moral relations; while in the order of physical consequences judgment is meted out to acts by physical law, with no definite adjustment to their moral quality.

What man was in his first estate, we know in part

from the law on which his bodily life was conditioned, and under which it passed away. The charter of a life to be nourished on the products of the earth is not without its limiting clause. Things allowed to be eaten imply things forbidden to be eaten; and the Hebrew idiom, "to eat thou shalt eat," or "eating thou shalt eat," has no more distinct reference to the common necessity of life than "to die thou shalt die," or "dying thou shalt die," has to the sure though possibly slow progress of death as a consequence of eating forbidden things. No sharp note of martial law or military execution here, but only the premonition of dying in the process of natural causation.

Further, we know in part what man was in the beginning from the fact that, while the preservation of his physical life demanded care first in the order of time, it was apparent at no very distant day that his chief danger was moral; that his chief woe was not natural death, but the violation of spiritual loyalty; and that the reactions of a mortal destiny were fitted to quicken attention to admonitions ministered from above, through reason and conscience, for the right conduct of life. Accordingly the command which man first disobeyed made its appeal expressly to the fear of physical harm, not to the dread of moral apostasy, — the finest indication of how spiritual training waits upon and appropriates the discipline of outward things.

As man's justification cannot prosper by covering his original infirmity or transgression, so neither can it prosper by any exaggeration of either. It is precisely at the point where physical law touches moral discipline in the history of the first transgression that our knowledge utterly fails; and at this point, also, men have always summoned poetry and speculation to their aid. The command laid upon our first parents as a simple epitome of physical law, a parable of life and death as pertaining to the bodily organization, we can well understand. The resources of life had so thoroughly developed their relation to the experience of death before the book of Genesis was written, that the law of nature, under which man must originally have received life from the Creator, could be set forth, certainly not with scientific exactness, but in a manner true to common sense and religious imagination. What we need to know, however, in order to appreciate, after the manner even of our poor judgments, the moral quality of "eating the forbidden fruit," is what only the Omniscient can know, namely, What did the first pair know? What sense had they of natural law and spiritual obligation? What were their thoughts of their Creator? What light had they upon their duty and destiny as keeping the first gateway through which their descendants would enter into life? When we weigh such questions as these, and think how slenderly we are furnished for judging even ourselves, is it strange if, on the one hand, we run into wild and extravagant guesses; or, on the other hand, conclude at length that our most impressive lesson is derived from the silence of our best Teacher?

Was Adam formed out of the dust of the ground and inspired with the breath of life to be presently taught that not only his own loyalty, but the spiritual life of all his posterity, was at stake on his obedience in one particular of duty? Was his religious sense awakened, and was he made to own his allegiance as a freely consenting party to the sovereign determination which placed him under such a responsibility? Was he taught, with more than the Sinaitic majesty and terror, that dying was not merely returning to the ground whence he was taken, but a spiritual experience of rebellion and coercion, relentless, persistent, unending? No such elements are found in the Scripture testimony. The sacred writer does not seem to "palter with us in a double sense" about dying; nor does he bring life and immortality to light for the purpose of extending the significance and perpetuating the reign of death.

But such elements have entered into structures of thought that men have built on the Scripture foundation ; and, there are theories of human nature that would in justice require such a character of divine teaching and procedure: notably the Augustinian dualism, which has so deeply colored religious thinking in later times, even to our day. The consequence is that our minds cannot take the story of Adam and Eve in its simplicity and sincerity, without asking if the vital tissue of fact can by possibility be made to assimilate the ordinary mystical interpretation of its poetic symbols. That man was made in the image of God, the symbolical serpent, the symbolical trees, the cherubim and the flaming sword, — all these elements combine in a significant penumbra to the verifiable elements of reality, on the simple condition of not being so interpreted as to destroy the reality. On the other hand, the constitution and calling of mankind, as known in consciousness and experience, cannot reasonably be contradicted by the figures of speech in which any part of human history is set forth.

What, then, had the Creator for the first human pair to do? For what calling in life were they well constituted and very good? To dress the garden or to till the ground, to know and to produce the means of life and to guard against life's dangers, to become the parents of children to be educated, as they themselves were to be educated, under the spiritual guardianship of their Creator: here is a calling for which man was originally gifted, for which he has always been gifted in some degree. For "the gifts and calling of God are without repentance."[1] Also, to learn what is genuine law and to act accordingly, to receive with joy the tokens of good, to respond with a dutiful faith to conscientious convictions of the divine teaching, though the teaching should point out errors and reprove sins: here is a calling of man as constituted for spiritual development under the influences of the creative Spirit. There has been no repentance of this calling. It survives, having reached its fulness in the man Christ Jesus.

But this calling contemplates "knowledge, righteousness, and holiness" as the fruit of experience and the attainment of life, — not as the original endowment of nature. What of that hypothetical calling which construes "knowledge, righteousness, and holiness" as the possession of undeveloped manhood, the spiritual image of God to be lost before the actual moral development of the race, as we know it, was to begin? Was Adam the first called to exhibit the sinlessness, the virtue, the victorious efficiency, of the last Adam, — to save his own soul and the souls of his unborn generations, — by not eating the forbidden fruit? Then it was a calling for which the first man was ill fitted, as was shown by his failure; a calling to be speedily repented of; a calling in which the magnificent imbecility of the first man is conceived as atoned for at the immeasurable cost of the final man,

[1] Rom. xi. 29.

while the infinite disaster is conceived as to be repaired only in part.

But no. By the law of being, one's calling is in one's gifts. The calling for which a man has no adequate gifts is the calling wherewith he is *not* called. Either Adam could have had no such calling as has been supposed, or his gifts must have comported with the calling. But if the calling was repented of and taken away, then the gifts must logically have been first repented of and taken away: in other words, Adam of the mystical image of God, "in knowledge, righteousness, and holiness," is undone before his eating of the forbidden fruit, or his eating would have been morally impossible.

Yet to make and straight unmake is as impossible with God as "to say and straight unsay." Therefore Adam was not undone. His gifts and calling remained, and he transmitted the same to his children.

But if we can believe that a divine economy transcending our knowledge might announce the seemingly impossible to be true; yet, in the sphere of our natural and necessary knowledge, the demonstrably untrue becomes, in its turn, impossible as an element of divine teaching. The Author of nature cannot contradict the truth of nature. Therefore the Scripture testimony about the first man and his calling in the world must be interpreted with due regard to the well-known elements and tendencies of human nature considered by themselves.

Assume the mystical calling, — the calling that transcends our knowledge and experience. Suppose an intellectual and moral endowment of the first man equal to a unique and incomprehensible responsibility. Fortified with " knowledge, righteousness, and holiness," he is required to do homage for himself and his posterity in one small matter of formal obedience, that concerns his physical welfare. Head of his race, his obedience is not merely in form, but much more in the homage and fealty he is asked to signify and seal. If he rebels, he gains no earthly advantage, but the reverse; while faith, hope, and love, the very elements of spiritual life, are definitively abjured. Will he, or will he not, be the loyal vassal of God for the physical and moral dominion of the world? Ask such a question about the Christ, the man of prophetic promise, the real image of the invisible Divinity; and let his temptation answer it. What is to be thought of millions of human beings who do not call themselves Christians, and yet habitually resist greater outward seductions, with no very exalted spiritual motives, and without feeling themselves in a critical position? Approximate the primitive man to the character of the spiritual man even in a moderate degree, — lift him to the range of ordinary Christian virtue, — and the story of the fall becomes at once incredible. It exhibits the mythical reason and the mythical unreason: it becomes a myth. The man of high intelligence and holy character, the spiritual image of God not in germ but in mature consciousness, does not fall into trivial acts of insubordination against infinite motives of duty and prudence.

Or, if it be conceived as within the possibility of personal determination that the creature of "knowledge, righteousness, and holiness" should do some distinctly forbidden thing with the deliberate and intelligent purpose of initiating a struggle with the law of the universe for his own independence; in other words, if a rebel is conceived as having wholly denied his original character and done the morally impossible thing, — he "falls like Lucifer, never to hope again." As ignorance and unconsciousness account for incidental errors, so they are incompatible with desperate transgressions. That sin which has no palliation of ignorance or unconsciousness is the sin which has no sequel of repentance and forgiveness. The sin which carries in it the potency of moral reprobation to a race is the sin which admits no benediction of fruitfulness, no commission to people and organize a world, no seed of promise, no hope of redemption. "For it is impossible for those who were once enlightened, and have tasted of the heavenly gift, and were made partakers of the Holy Ghost, and have tasted the good word of God, and the powers of the world to come, if they shall fall away, to renew them again unto repentance."[1] But though he thus wrote, the author of the Epistle to the Hebrews entertained, he assures us, a very different persuasion as to their character and prospects; and we are entitled to entertain a very different persuasion as to mankind, especially mankind in its earliest experience.

[1] Heb. vi. 4, 5, 6.

CHAPTER III.

ORIGINAL MAN AND HISTORIC MAN.

WHEN we have tried in vain to accept a transcendental hypothesis as accounting for a given order of facts in the Bible, we come back to nature, and are content to inquire how far a simple nucleus of well-known reality will harmonize the facts in question, and sustain the scriptural ideals of life and history.

To the author of Genesis, God only is great. All being, law, and discipline are from him. Man, though constituted to be chief of the visible works of God, is a very humble image of his Maker. No occasion is found to exalt him before his disobedience or to disparage him afterwards. He is introduced to us in terms of touching simplicity and candor. " A living soul," he is not sharply distinguished to himself from other creatures who also have "a soul of life," till by observation and comparison his pre-eminence is made to appear. Having known and named the lower species, he becomes aware that help and companionship suited to him must be found in his own species. Still, the infancy of all creatures is conceived as the absence of those antagonistic dispositions that are developed in the struggle of life; for to all, the vegetable products of the earth are given for food.[1] And when, on the presentation of Eve, Adam was awakened

[1] Gen. i. 29, 30.

to apprehend the physical nature, that approximated him to other animals, as the enshrinement of a social and spiritual capacity in which he was unique, "naked and not ashamed"[1] comes in as the mark of undeveloped nature not less than of undeveloped art.

Did, then, the clear knowledge of God antedate the acquaintance with God's creatures? This is impossible by the testimony; for not only is the distinction between man and beast faint, even after study and comparison, — the distinction between the serpent's temptation and the command of the Lord God is fainter still; and, what indicates the deepest ignorance, it is the suggestion of the beast which is preferred. At least, on the part of the woman the decision was in favor of the serpent; on the part of the man, it was in favor of the woman; and on the part of both, it was in favor of the fruit, — against the authority of God. As between the natural and the spiritual in human development, which is first and which afterwards, in our day? What was the commandment given? Did it regulate worship, or define social and civil obligations? Did it touch the standard of the Decalogue? No. The commandment did not unavailingly anticipate the progress of mankind. It was intended to aid that progress, touching the moral sensibility in due time.

We have brought before us in Eden, not the man of "knowledge, righteousness, and holiness," but the human creature enfolding the germ of spiritual life: native instincts and appetites to be directed from above, and a mind for prophetic and practical teaching, that appeals to faith. Exactly the being to fall a victim for a time to tempting fruit and subtle self-suggestion. Just the man, moreover, to hear by and by the reproving voice of

---

[1] Gen. ii. 18-25.

God, to be corrected, to learn faith, hope, duty. Such a man can fulfil a natural calling, and come at length to his spiritual heritage in accordance with his personal improvement of the Father's gifts.

And what was the sequel of his sin? The great practical problem of justification at once burdened his awakened conscience. How to be righteous, how not to disobey God, the inquiry of all ages, to which all revelation is addressed, suddenly emerged in its mysterious infinitude, as it emerges sooner or later in every personal experience.

But the first sign of something wrong is a changed action of man's mind. Having tried the experiment of judging for himself, he has become naturally sensitive and fearful at finding how poorly he is fitted to take his welfare into his own keeping. And since he has disobeyed the voice that was seeking to guide him, he is afraid of that voice, as well as afraid of himself. He has been rash, broken faith, and awakened a conscientious self-reproach. Still, what is done cannot be undone. And what is done? Something certainly quite different from the childish anticipation of the doers, — something to be justly appreciated only under the divine teaching. Hence God is represented as putting the question, in pursuance of his teaching. These children must learn how fatal is that self-assertion in which a man affects to be as a god; and that real godlikeness can only come with the spirit of dutiful submission, whose language is: "I am a stranger in the earth; hide not thy commandments from me." For already God had not hidden his commandment, but man had failed to keep it. Man had shown the tottering step that deviates to the right hand and the left from the straight line of progress, and still moves on. Man stumbled and fell. But was it that man should fall forever; or, rather, through the first fall did there not come to the first pair and to their children a discipline of righteousness and redemption?

Mark the sudden appearance and painful prominence of the moral man as distinguished from the physical man, after the fall. It is as if the moral man had been prematurely brought into the world by his own act; but having been once born to responsibility by the rash assumption of liberty, there is nothing for it but to give him a training appropriate to the high prerogative of freedom. The child's unfaithfulness is not to make the faith of the Father of none effect. Man is not abandoned to sensual suggestion and self-will; but in the administration of physical and moral law God comes to his aid. The command was to save man from physical harm; but, the command transgressed, all physical consequences are summoned to serve the end of man's moral correction and renovation. Every malediction is for man's sake; that the free spirit may be taught to distinguish and assert its true character by even the pain and decay of the lower nature.

Notice the gradation of inquiry on the part of God, with the corresponding gradation in the judgments pronounced. The investigation begins with the man, passes on to the woman, and ends with finding the source of temptation in the beast. Having thus passed downward from the highest to the lowest in its inquiry, the divine judgment passes upward from the lowest to the highest, — from the seducing serpent to the beguiled woman, that it may end with the more faultily consenting man. At the turning-point, where inquiry changes to judgment, the eternal discrimination is made between the serpent instinct and the moral law. No question is asked of the serpent. The serpent is judged as a beast, not as a moral agent. The malediction upon the serpent is the malediction appropriate to the most stealthy and venomous of beastly natures. It is the curse of enmity, deadly and enduring, between the animal seduction and the deceived humanity, between the serpent's seed and the woman's seed; the curse of bad pre-eminence among all cattle as the type of cunning and treacherous solicitation; the curse of utter destruction in the consummation of man's victory over the powers of temptation. For the conflict prophetically portrayed is not a doubtful one. The beast may injure, but is not to destroy the man; the man is to destroy the beast.

After this assurance of hope addressed to man's faith, comes the practical discipline for its fulfilment. It is a discipline of organic law pervading all the functions of life. Nothing here of "knowledge, righteousness, and holiness," as consciously repudiated by the sinning pair. They had confessed feebly and timidly, but upon the whole not disingenuously. They are not reproved for uncandid evasion or disloyal intention, but faithfully instructed and paternally chastened as the beloved of God. They had played with a delusive fancy for divine knowledge. They must learn how serious a teacher divine Wisdom really is; how careful of the spiritual law; how disenchanting and consuming to the desire of the flesh. No longer mere animal harmony, no more the living soul without the ruling spirit; but henceforth struggle with nature — pains, toils, conflicts, decay, dissolution — for the sake of the spirit now awakened, however abruptly, to the recognition of itself.

There is not a word to tell us that our first parents

committed any error foreign to the necessary liabilities of our experience in the world; not a word to tell us that the necessary liability of mankind to evil in connection with the earthly trial was fatally enhanced by the first transgression. It is not said that the gifts and calling of mankind underwent any revision to mankind's immense disadvantage. On the contrary, it is simply shown that the very inception of human history developed the identical tendencies that have belonged to it ever since. The revelation of Jesus Christ and the era of the regeneration pay the highest honor to physical tendency as well as to legal training in the development of our race, by admitting their primordial necessity and pointing out the limit of their claims. No animal nature, then no breed of men. No spiritual birth, then no Son of God.

First, that which is natural, — the man of the garden and of the living creatures; afterward, that which is spiritual, — the man of the divine Word and of the world discipline. First, the man of predominant physical motive, disobeying commands and not knowing what he does; afterward, the man of open eyes, salutary fears, and second thought. First, the man under special restraints for his physical good; afterward, the man enduring physical inflictions for his spiritual good. First, the man of greatest self-confidence and least faith; afterward, the man of greatest faith and least self-confidence. First, the man who is "of the earth, earthy;" afterward, the man who is "the Lord from heaven." The antithesis implies the progress from the first character to the last, and, of course, the contradictory moral phenomena resulting from the temporary struggle for ascendency between the two.

We are to consider, also, that to an undeveloped and uninformed nature confirmed unrighteousness is as impossible as confirmed righteousness. Infancy is not exposed to great spiritual dangers. The mistake of an initial trial cannot be a final crisis of character. No moral catastrophe is to be looked for in the cradle. But the discipline of life, guarding against physical danger, takes, of necessity, a moral risk. It is not enough that forbidden fruit should be kept out of sight. The natural appetites must be brought under control of a free spiritual loyalty. But spiritual loyalty is of faith, something quite distinct from physical tendency or gravitation. "Faith cometh by hearing, and hearing by the word of God." And since man's life is "not by bread alone, but by every word that proceedeth out of the mouth of God," shall not faith come, and come again, by hearing, and hearing as often by the word of God, until the prophetic soul shall take its proper attitude of attention and obedience, saying, "Speak, Lord, for thy servant heareth"?

The testimony of Irenæus is of interest in this connection as showing what understanding of the Scriptures was in the mind of a great defender of the Christian faith, whose writings were held by Eusebius to have made it clear that he stood in immediate relation with the Apostles. Far from allowing that moral character was bestowed upon man in his original constitution, Irenæus holds that "God made him free from the beginning," and adds: "But if some had been made by nature bad, and others good, these latter would not be deserving of praise for being good, for such they were created; nor would the former be reprehensible, for thus they were made [originally]. But since all men are of the same nature, able both to hold fast and to do what is good, and, on the other hand, having also the power to cast it from them and not to do it, some do justly receive praise even among men who are under the control of good laws (and much more from God), and obtain deserved testimony of their choice of good in general and of persevering therein; but the others are blamed, and receive a just condemnation because of their rejection of what is fair and good." [1]

Let any one free his mind from the bias of system, allowing the Scriptures to speak in their own simple way, and see how clearly throughout their whole extent the free yet imperfect nature of man is held to the guidance of divine truth by faith as the principle of obedience. The revelation of God comes down to the conditions of our trial, violates no requirement of reason, but awakens conscience in order to satisfy law.

[1] Against Heresies, book iv. ch. xxxvii. 1, 2, Ante-Nicene Christian Library, T. & T. Clark, Edinburgh.

CHAPTER IV.

THE PERFECT FAITH AND THE APPROVED MAN.

WE are given to understand, in the later Scriptures, that no law of outward conduct can be the rational measure or final test of righteousness; in fact, that no "law of commandments contained in ordinances"[1] was ever intended to serve more than a provisional purpose. The law of commandments is the instrument of instruction. Faith in God is the element of righteousness. The law of commandments is "line upon line and precept upon precept," — a thing of imperfect definitions and partial degrees. Faith is a permanent principle, that proves its quality both by fulfilling and by surviving the successive dispensations of law. It is good to keep the commandments of God as they are made known: now, "Eat not;" again, "Make no graven image;" again, "Do judgment, and relieve the oppressed." But it is better to go beyond these to other and nobler requirements of the perfect life by the law of faith. Faith is eternal, of the very essence of the perfect life, "the substance of things hoped for, the proving of things not seen." Faith gains a good report in spite of judgments adverse to many details of conduct, because it is working by love and working with God. Without faith

[1] Eph. ii. 15.

it is impossible to please God. With faith it is impossible not to please God according to the measure of faith, for faith is pleasing to God. A deficiency of faith on the part of a being who has had little or no discipline for the development of faith is not a deficiency to be mortally resented, since faith is born of the divine Word and Spirit, nurtured by gracious discipline, consummated in holy character.

As commands and instructions are given that we may not go astray in particulars of conduct, so faith is ministered to us that we may be justified from all things brought against us; even those things from which we could not be justified by formal law. Literal obedience to express directions can conclude nothing in our favor beyond those parts of conduct to which the directions refer. Faith in the higher authority may qualify actions mistaken and regrettable in themselves with the spirit of loyalty. Obedience to special commands does not of necessity prove a man to be sound in faith. A man sound in faith is in that very fact disposed to lawful obedience; and faith is what makes any act of obedience whole and acceptable to the authority obeyed.

Was there any other principle of obedience and life for Adam than faith in God? Law could be known to him only in parts, and the parts could be known but imperfectly. The whole law cannot be formulated in details. Law is the truth of God, to be communicated in the Word and received by faith. Faith builds up law as it builds up obedience and manhood. Revelation never says, "Obey in this particular, and you shall be perfect throughout your generations." But from Alpha to Omega we are called upon, as moving in a course of free development, to believe in God, to advance by his inspiration, and to be perfected. Yea, the principle of faith excludes justification on the ground of any particulars of obedience whatever. To seek righteousness "by the deeds of the law" is to lose it. If we find perfection in what we have done and are now doing, we give up seeking perfection in the better and ever better, which is our possibility by the law of faith. "He that seeketh findeth," by the law of faith. He will go on seeking and finding. But he that hath sought and hath found, by the law of works, no more seeketh, and findeth no more. Hence, though we have gifts and works, no matter to what heights and depths of achievement and sacrifice, if we have not love ever surviving, and still going on in faith and hope to more and better service, where is our justification? I do not say merely our justification for the past, but our justification for the present and the future. The principle of our justification must be a principle of eternal life, or our justification will fall into the decay, degradation, and death of transient ages. Through all dispensations the principle of our justification is one. Earlier than Moses or Abraham, later than Paul or Luther, faith abideth, like Jesus Christ the supreme Example of faith, "the same yesterday and to-day and forever."

Is it possibly because we hear so much of Jesus Christ as the Object of faith, that we fail to give him due honor as the Example of faith? We are taught to think of him as the Mediator of all spiritual benediction and grace; yet we frustrate the grace of God, unless we learn to think of Him also as the Leader of the war-worn hosts of faith, from the foundation of the world. It is only by bearing his cross and achieving the perfect example of faith and of the righteousness which is by faith, that our Lord passes into his glory and becomes Head over all things to his church, Chief of men as born to personal sonship in the holy family of God. Only by becoming the Son of man, born of a woman, made under law, subject to trial, learning obedience by the things that he suffered, fulfilling all righteousness, could he become known to us as Son of God and Saviour of the world. Having come into the house of our physical and social bondage, it was for him to lead captivity captive, and through the eternal Spirit to vindicate the faith in which he offered himself without spot to God, that he might open the way of redemption for mankind. The prophetic mystery and the Messianic revelation of godliness is summed up in these words: "He who was manifested in the flesh, justified in the spirit."[1] Here is an antithesis that rules in the earthly life, and is evermore a mystery. "Manifested in the flesh." Why? Was it that he might be justified in the flesh? Was the aim to exhibit the pattern and circumstances of the best earthly life, as if men were made for a terrestrial paradise and nothing better? Was the divine humanity to show an accurate conformity to moral precepts according to the limits of the average conscience and the requirements of existing institutions and authorities? Nothing of the kind. Manifested but not justified, in the flesh; manifested that he might be "judged according to men in the flesh," while living "according to God in the spirit;" manifested to declare not only the righteousness, but also the long-suffering of God; manifested to endure the contradiction of sinners, to be bruised and put to grief, to make his life an offering for sin, — above all, manifested that he might win the faith of those

[1] 1 Tim. iii. 16.

witnesses and messengers, who would bear his testimony to all nations, that he might be believed on in the world, having been received up into glory.

"Justified in the spirit," but not manifested in the spirit. "For who among men knoweth the things of a man, save the spirit of the man, which is in him? Even so the things of God none knoweth, save the Spirit of God."[1] The justification of Jesus Christ in the human conscience is of faith. The disciple believes in the righteousness of Jesus. He cannot demonstrate it by standards of law applicable to details of conduct. So our Lord ever stands before us as greater than the law, as justified in his own conscience by demonstration of the Spirit, not by demonstration of the Decalogue. It is by faith — by an assured persuasion of speaking the truth, doing the works, and suffering according to the will of the Father — that our Lord is righteous. He fulfilled the law and the prophets not by striking coincidences of the letter, but by believing in them so as to act out their perfect meaning.

Finally, on what principle or ground shall we conceive that the Incarnate Son is justified by the Eternal Father? Is it on the ground of his having fulfilled a certain prescribed work of self-sacrifice, until with respect to certain definite limits of that work, he can say, "It is finished"? Is it "after the law of a carnal commandment" requiring the Son of God to be put to death in the flesh, that the reclamations of divine justice might receive a formal or quantitative satisfaction, and sinners be saved from receiving the due reward of their deeds? Hear the Prophet. "When thou shalt make his soul an offering for sin" — what then? How is the

[1] 1 Cor. ii. 11.

Atonement to be atoned for?—"He shall see his seed, he shall prolong his days, and the pleasure of the Lord shall prosper in his hands." Of what avail to bear sins, if he could not save his people from their sins? Of what avail to experience the terrors of vindictive law, if he could not become the minister of peace, the mediator and pledge of regeneration? Is it punishment, and not sin, that is the evil and bitter thing? How does the Son himself vindicate the Father's government and his own submission? "Except a corn of wheat fall into the ground and die, it abideth alone; but if it die, it bringeth forth much fruit." Here is the faith of Jesus in the law of the spiritual creation. After his resurrection his word is, "Ought not Christ to have suffered, and to enter into his glory?" The testimony of the Gospel is, that "for the joy that was set before him he endured the cross,"—and, "thus it behooved the Christ to suffer," that the majestic purpose of Love might be fulfilled through the ages of ages in bringing many sons unto glory.

But take away the shield of faith, wherewith the Saviour is able to quench the fiery darts of the adversary, and what becomes of the sword of the Spirit,—the word of God? What becomes of the armor of righteousness on the right hand and on the left,—his active obedience? What becomes of the helmet of salvation,—his assurance of success? Nay; take away the persuasion of his resurrection and endless life, of the ages to come, of his all-subduing and all-reconciling reign, of the kingdom to be delivered up to the Father, that God may be all in all,—and is Jesus justified with God, or are the ways of God justified to man? On the contrary, we are simply brought to the unique demonstration of a pessimist world: the worst fate to the best man. If the Christ crucified be not the Christ risen and glorified, then of all men his followers are the most miserable — and most miserable are all men. If there be no resurrection of the dead, and no revelation of God and of the sons of God in an immortal life, then what is there to make good the word of promise, on which all righteous laws, all prophetic anticipations and benevolent sacrifices, have reposed? But grant that faith is the recognition, however feeble, of a divine reality and an eternal revelation, wherein faith has its own justification and guidance, and then faith will sustain and justify the human spirit in doing what faith demands. Thus faith, working by love, purifying the heart, and overcoming the world, becomes the organic law of citizenship and service under the government of God.

On this ground, it is true, faith cannot be confined to a critical act, in which, for example, a man takes it for granted that a mystical fall has its compensation in a mystical atonement. Such an act can, in any case, be only an incident of faith. Faith abideth, — a permanent principle of action, a vital relation of the finite soul with the eternal Spirit, or there is no faith and no justification. Faith is not only in itself the spiritual element of righteousness; it makes for righteousness also in the way of "good works, which God hath before ordained that we should walk in them."

Faith, in fine, determines its own antithesis, — unbelief. Unbelief expresses the evil that is in the world in its unity. Men, alike unknowing and unbelieving with respect to God and the ages of his revelation, are thrown back upon partial aspects of things. They find development and dissolution, immanent energy coming out in current consciousness, consciousness changeful, illusive, evanescent, lighting fools the way to dusty death, and opening the eyes of philosophers to the blackness of speculative despair. But while the struggle of faith and unbelief is ever bringing with it the comparative knowledge of good and evil, the revelation of God sets the bow of promise in the cloud, affirms the divine intention to be simply good, makes periods of darkness tributary to ages of light, gathers together in one all things in Christ,[1] and through the fashion of this world that passeth away[2] discloses the ever living universe to which we belong: —

> "One God, one law, one element,
> And one far-off divine event,
> To which the whole creation moves."

[1] Eph. i. 10. [2] 1 Cor. vii. 31.

PART FOURTH.

THE MANIFESTATION OF EVIL.

"HE that believeth not hath been judged already, because he hath not believed on the name of the only begotten Son of God. And this is the judgment, that light is come into the world, and men loved the darkness rather than the light, for their works were evil."

GOSPEL OF ST. JOHN, iii. 18, 19.

"THE highest enhancement of sin, the blasphemy against the Holy Ghost, is conditioned by the highest revelation of God ; only through Christ and the efficiency of the Holy Ghost proceeding from Him has it become possible."

DR. JULIUS MÜLLER: Christian Doctrine of Sin, vol. ii. p. 480.

"O DASS dem menschen nichts vollkommnes wird,
Empfind' ich nun.   Du gabst zu dieser wonne,
Die mich den göttern nah' und näher bringt,
Mir den gefährten, den ich schon nicht mehr
Entbehren kann, wenn er gleich, kalt und frech,
Mich vor mir selbst erniedrigt, und zu nichts,
Mit einem worthauch, deine gaben wandelt."

GOETHE : Faust.

PART FOURTH.

THE MANIFESTATION OF EVIL.

CHAPTER I.

OF SPECULATIONS ON ORIGINAL SIN.

IN the preceding study we found faith to be the principle not only of spiritual rectitude, but of spiritual progress; since righteousness is revealed in nature and represented in Scripture not as practical conformity with outward regulations, but as the development of personal life according to the revelation of God.

The Council of Trent was true to the principle of growth, if not to the economy of reformation, in what it declared concerning the increase of justification: "So, therefore, those justified, and made God's friends and servants, going from strength to strength, are renewed, as saith the Apostle, 'day by day;' that is, by mortifying the members of their flesh and presenting them as instruments of justice unto sanctification, by observing the commandments of God and of the Church, faith co-operating with good works, they grow in that righteousness received through the grace of Christ, and are justified more and more. Holy Church seeks this increase of righteousness when she prays, 'Grant us, O Lord, an increase of faith, hope, and charity.'"[1]

---

[1] Decretum de Justificatione, caput x.

This progress in faith and righteousness, depending upon the revelation of God, is always shaded in human history by manifestations of unbelief and unrighteousness, that affirm the animal appetites, childish judgments, and selfish wills of men. As there is the struggle of physical life, so above and beyond this there is the fight of faith, the conflict for spiritual enlargement, the effort to give reason and the will of God their proper persuasiveness and just ascendency in the dealings of men.

The advancing spiritual conviction has ever reflected with severe reproach upon our immature and complex nature for its proclivity to immediate enjoyment in preference to prospective improvement, and its obstinate adhesion to low habits in spite of noble ideals or moving examples that appeal for efforts and sacrifices in pursuance of the greatest good for all creatures.

What has been dogmatically laid down upon this subject in the creeds of Christendom need not be exhibited here. But in the reasoning of eminent thinkers we sometimes find a whole aspect of history in a few words, and so have an effective introduction to what we desire to examine for ourselves. The Duke of Argyle, through a series of elaborate studies in the "Contemporary Review," finds at length in man the solitary exception to "the Unity of Nature."[1] In the number for February, 1881, he says: "That which is really exceptional, and indeed absolutely singular, in. man is the persistent tendency of his development to take a wrong direction." Such a tendency, according to him, "cannot be reconciled with the ordinary course of nature or

---

[1] See also "The Unity of Nature," G. P. Putnam's Sons, pp. 355, 367, 372, 373, 544.

with the general law under which all other creatures fulfil the conditions of their being;" and this by reason of the general fact, "first, that man is prone to set up and to invent standards of obligation which are low, false, mischievous, and even ruinous; and, secondly, that when he has become possessed of standards of obligation which are high and true and beneficent, he is prone first to fall short in the observance of them, and next to suffer them, through various processes of decay, to be obscured and lost." The corruption of religion, as well as the corruption of morals, becomes intelligible, in his view, "on the supposition of wilful disobedience with all its tendencies and consequences having become 'inherited and organized in the race.'"

Cardinal Newman develops the same argument with intenser feeling.[1] "To consider the world in its length and breadth, its various history, the many races of man, their starts, their fortunes, their mutual alienations, their conflicts; and then their ways, habits, governments, forms of worship; their enterprises, their aimless courses, their random achievements and acquirements, the impotent conclusion of long-standing facts, the tokens, so faint and broken, of a superintending design, the blind evolution of what turn out to be powers or truths, the progress of things, as if from unreasoning elements, not towards final causes, the greatness and littleness of man, his far-reaching aims, his short duration, the curtain hung over his futurity, the disappointments of life, the defeat of good, the success of evil, physical pain, mental anguish, the prevalence and intensity of sin, the pervading idolatries, the corruptions, the dreary, hopeless irreligion, that condition of the whole race so fearfully yet

[1] Apologia pro Vitâ suâ, pp. 241, 242.

exactly described in the Apostle's words, 'having no hope and without God in the world,'—all this is a vision to dizzy and appall, and inflicts upon the mind the sense of a profound mystery which is absolutely beyond human solution. What shall be said to this heart-piercing, reason-bewildering fact? I can only answer, that either there is no Creator, or this living society of men is in a true sense discarded from his presence."

But since there is a Creator, Cardinal Newman argues that "the human race is implicated in some terrible aboriginal calamity. It is out of joint with the purposes of its Creator." "This," he insists, "is a fact,—a fact as true as the fact of its existence; and thus," he continues, "the doctrine of what is theologically called 'original sin' becomes to me almost as certain as that the world exists, and as the existence of God."

What is matter of inference in these quotations is introduced simply for the emphasis it gives to what is matter of induction. To highly developed and instructed intellects, to spirits trained in all the doctrine and discipline of religion, and characters ripened to pious susceptibility and devoutness, the facts of our mortal history are so fearful, the color of our fate is so sombre, that the passing generations, being plainly insufficient for their own burdens or their own duties, must needs refer their evils through unknown lines of natural descent back to "some terrible aboriginal calamity," some "wilful disobedience," on account of which God discarded man from his presence, and man was left as a race to inherit and organize the consequences of his transgression.

As the purpose of the present study is not to resolve

any mystery, but simply to deal with what is made known to us in nature for the clearer understanding of what we are taught in Scripture, and as we have already considered the beginning of man's history, we have now nothing to do with grounding man's present aberrations upon an original catastrophe; nor can we properly infer that man is discarded from God's presence from an induction of facts about man's sin and misery, without due regard to God's revelation for reconciling the world unto himself. That man does inherit and organize the consequences of his errors is true. That God does bear testimony against man's errors in the sufferings they entail may be taken as equally true. But as man's righteousness is simply his persistent progress in knowledge and obedience through faith in God's revelation, so man's sin has its development and aggravation through his continued resistance to the persuasions of the same revelation. Hence man's physical and intellectual error, inherited and organized through ages of comparative ignorance, supports his appeal to compassion; while man's moral inertia, or wilful reluctance to good under increasing light from above, opens the question of personal blameworthiness. First and last the spiritual movement of humanity refers wilful disobedience and judicial condemnation to the period of final decisions, not to the period of initial communications between God and man. The sin of ignorance is easily forgiven, however monstrous in its external aspect. The sin against light is promptly judged according to its inward quality, though it should violate none of the decencies of outward life. A "terrible aboriginal calamity" (if that be not a contradiction in terms), even though it were a "wilful disobedience," so its consequences be "inherited and organized in the race," would justly be pleaded by all the heirs of such an inheritance as a palliation of personal guilt, in just so far as it should constitute a native proclivity to evil. We are therefore to take nature as we find it, and to study the manifestation of evil in the concrete; that is, to study the so-called evil of life as related to the good. For it is evil as marking the whole course of nature, not as something perfectly definable in itself, that the Bible is persistently holding up to our attention. It follows that for us to attend to this, much as we may be baffled by the intricacies of the subject, is the way to throw the light of experience upon Scripture, and the light of Scripture upon experience.

CHAPTER II.

OF SPIRITUAL LAW OVERRULING PHYSICAL TENDENCY.

HUMAN nature is complex. The animal part of man has laws of its own, which are distinct from the laws of his spiritual obligation. In itself considered, the law of animal nature is very good. It wisely and kindly adapts and moves mankind to the fulfilment of a physical destiny. Equally certain is it that the animal nature indispensable to the fulfilment of our physical destiny is itself destined to pass away when its work is done. But if a mortal race is employed in the production and education of immortal men, then our physical organs, like other material objects, must come under the sway of spiritual law so long as there shall be any need of them as means and instruments of spiritual service.

Our bodily development is so vitally related to the quality and discipline of our spirits, however, that the race can ill afford a feeble physical organization. The physical motive has need to be vigorous, lest the struggle of life should be made uncertain or abortive by premature and overpowering spiritual demands. Infant saints are not thought of usually as hopeful candidates for earthly honors. If the child after the flesh is to die at an early day, the human race cannot be much indebted to him; and as for his own spiritual development on so faint and feeble a trial, what can it be but a precocious and puny product? The teaching of nature reduced to a proverb is a law of not too much on either hand: "Be not righteous overmuch, neither make thyself overwise; why shouldst thou destroy thyself? Be not over wicked, neither be thou foolish; why shouldst thou die before thy time?"[1] The way is narrow. There is danger on the side of excessive spiritual exertion, as well as on the side of excessive physical indulgence. To wrong the lower nature is to wrong the higher also. But first in the order of time comes that which is physical, — to be handled at short range, to be wisely indulged or restrained, not under moral precepts, but according to natural law. To foster and develop the energy which in its various functions the spiritual man will by and by responsibly employ, meanwhile waiting to salute the youthful spirit for the purpose of introducing it gently to its appropriate moral lessons, — this is what it means to bring men forward in the world.

But while there is a period to which moral training is inappropriate, and nature is its own law, there is still a higher nature to which law is to be communicated from above, and the word of the Lord comes by and by in a peculiar sense. A command authoritative, prophetic, divine, — not less so for being familiarly uttered by parental ministry, — requires the child to abstain freely from some natural pleasure because the indulgence, or too much of it, would be injurious. The well-known conditions of life, the laws of nature as long experience has taught society to apprehend them, become matter of moral discipline to the untaught and the unwary. What cautious and watchful guardianship about forbid-

[1] Eccl. vii. 16, 17.

den fruits! And how much instruction has to be given before the child of nature can be counted upon as having grown to such spiritual faith as will insure a moral obedience! Efforts and actions that are perfectly and innocently spontaneous, yet contrary to the superior judgment, have to be reproved and corrected, as a means of awakening the conscientious feeling and confirming a conscientious habit. At the first the natural alienation of childhood from this kind of training is total. Why? Simply because the child has its law of spontaneous movement in the line of physical motives. Is this law sin? Certainly not in the moral sense, though it may express the natural inheritance of morbid tendencies. But when the higher law comes, then comes the demand for faith; then comes proof of a practical potency of foolishness and impiety bound up in the child's constitution. The child seems a creature of mere animal desire in opposition to the divine word opening the way to new obedience. Infantile rebellion is outspoken and unscrupulous just in proportion as it is ignorant, unapprehensive, and irresponsible. The will of the flesh is not informed as to the higher range of man's life, until the very teaching that begins to point it out is understood and felt as overruling the law of the lower nature. When the commandment comes in this sense, the natural motives, in proportion as they are thrown into practical opposition to the law of faith, begin to take a relative character of unbelief and unrighteousness. That which was innocent and excellent as the original creation of God, and which is still innocent and excellent, so only it be kept in just subordination to every spiritual word of God, imports evil, and liability to more and more of evil, when it is allowed to assert itself as so much mind of the flesh — so much prejudice of animal habit and desire — against the higher ruling. That physical tendency which is not in itself subject to the spiritual law of God, neither indeed can be, is to be subjugated by the spirit of faith in man. For by faith man is subject to the spiritual reign of God, and can become subject to the same more and more. Low down in our career we are all in innocent unbelief, in the nothingness and vanity of our ignorance, by no will of our own. Our destiny for good depends upon the commandment that shall come, upon the word of truth and grace that shall visit all; albeit why some are so tractable, and others so intractable, seemingly, to the heavenly guidance is a secret that merges in the mystery of being, while the fact revealed in experience is that "all we, like sheep, have gone astray."

But the new commandment demanding faith, — does this throw us from the track of obedience to our destruction, because it acts as a brake to check and regulate a native tendency liable to unconscious and fatal excess? By no means. For this very reason the new commandment is good. It comes forth from a perfect law, and ministers to a divine order; it is not opposed to the physical tendencies as such, but only to their transgression of salutary limits. The higher law enters not only for its own sake and for the sake of the higher man, but because of a dangerous liability to transgression even in the lower sphere of physical requirement. The Creator declares himself as the Guide of the human soul for the sake of the body; and by that means he becomes the Saviour of the body for the sake of the soul. He points out our natural weakness, appeals to a wholesome fear, solicits faith as the principle of obedience, and hence the condition of all blessings he desires to bestow. All the contents and endeavors of our being are continually coming to judgment in accordance with the progressive demands of the truth as apprehended by faith. It matters not what the requirement may be, — does it express a claim of supreme law? Then to believe and to obey is good. Unbelief in all conceivable degrees of disobedience is relatively evil. Hesitation, reluctance, delay, resistance, — all that is not of faith is of evil. This antagonism of unbelief and faith holds through all gradations of intellectual and moral development, and is quite distinct from any judgment as to degrees of personal responsibility. Granted that the supreme Wisdom is moving men with counsels or commands, — then, as certainly as faith and obedience are their only righteousness, so certainly unbelief and disobedience are the measure of their unrighteousness. The common aspect of evil, in individuals and in society, is the aspect of something negative to the best suggestion, to the wisest teaching, to the most beneficent example, — something negative, in a word, to the divine inspiration. For if a little advance in knowledge and experience is enough to bring a person into a critical attitude of mind towards whatever is behind, so that to excuse is also to accuse the more ignorant, how should not that all-searching inspiration of God, which ministers instruction in righteousness to the human spirit, cause even the fine gold of natural virtue to grow dim by comparison with the virtue that excelleth, — to say nothing of those grosser exhibitions, wherein animal appetites and lawless passions conspire with headstrong self-will against admonitions of authority and persuasions of conscience?

Infancy does not grow to a spontaneous fulfilment

of the tasks and graces of childhood; nor is the child invariably met with a discipline to charm it into perfect action. Youth, maturity, old age, — each period has its peculiar tendencies that are distinctly against the best thought and hope; though they are as distinctly of nature under the existing stress of conditions and motives in the lower sphere of life. Always, however, there is the law and mastership of life calling men onward and upward. Prophecies of intellectual, social, and spiritual attainments utter themselves in the soul. Yet there is ever a preoccupation, some concrete expression of unbelief, by reason of which, if it may be deemed that some are excusably late in reaching the land of promise, it must be confessed that there are others who do not for the present appear to enter in at all. And who can be sure of having exerted his powers to the best practicable effect?

As one man's lack of faith in life's promises and possibilities makes its contribution to a general average of failure, which becomes a mode of social existence, so the manner of living in society becomes a clog, or prohibition, or bias, to individual progress and influence; though the need of reformation may be to prophetic souls as a very fire in the bones. The illuminated, the elect, through whom the higher calling is brought to the knowledge of meaner men, are apt to become jealous for the Lord their God, but incommunicative, severe, condemnatory, toward their fellow-men. They make a virtue of despising the very conditions of virtue. That the higher law should respect and vindicate the claims of the lower law seems too great a condescension; and so the lower law is disparaged and denounced as interfering with the demands of the higher. The earthward gravitation is accused of hindering the heavenward motion. The man of lofty contemplations, who cannot take others upon his flights, conceives their heaviness as infinitely more odious to their Maker than burdensome to him, and finds it the part of piety to construe the universal trial as universal apostasy from the very beginning. In this way he thinks to give God glory for all aspects of good, while to man he assigns the responsibility for all aspects of evil.

But the Creator does not reveal himself as wholly on the side of those who seem called to take his part. If error besets the lower functions of our nature, does it not beset the higher also? Has not man erred as disastrously in the over-assertion of spiritual prerogatives as in the over-indulgence of animal tendencies? Is it not the part of the infinite Judge to correct error in all and for all? How shall the prophet of improvement even in art be ever recognized as such, if he have no patience with the cool stare of unbelief or the active persecution of vested interests? What, then, shall the prophet of enlightened conscience and of moral law expect? Relatively to each other it is not the prophet, but the world, that is lying in wickedness. But the prophet is also of the world, and the world is prophetic with the prophet, however it may seem to be against him; while prophet and world, the whole race of men, are in that error and faultiness out of which slowly and painfully the way is opening toward the world that is to come. As this progress in its very nature implies the better thoughts and nobler faith that lead the way to unseen good, so by a necessary correlation it implies the lower habits and short-sighted affections that are judged as evil and doomed to pass away.

The absolute good is not in creatures. But given the absolute good in the Creator as the Object of faith, and the absolute evil is impossible in the creation. Evil comes out as a mistaken or perverse determination of life, — to be corrected by the further discipline of life lest it should defeat the consummation of life. This is not theory; it is history, — the divine teaching in the facts of existence. As faith embraces the divine motive and guidance in nature, and thus stands for life in relation to its possible good, better, and best, under the inspiration of supreme Wisdom and Benevolence; so unbelief, indifferent or oppugnant to the light and leading from above, because seeking good in obedience to animal instincts or personal calculations, stands for life in relation to its possible progress in error and the natural consequences of error, — the bad, worse, and worst of illusion, abortion, and destruction, which are the historic mark of works not wrought in the spirit of faith and obedience. As the way of wisdom is the way of peace and pleasantness, no matter with what incidental sufferings, so the way of indocility is the way of prohibitory and punitive discipline,—the hard way, no matter with what incidental pleasures or advantages. Unbelief, as the error of immature intelligence, is corrected by larger experience. No one is allowed to commit himself finally to a wrong choice without trial of that servile apprenticeship to transgression which opens the eyes to the majesty and freedom of law. The "evil, be thou my good," of unconscious, inconsiderate, and ignorant preference, cannot grow in personal development to the "evil, be thou my good," of ultimate spiritual determination, except the person travel all the pathway of contradiction under the lightnings of divine law, which measures the moral distance between an infantile deviation from the truth of life, when as yet the inspiration of Wisdom has hardly indicated its motion in the soul, and a deliberate alienation from God after the most persuasive proof of his goodness has been brought to bear upon the spirit. It is in multitudes, as flocks and herds, that men try the first stages of the broad way leading to destruction; but one by one, as spiritual persons admonished and taught of God, are they turned into the way of eternal life.

CHAPTER III.

OF PAINS AND PENALTIES AS RELATED TO CONDUCT.

THE sketch just given of unbelief and evil among men stands for a condition of things that antedates all generations of historic humanity; a condition of things, consequently, with respect to which no man holds himself to be personally responsible, except for his own contribution to the general result.

The world presses upon every human being different objects and aims, which, appealing to different orders of motives not of equal authority, demand of every one in the exercise of his constitutional freedom to choose wisely for himself and for others. In this way we come to our type of personal responsibility. Other men, who by their conduct have helped to make the world what it is of good or bad, must personally answer for themselves, as we in our place and order shall answer for ourselves; and when every individual of the human race shall bear his full personal responsibility, there is much reason to think that speculation about sin will be out of date. The good or evil of our history will have been personally accounted for, with perfect honor to the wisdom and benevolence of the Creator.

In the mean time we need to study the evil consequent upon our manifold errors in its relation to the development of individual and social responsibility. We have seen that the elements of our trial are brought slowly and prudently to our apprehension. Nature shields us at first by our very feebleness from the possibility of precipitate determination to wrong-doing. The creative teaching takes advantage of our growing moral sense to point out to us that we cannot be made the victims of any inherited depravation except by a voluntary surrender of our better selves. As long as the apprehension of truth is childishly feeble, and practical mistakes are the only way out of intellectual and moral limitations, it is clear that there can be no decisive trial of faith, no fatal unbelief, no final determination of the spiritual career.

But while faith in all its degrees is an element of personal responsibility, unbelief grounded in ignorance is of a nature to excuse a certain bondage to practical error. Faith and unbelief refer to motives of conduct, not to specific and mutually exclusive moral qualities. The men of unbelief and the men of faith are only relatively distinguished; they are not separate hosts under different colors. A man's faith is nothing less than his spiritual relation to universal reality on the side of knowledge, suggestion, inspiration: it is all that makes for personal progress in harmony with divine law. A man's unbelief, on the contrary, is his spiritual relation to universal reality on the side of ignorance, doubt, contradiction: it makes for degradation and failure, from mistaken devotion to partial views in opposition to universal truth. In the struggle of opposing arguments, a man passes, it may be, from an action having the mark of unbelief to an action having the mark of faith by simply modifying his conduct in accordance with new convictions as to the grounds of his responsibility. He shifts the line, so to speak, between what he takes to be true and what he takes to be not true, just as one changes the limits of one's horizon by moving to a higher point of view. There is no faith without a correlated unbelief, no unbelief that does not assert itself as a limitation of an existing faith. Faith and unbelief, like positive and negative electricity, are developed at the same instant and in the same action; are indeed opposite polarities of the same voluntary effort. Faith and unbelief, in the normal action of the spirit, determine that necessary mental oscillation which is the note of progress. The evil unbelief is that general distrust which finds oscillation disagreeable because the onward movement is held to be undesirable, and the alternative of rest, at whatever risk, is voluntarily preferred. The whole development of personal responsibility turns upon what a man takes to be true as distinguished from what he decides to treat as untrustworthy; while the consequences that naturally ensue upon one's determinations are simply testimonies of the universal Governor as to the merits of the belief, or of the denial, that is brought into judgment.

Is it likely, then, that man was ever intended to pass from the ignorance and helplessness, which would be speedy destruction were it not atoned for by parental love, to freedom and security as a prince in the household of God, without the excitement and discipline of pain, whether physical or spiritual? Would it be good, I do not say for the economy and success of life in general, but for the conscious animation and pleasure of the hour, — would it be good that no bitter herbs should flavor the feast of existence; that, come what might, there should be no sensible discords to awaken and remand us to the concords of being? Such insensibility is the mark of death, — the way of inorganic matter.

To rational life, on the contrary, in a universe vital and infinite, wherein all parts and syllables of truth are precious by reason of their relation to truth as a whole, pain is the magisterial expression of Goodness, bidding us to pause when we falsely think we ought to go farther, or to move on when we falsely think that our rest is gained. What is precious must be costly in order that we may appreciate it as precious. If man is compelled to rally his invention, to combine the resources of many individuals in the struggle of life against animals of superior physical energy and agility, until, at no trifling expense, he becomes what Aristotle defined him, — "a political animal," — will he win his proper degree in the spiritual kingdom of God without danger, by mere social assent or listless submission? To know in order to believe, to believe and make trial in order to know, — is this, or ought it to be, an easy and painless endeavor? To say so would be to deny to our spiritual calling the character of an exciting and honorable career.

Experience teaches us that faith has its faults and misdoings, which originate in the very action of faith as related to its limitations. Faith, therefore, is under correction to the wisdom and love of the Father as manifested in the government of things; and the very leaders of faith, the heroic exemplars of virtue, submit joyfully to a discipline of pains and penalties comporting with the majesty of the divine service contrasted with the poor results of the best human effort. The cost of wisdom must be paid, whether in the chastisements of sloth or in the pains of effort; and even the well-authenticated dictates of knowledge, "thou shalt" and "thou shalt not," do not become a firm persuasion in the minds of the ignorant without more or less of bitter experience in the hard way of transgression.

It is not merely that the real faith has at times to substantiate its claims against an unbelief that inherits the effects, wears the regalia, and rules in the name of an elder faith; but the apostles of truth are brought by varied experiences of suffering out of dangers incident to their own interior progress in the experience which is their peculiar glory. Faith does not enable a man to demonstrate the ultimate patterns of duty; it inspires him to divine and to enter upon the immediate efforts of duty. But faith, as it implies limitation of intelligence, so it does not reach the safe standard of divination, except as it shares in the divine motive of love. Too often the intellectual assurance and practical zeal of faith are in the inverse ratio, both of instruction and of charity; while, on the other hand, at whatever height of attainment a man presumes to think that he has nothing further to gain, in that very fact he denies faith, and according to that denial the infinite truth is not in him. To be self-satisfied in view of what we know, is so far to be unready for the new word of faith. To run credulously after every novel teaching, is to indicate no trustworthy appreciation of the truth already given us in charge.

The illusiveness of finite knowledge, the indeterminateness as to practical form of relative duties, the liability of all good qualities in human nature to run into bad qualities by unconscious transgression of their proper limits, — how would not this constitute a relative manifestation of evil and a necessity of corrective discipline even in the experience of the elect of the race, no matter how much time might be allowed for attaining and manifesting the best type of character possible to each individual? But when we consider that the elect are chosen in order that others may be called; that no character reaches its ideal glory here, for the reason that spiritual development on this side immortality is arrested by physical decay; that the heavenly vision of the seer is simply his commission to struggle with the earthly vision of the multitude, and learn by trial how great things he must suffer in the name of the truth, which other men have as much need to appreciate as he has: when we weigh all this, I say, are we not prepared for a manifestation of evil on a scale commensurate with the development of good, — evil of a force and color in no faint contrast with good? For, as there is no power, motive, or passion in the race which has not its counterpart in every well-constituted individual of the race, so there is no array of embattled hosts that is not determined by personal tendencies. If the heavenly vision of faith is liable to sin by over-exaltation against its commission of service, and to suffer accordingly, certainly there is danger that the earthly confidence and the earthly struggle may sin by sensual indifference against the heavenly gift, and suffer accordingly.

Indeed, so important is suffering in the discipline and struggle of life, that men are continually inflicting it upon themselves and upon those they love, as well as upon others whom they dislike or desire to overcome. In this way they accumulate figures in which they not only represent, but misrepresent, the divine chastisements. The inflictions that come unbidden of personal wills and by the secret dispensation of God in nature, compared with the pains and penalties referrible to positive enactments and settled administrations of men, are as the common law of a remote imperial government compared with the petty tyranny of an officious and mercenary police. The man who proposes to govern himself according to a high aim makes light of pains. It is his delight to "scorn delights." He toils for the present, that he may live more strenuously laborious days in the future. He keeps his body under severe training and brings it into subjection. St. Francis called his body "the ass," and confessed at last that he had treated the creature harshly. Those who construe themselves, not as man and beast, but as two men — the spiritual man and the carnal man — in like manner lord it over the subject nature; and, while taking moral responsibility and blame as appropriate to the master, accuse the servant of fatuous dereliction in not helping them to do the things that they desire to do.

Meanwhile the ascetic virtue has fallen as far short of perfect spiritual manhood as of doing full justice to physical demands. Childhood cannot seize maturity by violence, and there is a force by which the kingdom of heaven is not taken. Conscientious faith has jurisdiction, but not supreme jurisdiction. The most sensitively conscientious man, feeling how much error abounds in his best endeavors, how it needs repression and correction in order that grace may much more abound in the way of free forgiveness and new obedience, will be led to appeal from his conscience to his Judge, and to rejoice most of all that the distinction of right and wrong is too vital and sacred to have its claims finally adjudicated, even as respects the most common details of conduct, by any but the highest Authority. And if the good man cannot do justice to himself, still less can he estimate justly, except in a very general sense, the man who exhibits according to his natural gifts, his period of life, or the society by which he is moulded, a manner of living very different from his own. Only of this we are sure, — that the pre-eminently good man, finding evil in himself and in those like himself, will find evil abounding much more in the world. He will deem himself the organ of the divine truth, commissioned by the indwelling Spirit of God to "convince the world of sin, of righteousness, and of judgment."

But the world, — the world that stands for vast societies knowing little of righteousness and sin because believing little in God and truth, the world that being already unchristian only awaits the revelation of the Christ to find itself antichristian in its habits and tendencies, the world that dismisses souls of men by death that new bodies of men may have a chance in life, — is it a world to take easily, and without any violent reaction, a spiritual discipline, wherein every untrained nature is "a bullock unaccustomed to the yoke"?

If, again, the physical foundations of society are given to decay, what is to become of the best political and religious structures erected upon them? Must they not be evermore shaken, transformed, and superseded in the progress of new operations? How is the Master-builder conducting his work here? This present world at any moment contains a vast accumulation of things venerable for age, that stand in the way of new outlines and inspirations in which required improvements are set forth. It is not only the world of the usurping beast, but the world of the usurping prince, prophet, or priest, as well; a world not to accept easily and peacefully the reforming legislation of the true King. Usurpations fortified by habit are likely not to be thought of as usurpations, and the man who simply bears testimony to the truth is not at once recognized as supreme authority. The world made only to be changed is of necessity distinguished from the Power and ruling that are to change it. It is ever the "present *evil* world" from which souls and societies are to be redeemed to ages of peace and immortality.

How vast the range of evil! It is vast as the range of the human mind, — vast as the possibility of human error. If man is exceptional and singular in his apprehensions of reality as compared with other animal natures, he is equally so in his liability to error and transgression, with all their consequences. The most awe-inspiring apprehensions that can visit the human mind have given birth to the most mistaken and hideous practices. The mystery of religious fear, devotion, godliness, works through errors of authority and errors of submission which no outward word, but only the inward revelation of God, can correct. From the barbarian of the barbarians, who thinks to appease his divinity and escape punishment by human sacrifices, to the Hebrew of the Hebrews, verily thinking he ought to do many things contrary to the name of Jesus of Nazareth, against the lives of his followers, and on to the Christian of the Christians, who in the name of Jesus of Nazareth persecutes unto the death the disciples whose confession of faith is not in accord with his own, we have the same story of partial enlightenment, spiritual assumption, illusive expectation, and practical zeal not according to knowledge.

Grant that the world grows better in parts, that there are ever coming down out of heaven from God the working plans of a heavenly city; still the world grows worse in parts, — quarries and workshops are not the city. The polished stones in the eternal mansions rear themselves to other music than the sound of our hammers. There is one clear voice, that of sublime prohibition to all fulfilment of human hopes and possibilities in the present order of nature; but in other respects the triumph of death is full of mysterious uncertainty. Now premature, quenching the kindling dawn of existence with a touch; again, languid and late, compelling the active powers to lie in cold obstruction and refusing the stroke of grace, the conqueror rules with a capricious and tyrannic terror. Under the reign of mortality good is ever eluding our grasp, evil is ever seizing upon our possessions. Good disappears in the past, hurries forward to the future, hides in the darkness of fate and in the mystery of God; while in the same degree evil thrusts itself with obtrusive violence into the present sensation and consciousness, — a harpy to pollute the feast of life. Evil is of experience: good is of faith. Evil is a palpable precipitate: good is an invisible reagent. Evil salutes us at our birth: good withdraws by the gate of death. But neither good nor evil reaches any final definition or conclusion. Evil discovers itself in what seems to be good: good is latent in what presents the aspect of evil. The knowledge of good and evil inextricably mixed, as we naturally know good and evil, involves a discipline of bodily suffering in the ratio of individual and collective error. Again, to know good and evil as we are spiritually learning to know them, involves a discipline of spiritual pain in the ratio of responsible disregard of personal obligation in view of recognized truth. The secret of life and immortality is for those who, having paid their physical penalties and having realized the love which is the perfection of responsibility and the fulfilling of law, no longer need the monitions of pain, — no longer learn obedience by suffering.

But it must be admitted that if the manifold afflictions of the present life are part of a necessary discipline for the correction of human error and the development of personal responsibility, they are also a trial of faith, and are appealed to in the conflicts of thought as arguments and apologies of unbelief.

It is not that the plagues of humanity are specially mysterious in detail, — whether they come by the arbitrary dealings of men or according to the unvarying laws of nature. "The curse causeless does not come;" and the law of its administration may be traced in part, or its teaching could not be rationally appropriated. Human conduct is ordinarily something to be understood and appreciated, both as to its motives and its results. A low nature is not mysterious by being low. A sensual man is not a mystery in so far as he is indifferent to spiritual aims; nor is worldly ambition a mystery in being alien to the revelation of divine law. The wars and tumults of men are on a different scale from those of insect nations; but they can be just as clearly accounted for. They increase the variety within the unity of nature.

On the contrary, mystery is the source and the refuge of faith. Absolute truth is absolute mystery. God is the mystery of the universe. Life is the mystery of creation. The eternal revelation of God in the progress and consummation of his intelligent offspring is the mystery of redemption. There is no series of growths wherein every part is not bound in the vital chain of organic law to the Source of being. No interweaving of voluntary efforts, no combination or movement of political powers, no determination of successive events, wherein both the law of personal agency and the law of physical limitation do not lead directly up to the Centre of government. But we know only in part. Our judgments, too little instructed as to the nature and meaning of facts, are also biassed by a strong feeling for ourselves. Then, too, imagination revels in poetic grouping and coloring, — representations tragic and comic, that confuse the sense of reality. We are prone to morbid brooding over what we call "the mystery of evil;" by which is usually signified certain kinds and aggregates of human misery, — visitations of destruction, reigns of terror, agonies of pity, tortures of oppression, outbreaks of crime, — blended into massive horror without reference to law, and spread as a pall over the cheerful day that is uttering its speech about the mystery of good. Notwithstanding so much that is cheerful in life, not only the passionate soul but the much-enduring race of man is restlessly heaving to and fro, its thoughts running this way and that way in anxious suspicions and sacrificial inquiries as to why the Power that rules in the world should mark his administration with such and so many tokens of opposition and displeasure towards his utterly dependent subjects.

Is it that the Demon of the world is malignant or envious, and will not tolerate happiness among men without a tribute of blood in purchase of his forbearance? We can point to plenty of sinister conceptions for divinity, whose names and worship support no better meaning. But this will not do. Man may be an object of pity, but a divinity must not be an object of reproach under a form of homage.

Then, may it not be that while God is good and just, man is unconsciously and immeasurably rebellious? We in our ignorance have wrecked the creation; and the Spirit that moved upon the face of the waters at first with the fiat of all-animating order, is left to brood over the chaos come again, the moral ruin of the world, with the forlorn hope of saving with infinite difficulty a remnant from destruction.

But is not this to defend the divine goodness at the expense of the divine power? The world must be still in the hands of its Creator. He is equal to whatever he may desire or determine as respects the destiny of mankind. Must we not infer, therefore, with St. Augustine, that his purpose is to make use of our already condemned race for the practical exhibition of two phases of the divine character and government, — namely, the phase of vindictive justice in the majority as a manifestation of what all deserved, and the phase of gratuitous mercy in a considerable number as a proof of what grace he was able to bestow;[1] and that this life is simply the

[1] Hinc est universa generis humani massa damnata : quoniam qui hoc primitus admisit, cum ea quæ in illo fuerat radicata sua stirpe punitus est, ut nullus ab hoc justo debitoque supplicio, nisi misericordia et indebita gratia liberetur ; atque ita dispertiatur genus humanum, ut in quibusdam demonstretur quid valeat misericors gratia, in cæteris justa vindicta. Neque enim utrumque demonstraretur in omnibus : quia si omnes remanerent in pœnis istæ damnationis, in nullo appareret misericors gratia redimentis : rursum si omnes a tenebris transferrentur in lucem, in nullo appareret severitas ultionis. In qua propterea multo plures quam in illa sunt, ut sic ostendatur quid omnibus deberetur. — *De Civitate Dei*, lib. xxi. c. 12.

preparation for these unchangeable distinctions of the endless future?

But this dogmatic distribution of human destiny in the unknown future is an affair of limited knowledge and feeble judgment. It assumes that the divine attributes are to realize their eternal satisfaction in separateness and distinction, not in reconciliation and oneness. What, then, is the glory of just punishment conceived as an end in itself, if it be not the glory of a final and magnificent failure in disciplinary moral government? Rather than distinguish the moral perfections of the Creator by such contradictory issues of his tutelary administration, how much more natural and less terrible to suppose that having made the worlds he has left them to go very much their own way; and that man, with all his intelligence, is to work out his own little measure of life and enjoyment as simply the head of the great family of beasts that perish!

These alternative extremes of thought, it must be confessed, are extremely forbidding. They are, all and several, open to the objection of representing the whole system of government to which we belong as an immeasurably worse thing than the little province with which we are acquainted. Either on the one hand we are filled with foreboding of lasting evils that we know not of, which make the ills we have seem trivial except as premonitions of our doom; or, on the other hand, the unknown but not unhoped-for career of personal service and enjoyment, in which the ills we have might be accounted for and compensated, is taken away.

But the alternatives from which we recoil have their rational significance with reference to that middle way on which we go forward in the experience of life. Finding physical pain to serve as sentinel warning us against greater pains to which we are liable, we learn at length to construe all our sufferings according to a law of benevolence. We infer that our liability to error and consequent correction, as individuals and as a race, is related to the measureless orbit in which we are moving; according to the expression of Origen that "God governs souls not with reference to the fifty years of the present life, but with reference to an illimitable age."[1]

[1] Origen, De Principiis, lib. iii. c. i. 13. Ante-Nicene Christian Library, T. & T. Clark, Edinburgh.

CHAPTER IV.

OF PHYSICAL DEATH AS RELATED TO SPIRITUAL DEVELOPMENT.

OF late we have become familiar with the thought that throughout the whole range of animated nature on our planet the war for subsistence would be waged only the more violently, other things being as they are, were a longer lease of life given to the various species by their organic law. From the cosmical administration which supports life with life and gives scope to reproductive energy by cancelling outworn organisms, there is no appeal. If all generations, animal and vegetable, for so many ages have gone "the way of dusty death" that the creatures of to-day might have their turn in the light and air, the creatures of to-day have no choice but to follow their predecessors when the signal shall be given.

Death has been called "the debt of nature" and "the wages of sin." These allegorical phrases are plain enough in their general significance. It is their particular application that brings us into difficulty. Why should nature exact her debt from myriads who have had no time to contract personal obligations? Why should the wages of sin be paid to myriads who have had no opportunity to sin after the similitude of any moral transgression?

A difficulty in the application of a figure of speech will lead some minds to construe nature according to the figure, while it will constrain other minds to accommodate the figure to nature.

Whatever debts contracted or transgressions committed may come to judgment in the dying of individuals, it is certainly proper to look at death as first of all something in the physical order. A man may be more or less responsible with respect to many misdoings whose effect is to hasten or imbitter his dying; yet for his dying itself, as a physical claim enforced by physical process, he is no more responsible than for his birth.

Our physical economy has a sphere of its own distinct from the sphere of moral determinations. Intellectual efforts and agitations of feeling have their effects upon the body in accordance with physical law; and these effects are not at once distinguished or measured by moral motives. The noblest intention cannot save a man from the physical cost of his zeal. The basest motive has no immediate and characteristic tendency to cripple or exhaust the physical resources. Whether a man is serving righteousness or sin, he serves with a certain expenditure of natural force which is never mistaken for the exaction of moral law. And even when vice inflicts in process of time a characteristic stigma upon the body, this only indicates in what way moral delinquency has connected itself with the transgression of physical law without in the least identifying physical suffering with moral retribution. In fact, so sharp does the distinction at length become between one's moral personality and one's bodily organization, that the latter is looked upon as merely a possession and instrument of the former. The flesh is not only heir to natural shocks, it is brought into peril and suffering in all commercial, political, and moral struggles; while death is defied as aiming its shafts, according to the saying of Epictetus, at "not you, but that insignificant body of yours."

The general fact of our history as part of the animal creation is this: since the life of the race depends upon the life of individuals, while the life of individuals is conditioned on the persistency of the race, it follows that death is indispensable to the general economy of earthly existence in order that the function of the individual and the function of the race may be attempered to each other. If, therefore, we see mankind wisely and benevolently constituted with respect to their environment and all the natural resources on which organic existence depends, how can we reasonably doubt that the laws which limit organic existence are adjusted and administered with equal wisdom and kindness? Do we not take social order, the absence of prevailing violence, as proof of how far individuals and parties are held in check so as neither to tower threateningly above, nor to linger fatally below, their serviceableness to the general welfare? On the other hand, we interpret the agitations that affirm prevailing discontent as evidence that the social mass is seeking to throw off some incubus of personal power. But everywhere and always men are held together in mutual helpfulness and common welfare by the practical working of the law which takes all in succession away from the present struggle. By the teaching of this universal mortality the personal being is consecrated as a mystery of faith and sacrifice which can give no adequate account of itself except as destined to survive the physical dissolution and to move onward in a career of its own.

One's earthly life is precious because there is so little of it. Life could not be the spiritual reality that it is, without death; and death ceases to awaken fear, when faith has grown strong in the rational conception of life. Indeed, the natural dread of death is the negative testimony to the value of life. If the loss of life is looked upon as the symbol of all evil, what can life be but the essence of all good? If the common consciousness of mankind contemplates physical life as a boon worthy of being distributed through a race, is it something other than a boon because individuals cannot have it forever? And then, why judge of death without experience of what it is, not merely in relation to what is agreeable to us now, but in relation to what may concern us hereafter? If the anticipation of death makes for our higher personal life, why not assume that our personal life shall be much more indebted to the experience of death? At any rate, we are not merely entitled to put the best rational construction upon what we know, in the interest of the present as well as the future; we are bound to do it. We cannot, without violence to reason, adopt a working hypothesis which discredits and discourages the noblest efforts we are constituted to put forth, not less than the best hopes we are constituted to entertain.

It is certainly remarkable that all the proneness of human nature to the animal life has never been able to nullify the spiritual suggestion of personal existence after death. This appears in the animism of "primitive culture" as set forth by Mr. Tylor not less distinctly than in the philosophy of Plato and Cicero, or in the forecast of religious faith among historic peoples. Everywhere there is the deep human longing for redemption from the power of the grave, the instinctive persuasion growing into rational conviction that man shall somehow, under new conditions of life, find indemnity for the darkness and deprivation that settle down upon the senses in death.

Equally significant is the testimony of experience that, as the belief that death belongs to an economy of universal good-will justifies itself by its practical tendency to raise life to its utmost value while correspondingly reducing the fear of evil in dying, so the contrary assumption, that death is of a malignant intention, is set to demonstrate its own absurdity by its necessary tendency to wither the joys and aggravate the troubles of existence, till life under the shadow of death is apprehended as the evil of nature, while relapse into nothingness represents the fulness of hope.

Nature with infinite patience is evermore vindicating the intention of the Author of nature: holding up to the wise a good toward which they are to aspire, in contradistinction to the relative not good, or evil, from which the foolish are called upon to escape. In the physical economy pain cannot do its work as an instant admonition for the preservation of life without the instinctive fear of something in which bodily injuries may end. But this really means that it is our spiritual career which is most deeply indebted to the admonitions addressed to us by the suffering and dissolution of the body. Our physical organization is not only in the interest of the race, — designed for the propagation and distribution of life, and constituted to pass away lest life should exceed the limits of common well-being; but it is also and equally the servant of the individual, — suited to the working out of a spiritual intention, and dispensed with when it can no longer answer that purpose. We do not have our personal progress here, which is life, without something to change and pass away, which is death. We are given something to sacrifice, something with which to pay our entrance-fee to the higher departments of experience and effort, something outward to be at stake upon our inward determinations. The Power that exacts the fee or the sacrifice may well be trusted as to the reason and usefulness of his law.

But although to mistrust and to misconstrue the good is the real evil as well as the aggravation of all incidental aspects of evil, certainly the outward semblance of evil in the development of mankind is something not to be argued down. If faith cannot penetrate the secret of good, neither is unbelief wholly without reason as to the signs of evil. What but immortality revealed in the Christ and in humanity can put any one into the right relation with that vicarious suffering in which the race serves the individual and the individual serves the race? How many have to die before they are born, or very soon after, — "martyrs in deed though not in will" to the truth that mankind must study and obey the laws of life, in order that other generations may come forth under better conditions! How many have their days shortened or their strength weakened, in order that they may be pricked on intellectually and morally to the duty they owe to even the physical well-being of themselves and others!

In human nature the physical organization is all the time addressing itself to a conscious intelligence and moral sense. It is by physical nourishment and stimulus that there grows up gradually a responsible agent, with spiritual relations and under spiritual law. The human creature, child and heir of its race, moves toward the fulness of being as the child and heir of the Creator. The process is the development of personality. Humanity exists, works, longs, and suffers for the personal man. The personal man is held to the payment of a reciprocal debt to humanity, whether in the use of powers or in the surrender of life. He must read Scriptures, consult oracles, offer prayers, and not decline the benevolent demand for sacrifice. He cannot have his capital of truth all at once, nor duly estimate his obligation in the use even of what is given him. Gradually he must win his way, invent his apparatus, prosecute his experiments, and accumulate his gains. It is for him to move in the direction of the hint, suggestion, or premonition of truth, — that is, to move by faith; or else, missing the alchemy that transmutes all things to gold, he is in danger of falling into the error of unbelief, which, disregardful of commanding motives, is unequal to successful experiment, allowing the choicest elements to be lost in dross and slag.

Turn the horse's attention towards the precipice by the wayside, and he will be stimulated to avoid it. In like manner the immediate sense of personal duty is quickened by vague apprehensions of remote catastrophes that beset the path of life, until as life approaches its end the prudential shrinking from danger is no longer needed. The law of the Creator, under which we are trained to our responsible activity, "is perfect, converting the soul." Thought is occupied with reasons more or less convincing, for this way or that way. Different pleas are presented to the judgment. Persuasion and dissuasion end in one determination and one action. Personal autonomy, self-direction, under the law which governs all, — this is the great distinction of man, and, in connection with limited knowledge and imperfect character, his primal danger. Law regulates the alternatives to be presented: the free soul makes choice of the alternative to be accepted. Law points out the steps by which men go up or go down, — the degrees and means of advancement or degradation: the free will determines the attention, zeal, and effort of personal progress. More and more the personal sovereignty asserts itself in each separate man. He possesses and uses not only his own body but material nature in general; and, though subject in a way to both, is not of necessity servile to either. But do something he must. Either as a man of faith, finding life limited and death certain, he shall subordinate physical existence to spiritual law, and make both his living and dying a testimony to supreme reality; or else he shall have his ruling interest in the physical and worldly life to the disparagement of spiritual considerations, despite the certainty that his coveted happiness will be cut short, and his expectation for the future darkened. Benevolent, impartial death is the angel of redemption to both the faithful and the unbelieving. It is death, whose unmistakable nearness and steady approach makes the self-sacrifice of enlightened and prophetic spirits not too great for their virtue; and it is death that limits the temptation to disloyalty and apostasy, since, though any should be willing to deny their souls for the sake of their bodies, it can avail but little. Death is still certain and still near.

In short, man in the body is like the lamb in the fable, that fled into the temple to escape the wolf. The lamb's blood was sure to flow; and so the lamb might choose, not indeed between living and dying, but between giving his blood upon the altar of divine service and giving it to feed the hunger of his natural foe. To die is the common lot. To yield up the spirit piously is the free choice of the faithful. To fall into the jaws of the devourer is the fatal alternative of unbelief. To reach the end of sufferings incident to the processes by which death is reached, is the constitutional privilege which faith cannot dispense with and unbelief cannot forfeit.

We find, therefore, that use of our resources and opportunities under correction of natural law is to teach us how not to abuse them. Our first trials are most prone to error, while our later conduct is usually ordered with more prudence. The whole period of mortal existence is employed in starting the personal being, which can attain to completeness only by being transplanted. The revelation of God in man's spirit must needs transcend the present weakness of nature, or come short of its rational fulfilment.

Meanwhile, when it is considered that individual and social habits form themselves in advance of the ripening judgment; that veterans in the experience of life cannot so instruct raw recruits as that they will not have to learn their duty through error and suffering; that the physical struggle, the momentum of material interests and national enterprises, implies a necessary preoccupation of powers intended ultimately for better things, — it may well be feared that man will not soon escape from what seems "the persistent tendency of his development to take a wrong direction," however "exceptional" or "singular" the tendency may be regarded as compared with the way in which other orders of living things "fulfil the conditions of their being."

But when we come to the marks of a wrong direction

in man's development and find that they are manifold and repulsive, is it for us to ask: Why are so many products of human intelligence and energy given over to destruction? Why is personal discipline so severe? Why is the world always travailing in pain that the world to come may be brought forth? Why so much evil in the endeavor to realize good? Should we not inquire more wisely if our questions were guided by religious confidence rather than by natural distrust? How is it that human societies, imperfect as they are, rule without ruining the individual destiny? By what genial spirit of law are conflicting interests and struggling powers held in a certain equilibrium, so as to secure a constant trial rather than a mere foregone conclusion of personal conduct and character? What is the check upon the strong man's usurpations, when he has become the idol of his tribe, if it be not the limitation of individual life and the development of the popular power? What adequate restraint upon the insolent demands or ignorant aspirations of a populace as against the necessary personal offices of sober government, if there be no death to dissolve adventurous compacts before they can be completely formed, while society is renewing itself according to a traditional and necessary order? How otherwise shall the true leader have his opportunity and influence with the people, and the people have their trial in appreciating the serviceable man? How otherwise shall so much good be realized with so little evil?

Seeing that death and destruction enter so effectively into the economy of nature, men learn to appeal to them as motives. They combine, that they may wield more effectively the power of death. They develop organs and engines of destruction to be employed in the conduct of affairs. Opposing forces are discharged, not in the quiet order of nature, but in the shock of battle, that the forces remaining may rearrange themselves under new conditions. The divine Providence is often construed, not with reference to a universal intention, but as on the side of the strongest party. But then, the cost of war calls attention to both the prudential and moral considerations that forbid the appeal to arms except as a measure of last resort; and thus violence without law and without religion becomes the part of savages and enemies of their kind. The hero is known by his risking his life for those who need defence against the giants of arbitrary cruelty. The moral rank not only of an individual but of a people is marked by the manner of reducing death to the service of life. Death and destruction never say, It is enough, — so long as there is wickedness to be punished, unbelief to be convinced, faith to be tried, or virtue to be glorified, upon earth. Grant that the sacrifice of life imbitters the experience while it chastens the characters of men, — who can say that it is not also for the relief of man's estate in provisionally adjusting or seasonably adjourning the conflicts that signalize the progress of society? How else could old prejudice and prescription be so safely withdrawn, giving to untried disciples of Truth and Love a sober and moderate success befitting the state of discipline, wherein the struggle of faith and loyalty against appetite and ambition is ever to open anew?

We are not, therefore, to contemplate death as having exclusive reference to man's cosmical conditions, and to the *æon* of man as one of the animal races in the struggle of physical life. It has a bearing of the utmost importance upon his spiritual discipline. If the present life is childhood and schooling, how needful that the days of this tutelage should be shortened to such a period as would not forbid man to bring the elements of his training within the compass of his intellectual faculties and moral sensibilities. Life being short at the longest, man feels the demand for prudence and diligence in the conduct of life with a view to its immediate value and longer continuance. An apprehension of the nearness of death reacts in favor of good personal aims and efforts; while, as the passing days diminish the body's time and deteriorate its functions, the temptation to sacrifice conscience and faith — the tokens of endless life — for the sake of a poor remnant of animal existence, is losing its power.

Let us imagine now, instead of our common experience of nonage and decay, an experiment of vastly greater persistency and accumulation in all the powers and products of life. Let the organic law be capable of bearing a very great strain. No fruit inflicts immediate pain or suggests remote danger. No ordinary violence shows any tendency to snap the thread of life. No pressing appeal is made for prudence or science in observing or ascertaining the conditions of health; and hence there is no immediately effective check upon the struggles of selfishness and ambition. The demigods of former generations — *dii majorum gentium* — keep a mighty hold upon their sceptres. More and more the new life is compelled to take the shape and motion of the old. Society becomes a thing of conditions and fatalities, into which it is the more a misfortune to be born the remoter is the prospect of escape by the door of death. And if the patriarchal power is ever to be checked, if the party of more recent generations is ever to bear sway, how should such a revolution come but by terrific explosion, by calling upon death through all conceivable energies of destruction as a release from the stricture of unrelenting time? If we were to take the life-periods of the antediluvian patriarchs as exactly expressed in terms of our modern reckoning, and withal as wisely adapted to the world-work of their age, would it not give a vivid and terrible meaning to the statements that "there were giants in the earth in those days," that "the wickedness of man was great," that the earth was "filled with violence through them;" — a meaning such as would make the Deluge appear a mercy not less than a judgment, and the shortening of man's life the note of a new and more hopeful era?

CHAPTER V.

DETERRENT CONSEQUENCES OF DELIBERATE UNBELIEF.

WHAT is essential to peace and hope as respects the manifestation of so-called evil is to distinguish between evil as the error and misconduct incident to moral development, and evil as the unhappy experience naturally ensuing upon such error and misconduct.

Evil of the latter kind, being fitted to convey salutary rebuke and warning, is transferred by the law of reason and faith to the account of good. It is held to be good in the creative purpose, and good in its bearing upon human destiny as a whole.

Unbelief — indifference to ideal truth through preoccupation in common affairs, distrust of the infinite unknown, treating inspired prophecies as a deceptive mirage, and stubborn facts as the unchangeable type of reality — can neither do nor suffer nobly. It involves a voluntary predetermination not to take advantage of life's disciplinary purpose in its highest sense. A weakness for scepticism, a mood of mind and habit of argumentation which refuses to entertain, and of course does not keep pace with, the rational intimations of personal immortality in communion with the Author of being, ought to bring the unbelieving man in the process of his experience to a sense of his self-imposed limitations. How can he avoid coming at length to regard his material organization, not as a tent to be struck on the march to higher destinies, but as a prison to shrink and fall, burying the nobler manhood in its ruins? As personal consciousness becomes more and more the centre of a distinct and unique interest, how should it not, in that very fact, more and more abhor the prejudgment which dooms it to destruction under the pressure of physical change? For such a prejudgment imports more than the loss of personal consciousness in the measure of one's present capacities; it is the negation of an infinite progress, in which the ideal of man is conceived as fulfilled through the operation of God.

To disregard the boundless possibilities of being in attempting to define a certain nucleus of knowledge is, of course, to impose upon knowledge a character and meaning according to the limits defined. Deny all ideal fulfilments of things, and the partial elements of reality have nothing to atone for their repulsive features. Unbelief in this way can make for itself not only a bad world, but the worst. It can prostitute all the beneficent correlations of the cosmos,—infinite skill and infinite kindness,— to support the hypothesis of a world-will carrying on the poor play of life through an illusive and tantalizing consciousness, that acts its personal part only because it is the victim of false visions of faith and hope. It can construe all success as being only in order to realize the more astounding collapse and failure,— turning the triumphs of mind into trophies of decay. That which is ideally the best becomes a fascinating dream; that which is practically the worst, a frightful reality. The anticipated lapse into unconsciousness is soothing to fraud and violence in the enjoyment of ill-gotten gains; for judgment to come is their dread. On the other hand, self-sacrificing virtue intent upon the welfare of mankind bears its last testimony against an adverse judgment here, and is denied the life to come. "One soweth and another reapeth," — the saying is as true of ages as of individual men; but the empty eternity of unbelief has no season of common fruition, when " both he that soweth and he that reapeth may rejoice together." The incarnate humanity is dissolving day by day; it never fulfils its spiritual promises. Unbelief is positive about dissolution, negative as to the spiritual consummation which is the higher meaning of life. The fathers cannot reach perfection without the children, nor the children without the fathers. Unbelief sees a race continuing for the sake of individuals, and individuals consecrated to the service of a race; but either cannot admit, or sets itself to deny, the spiritual ages, when they neither marry nor are given in marriage, but have come to a personal equality with the ideal angels, as children of God and of the resurrection. All this violation of the essential proprieties of thought is on the way to a last contradiction of reason, when it comes to the necessary idea of oneness, — oneness of cause and oneness of intention, — accredited in the constitution of things.

Unbelief in its moral sense cannot exist without some degree of personal responsibility with respect to the revelation of rational truth. That absence of belief, which is the absence of knowledge, power, experience, responsibility, while as yet the personal embryo has not come to self-consciousness, is a condition privative with respect equally to both the evil and the good of moral agency. Not till the polarities of thought begin to be developed by contact with reality, does unbelief become the name for all our moral evil in contradistinction from faith, the principle of all our righteousness. Only as the antithesis of faith, — as the reluctant and disobedient action with respect to what is giving proof of itself as the true personal calling, — does unbelief sum up our moral delinquency, so as to stand for the spiritual man neglecting his spiritual duty in a wilful addiction to something else as more gratifying or advantageous for the moment. The unbeliever is aware of his birthright; and for that reason alone is he profane in his exclusive regard for the mess of pottage. The simple animal is not the partisan of the animal nature, for that comprises its whole motive of life. To the animal there is death, but no exasperated ghost to trouble it with the dread of something after death. Only the inner darkness of partiality, indocility, and deeds that shrink from light has for its necessary correlate the outer darkness, the eternal negation of true life, from which the spirit recoils.

Indeed, it is because unbelief is negative to truth possessed, as well as negative to the truth to be imparted, that it is so positive in its personal manifestation. Often it acts with an arbitrary intensity which indicates the force of argument and persuasion against it. There may be a natural disinclination to take the next lesson; but it requires an energy of will to resist the demand of faith when it comes with the authority of a teacher. Yet as faith is free or it is not faith, so coercive processes for the propagation of faith may provoke a violent resistance to the sway of truth. The promulgation of truth rouses human nature, not only in so far as there is in human nature an affinity for truth, but in its whole range of motives. All interests have to assert themselves in order that all may have their due consideration; for so only can patient reason do its perfect work.

The prophet of new and nobler things is the man who proposes to move the universal human life, not merely to readjust a few practical details. He intends to awaken the higher energies and to shatter the popular idols,— to cleanse the very temple of God. If heavenly thought is higher than earthly habit, for that very reason shall the children of light be found awkward and unequal to their tasks, while the children of a commonplace world are wise and accomplished in their affairs. If men are startled from their religious repose, their first impulse is to appeal from the quickening teacher to their holy books. If a moral reformation is the demand, men make haste and delay not to take counsel of their material interests.

In the higher ranges of disciplined thought, least of all is progress by unquestioning assent. Philosophers debate in order that prophets may divine; and statesmen know not how to salute the new doctor till he has triumphed over the old doctrine. The forces of criticism and contradiction rally promptly, that the power of truth may bring the argument to a more decisive conclusion.

CHAPTER VI.

EVIL AS SET FORTH IN THE CHRIST'S TEACHING.

THE Scriptural rendering of human history as respects the distinction of good and evil is through human nature. It is supernatural only as it involves the divine suggestion and energy moving in nature for such a progress and consummation as shall fulfil the creative purpose. The divine witness against the manifestation of evil is through the correlative manifestation of good. The whole revelation of God in the world, including those aspects of it which are regarded as miraculous, is through nature — not outside of nature; while the eminent expression of a creative reason is found in those inspirations, instructions, examples, and vital influences, that make for the harmony and perfection of mankind.

Inasmuch as the Scriptures are found to exhibit an historical testimony to one only Creator, conceived as moving in universal nature, but declaring himself as a personal Ruler and Providence in the convictions of mankind, and finally speaking through one man as the Word of God, — it is evident that their claim to universal acceptance and authority is in the reality which they represent. Whether they be counted true or untrue, the spiritual intention apparent in them, which construes them sacred Scriptures in distinction from ordinary writings, cannot be denied. As the faith in God, which the Scriptures illustrate, rests upon the evidence of universal reality, so the faith of Jesus Christ, in which they culminate, rests upon the absolute fidelity of Christ's testimony to the divine working in human nature. Always it is the universal reality which governs faith, — not faith which constitutes any reality but its own. If the sense of reality be weak, faith is feeble. If the sense of reality be limited, faith is limited. The miracle which accredits the commission of a prophet, or the striking object in nature which excites imagination as the enshrinement of a god, — what is either compared with the miracle of universal nature which affirms the one God?[1] Those are not justly called the ages of faith which exhibit great credulity, and equal error. Not that they are without faith, but their faith is as meagre and vague as is their knowledge of the truth. The times of ignorance are times of necessary and excusable unbelief. But when the personal Revelation of truth appears, then comes the command that all men everywhere should change their thoughts and become his disciples.[2]

There was faith and there was unbelief under the old dispensation; and the distinction between personal righteousness and personal unrighteousness was ever inwardly the distinction between faith and unbelief, as principles of conduct.[3] But the world-history was cut in twain by the coming of our Lord. He introduced the new age of faith, which was the day of judgment to a whole æon of unbelief. The world that "knew him not," his own that "received him not," the empire and the hierarchy that combined to resist and crucify him, — all are thrown by the crisis of his revelation into the era of

---

[1] Rom. i. 20.   [2] Acts xvii. 22-31.   [3] Heb. xi.

ignorance. They are shadows of a by-gone history. The great mass of mankind was found to be in the darkness not merely of partial knowledge, but of unfaithfulness in some degree to the light that is in every man. The world was wise in its conceits, accomplishments, routine, — not wise in faith, foresight, hope. While, therefore, Jesus was setting himself to fulfil the law and the prophets, as to their divine intention and positive meaning, the world was set chiefly upon that literal and conventional obedience which is prone, by making void the law of good, to fulfil the prophecy of evil.

As important as was the coming of our Lord to the revelation of the Father, so important was it, according to the New Testament, in the history of all his human children. It is conceived as that turning-point of universal experience which, by perfectly marking the difference between humanity in its initial imperfection and humanity as partaking completely of the divine Spirit, marked also, and just as perfectly, the necessity, possibility, and method, of man's reconciliation, whether with his Creator, his race, or himself. Only through the revelation of God in man is it held to be possible for man to fulfil the law of his being.

But inasmuch as our Lord's mission was to draw all men unto himself, — not to pronounce at that day a final sentence upon any, — the arraignment of men was provisional and disciplinary. The judgment against them was that, light having come into the world, "men loved darkness rather than light because their deeds were evil." Men of the world would go on according to their worldly momentum, and fill up the measure of their iniquity before apprehending the immeasurable condescension and patience of God, on which their eternal redemption was depending. Yet this moral condemnation takes just account of palliating considerations in its estimate of sin. It tones down the blood-red hue of most fearful crime to the duller complexion of pervading unbelief. "Of sin because they believe not on me,"— what other conviction need the Spirit of truth beget in the spirits of men, in order to save them from their sins? "Father, forgive them, for they know not what they do,"— infinite considerateness for the blind offender, that he may not despair of pardon when he shall come to the sense of righteousness! Such is the revelation of grace and truth as conceived in Scripture, through which the Prince of life judges and casts out the power that is contrary to life, and introduces the reign of God to the knowledge and faith of mankind.

But the dividing of the old world-age from the Christian era implies no sudden revolution, to be recognized on the day when it occurred. Our Lord describes the reign of God as not coming with observation. It is too vital, too deep within. Like the leaven, like the seed, its progress is according to its own law. The reign of God distinguishes eras only because it distinguishes society, — yea, divides asunder the very soul and spirit of the individual man. The point which indicates the line of distinction between the spiritual reign of God and what is negative to it, whether in general history or in personal experience, is the point where the action of faith meets the counteraction of unbelief, as respects the movement of divine revelation. No geographical, political, or family demarcation is of any permanent significance. The kingdom of God is all-comprehending as well as all-discerning. The Word of truth is for every creature. But as certainly as faith is the law of human fellowship with the Lord's mind, will, effort, suffering, and success, so certainly is unbelief the correlative measure of alienation from his spirit and work. Faith brings men from the four quarters of the globe and gives them seats with Abraham, Isaac, and Jacob, in the kingdom of God. Unbelief keeps the so-called children of the kingdom in outer darkness, though they should inhabit the very penetralia of the visible sanctuary. Faith is assured "that in every nation he that feareth God and worketh righteousness is accepted with him." Unbelief has respect of persons and prescriptions: "Except ye be circumcised and keep the law of Moses, ye cannot be saved." Jews as such continue to require signs, and Greeks before the coming of the new faith are seeking after wisdom, — neither at first finding anything but scandal or folly in the cross; but to every one that believeth, whether Jew or Greek, Christ the crucified is "the power of God and the wisdom of God."

Thus, according to the New Testament, the new world-age takes color gradually from the truth of Christ, while gradually the old dispensation is thrown into a background of darkness; and not until the new times are fulfilled can the distinction between the old and the new have been exhibited in full historic detail. As the dispensation of law was prophetic, so is now the dispensation of the Word and Spirit. Young men see visions, and old men dream dreams. But the ruling fact declared is that the Seed of promise has been approved and glorified of God. And now, to call on the name of the Lord, to make the appeal of faith according to the inward revelation of truth, — this is the eternal law of salvation.

If, however, we look to the Scriptures for Christ's estimate of human behavior under divine discipline, we find that the grosser elements of man's nature, which stand for unbelief, are recognized as in necessary correlation with the higher faculties concerned in the actions of faith. We may figure this correlation by the wave that rises not only before but also against the wind that is moving upon the face of the waters. The Word that is spirit and life discerns the thoughts and intents of the heart, and brings out their polarities. "Follow me," says Jesus; but did any disciple so follow as to indicate no contrary tendency? "I will follow thee whithersoever thou goest," says a man of forward faith, without waiting to be specially called. But Jesus bids him pause. It behooves to consider what that following means: "Foxes have holes, and the birds of the air have nests; but the Son of Man hath not where to lay his head."

To enter upon the discipline of faith, is that to reach the end of discipleship? On the contrary, every pulsation of faith has its natural reaction of unbelief; and the most confident profession of fidelity may be to the deeper moral insight a natural premonition of failure. "Blessed art thou, Simon Bar-jona; for flesh and blood hath not revealed it unto thee, but my Father who is in heaven," — ample recognition of faith! "Get thee behind me, Satan. Thou art an offence unto me. For thou savorest not the things that be of God, but the things that be of men," — prompt rebuke of unbelief! "Though I should die with thee, yet will I never deny thee in any wise," — free intent of faith! But he began to curse and to swear, saying, "I know not this man of whom ye speak," — fearful recoil of unbelief! But there cannot be these opposite extremes without the constant antagonism of spiritual and carnal principles. "Thou canst not follow me now," — the moment is too critical, the trial too hard, — "but thou shalt follow me afterwards." For, not until Peter shall have taken the last lesson of his Master's passion will there have been given him the full victory which as disciple and apostle he was invited to win.

Thus it is that Jesus appears chief of the many to whom the Scriptures bear testimony that they "wrought righteousness," in the fact that of him alone it is affirmed that he "did no sin." His oneness in spirit with the Father is held to assure the perfect consecration of physical life. Acting under the guidance of universal love, he does not fall under the bondage of animal instincts nor into any complicity with selfish habits. In his estimate of the practical alienation of mankind from the Father, he is conceived as the truth itself. Of course, his teaching in this regard would naturally be as unique as his character, and supremely important.

It is remarkable that the great Teacher nowhere refers us back to the first man, by way of accounting for the evil that is in the world. On the contrary, he points us to the paradise of infancy for our instruction as to the reign of God. He blesses little children. "Of such is the kingdom of heaven." "Except ye be converted and become as little children, ye shall not enter into the kingdom of heaven." "Whosoever shall humble himself as this little child, the same shall be greatest in the kingdom of heaven." "I thank thee, O Father, Lord of heaven and earth, that thou hast hid these things from the wise and prudent, and hast revealed them unto babes." "Out of the mouth of babes and sucklings thou hast perfected praise." Yet the paradise of childhood is not without its dangers. It is beset with evils. Not only are little ones, exposed in their weakness, liable to be despised and led into sin; they are in danger of destruction. They are lost, without protection and guidance. Hence that gracious teaching in the eighteenth chapter of Matthew, of "their angels" that behold the face of the Father, — and of the Son, higher than all angels, coming to seek and to save them, since it is not the will of the Father "that one of these little ones should perish."

The great Teacher brings Eden to every household. The story of Genesis alleges the perversion of man's action, while affirming the goodness of his original nature. It has been a fashion of later times to affirm the corruption of man's original nature, in order to account for the perversion of his action. The teaching of Jesus is in harmony with the teaching of Genesis. No spiritual corruption is charged upon the fontal creation. "That which is born of the flesh is flesh." The animal nature can neither transgress nor obey in the moral sense. "That which is born of the Spirit is spirit." The spiritual man, born from above but conditioned in the flesh, is recognized as not only liable to be more or less involuntarily subdued to the lower elements in which he works, but as in danger also of being more or less wilfully addicted to the same. Jesus would convert the man of low experience from the sophistries of the world to the sincerity of his original nature, in order to his receiving continual inspirations of divine truth, and so coming into spiritual communion with the Father. The Prodigal comes to himself that he may go to his Father. The Sun of righteousness pierces the blinding fogs that enshroud society, that the single-eyed and simple-minded child of humanity may awake to the fulness of light.

Always in our Lord's ministry the appeal of the miracle, of the parable, of the exposition, allusion, action, is to faith, against unbelief as summing up all that is adverse to truth and goodness. By this sharp point of distinction, as it moves on from moment to moment in personal trial, is generated the line of separation between the predominance of light and the power of darkness, between godliness and worldliness, between the foregleams of immortality and the shadow of death. Christ makes nothing of old scores, except as past history enters into the present determination of duty or danger. Setting forth the conduct of his relentless adversaries, he says: "If I had not come and spoken unto them, they had not had sin." There can be no responsibility accruing from revelation that does not imply the plea of ignorance in palliation of temporary unbelief. That sin is exceeding sinful which declares itself as a voluntary persistence in wrong, despite the persuasions of Truth and Love in behalf of the right.

The Apostles, taking up the testimony of their Lord after his departure, were left in no doubt as to how far-reaching was His authority whose commission they bore. There were distinctions that had had their day. It was now declared that God was not the God of the Jews only, but of the Gentiles also. The Word of God was addressed to all nations, was to be proclaimed to every creature. All were called to be disciples. The elect were those who voluntarily obeyed the call and thus distinguished themselves from the unbelieving world, no matter from what nation, family, or caste, they might come. The reprobate people were the knowingly unbelieving and disobedient, — no matter what worldly distinctions might be theirs. The King, who was the personal enshrinement of divine law, could recognize only this antithesis in the relations of men to himself. But the antithesis was not as yet absolute. There was no personal faith without its alloy of unbelief; no personal unbelief without a potency of faith. Men were changing moment by moment. Society was changing. The distinction of believers and unbelievers was not marked by any hard and fast line, but was moving according to free personal determinations. The process of change was invisible. The remote issues of the great regeneration were inscrutable. They were referred with equal awe and confidence to depths and riches of divine wisdom and knowledge — judgments unsearchable and ways past finding out.

What the Apostles saw before them was simply the world, — the humanity of past efforts and accumulations, — out of which was slowly to be moulded the better world that was looming up in inspired imaginations and benevolent desires. They discriminated between the fashion of things that is passing away, even while claiming to hold out, and the law of things that is growing strong, even in the very souls that seem to resist it. They apprehended the difference between the natural man, coming by ordinary generation, and the spiritual man, child of the life-giving Word; and, consequently, the difference between universal humanity on the side of a common mortal nature, represented in Adam, and universal humanity on the side of its spiritual responsibility and personal heirship of God, represented by the Christ.

It is impossible to hold up to view the better without accusing the worse; impossible to call men to their Christian discipleship as the supreme good, without exposing the evil and danger of going on in old ways; and it is important to remark that this was in fact the Apostolic way of finding fault with men and with the world. The Apostles addressed themselves to society as it was. They were not metaphysical or dogmatic; did not busy themselves with speculations tending to ground human error and transgression in a transcendental original sin; did not set themselves to nice discriminations of different degrees of personal responsibility or different shades of personal guiltiness; but with magnificent comprehensiveness and impartiality they appealed to the revelation of God's goodness, made more distinct by the tokens of his severity, and represented the future apocalypse of evil as having its whole secret in misappreciation and resistance of offered blessings.

St. Paul could account on natural principles for the first man's falling into sin, because he himself, under far greater light, and delighting in the law of God after the inward man, still found a law in his members warring against the law of his mind, which in kind is exactly what Adam was conceived to have found. But with a conscience more disciplined than that of humanity in its earliest moral experiment, St. Paul was learning not to confer with flesh and blood as to what concerns the fulfilling of a requirement which is above the sphere of physical law. As a spiritual man, he owned allegiance to the spiritual Word, and set himself to bring his body into subjection.

As it was in the beginning, so now in St. Paul's day God's judgment upon man's conduct is conceived as inseparable from knowledge of the truth brought effectively to bear upon conscience for man's spiritual direction. It was the prerogative of God to overlook the sin of ignorance that he might correct it by the unfolding of law, and to watch the effect of unfolding law in order to vindicate it against unbelief and transgression by proper tokens of his displeasure. Hence the postulate of the Epistle to the Romans is that God can do no wrong. He judges the world and is judged of no power. Let God be true, though every man be found a liar. The gospel, in its application to men, was simply the expression of a divine intention whose fulfilment had never lingered for one languid instant on the part of God. God's righteousness, the moral development of human nature, which God was seeking to realize through his Son, was from faith to faith, — from the faith of the past to the faith of the future; according to the Scripture which declares, "The just shall live by faith." Here is St. Paul's impregnable position and line of defence: "no replying against God." Impossible to understand or demonstratively to justify his ways? It matters not. The revelation of his Son is the Father's vindication, whether as regards his economy of mercy or his edicts of judgment. Refer everything to the Sovereign in so far as his dealings are beyond the range of the human understanding. Say that he hath mercy on whom he will; say that whom he will he hardeneth, — since no moral reaction is independent of his law, — but let not the thing made call in question the Maker. Faith, not fatalism, however, is the element of reason with regard to the unsearchable things of God. Though the calling and election of God, as determining temporary distinctions among men and nations, cannot be accounted for on the ground of individual merit, yet, as to the great future, judgment does not anticipate trial. For all men the day is a day of salvation.

The defensive motive and action in the Epistle to the Romans is incidental. It comes out sharply in the fifth and sixth verses of the third chapter. It pervades the ninth, tenth, and eleventh chapters, where the appeal is to faith in the sovereign Wisdom, that the dangerous partialities and groundless pride, whether of Jews or Gentiles, may give way to a common submission and pious awe. But St. Paul would have no such occasion for a defensive vindication of the divine rectitude, were it not for the "sword of the Spirit," — the invading Word, which declares God's benevolent hostility to man's unrighteousness. The gospel of salvation is not without a necessary note of aggression; and this meets us at the eighteenth verse of the first chapter: "For the wrath of God is revealed from heaven against all ungodliness and unrighteousness of men who hold down the truth in unrighteousness." And then follows, as far as to the twenty-first verse of the third chapter, a bold sketch of the evil to be overcome, in its actual details.

The truth of God, affirmed in nature but turned into a lie in the popular idolatries, the shameful crimes, the odious sensualities, the unnatural and destructive self-abuse, the malignant dispositions of men in relation to their fellow-men, — these were not sins of ignorance alone; they were offences against the natural conscience in every man, insults to the better sort of people who in a greater or less degree were showing the effect of God's law written in their hearts, outrages against precepts, laws, institutions, that contemplated the punishment of evil-doers and the honor of those that did well. In a word, the crying sins of the time were such as men would judge and condemn in others without even stopping to think how far they might themselves be implicated in the same.

If the Gentiles were in a bad way, how was it with the Jews? The Jews boasted of their law, and thought themselves able to instruct the unwise world. But what things their law said, it said to them that were under the law. Had the law no fault to find with Jews? When had not the name of God been blasphemed among the Gentiles by reason of Jews? Of Jews no more than of Gentiles could it be said that their moral habits were good enough, and should be let alone. It was plain, on the contrary, with regard to both, that the rudimentary moral discipline under which they had lived, far from leading them to the maturity of virtue, had brought them to the knowledge, if not to the acknowledgment, of sin. And if they were judged of their own consciences and their own laws as transgressors, much more must they find themselves to have come short of the moral glory of God revealed in Jesus Christ for the obedience of faith and the perfecting of life. On the other hand, supposing all men to have faithfully fulfilled the law of their being thus far, of what avail would be this foregone personal righteousness, if instead of perpetuating itself in more abundant fruits of good living, it should wither like a flower before the rising sun of a brighter day?

Therefore, unless the whole Apostolic persuasion about the Lord Jesus were a mistaken one, he, the Christ, was the end of law for the attainment of righteousness, whether as regards spiritual evil to be overcome or spiritual good to be realized. This simple issue the Apostles were pressing to a historic trial at every sacrifice, even to that of life itself; and the banner of their Leader was to be their sign of conquest in all the world, even to the end of the world-ages. To all men without distinction they said, Man's spiritual consummation was in the beginning, is now, and ever shall be, not in a more or less scrupulous fulfilment of limited conceptions of law, that are themselves shadowy and transitory, but in spiritual communion with the Father, through whose only-begotten Son there is mediated a constant teaching of the eternal Spirit. This is the "living way;" and, since the Word made man is the fulfilment of all previous laws and prophecies, it is, relatively to the old dispensation, the "new [or recent] way." You, Jews, who would not receive your own proper Prince, you of the Gentile world, who have not recognized as yet the Lord and Master of life, — you have all come to that moral test according to which the divine government is proceeding, and under which every man shall work out the practical demonstration of his own character, whether for weal or woe.

There is no avoiding the significance of a standard. God's law is the truth. The truth of manhood cannot help vindicating the divine reality against the counterfeit presentment. The reign of divine law would cease were it to make terms with falsehoods and illusions. The whole world presents of necessity a relatively darker aspect of evil, the moment the heavenly reality conceived as salvation — development of life in communion with God — is held up to view. Then it begins to appear what unworthy contentment there is in men with things as they are, what powerful interests array themselves against changes that make for ultimate good but involve immediate suffering, and what violent resistance abounding sin offers to superabounding grace. The sign of the Son of Man is that all aspects of evil, all energies of self-will, all shades of prejudice, are for a time quickened in the human consciousness when he comes. He is content with no easy and barren victory. It is for him to struggle with the unbelief that dates from his testimony, — an unbelief more violent and more blameworthy than any which could meet an inferior witness. Yet divine justice recognizes the condition of unbelief as a plea in excuse for acts of unbelief. St. Paul is permitted to say, in view of his persecution of the church, "But I obtained mercy because I did it ignorantly, in unbelief;" and St. Peter, speaking to men whom he charges with denying and killing the Prince of life, adds: "And now, brethren, I know that through ignorance ye did it, as did also your rulers. But those things which God before had showed by the mouth of all his prophets that Christ should suffer, he hath so fulfilled."

Thus the faith of Christ is not only an ever-living persuasion of God as working in nature, but an ever-enlarging apprehension and deepening impression of universal nature as God's workmanship. To this faith, as it speaks in the Scriptures, moral evil appears as an irrational factor, unavoidably incident to the voluntary working of imperfect moral agents in a process of development under stress of life's struggle, but disappearing when the consummation of personal being is reached. The disregard of right moral suggestion, through personal ignorance or slowness of faith, is ever proving itself at length to be as foreign to the meaning and purpose of man's nature as it is to the teaching of inspired seers and prophets of God, who best interpret for their day the divine intention to which nature is evermore giving utterance.

It might seem, at a moment of sudden conviction, as if the personal revelation of truth and love, in the very fact of its divine authority, could admit of no deliberation or delay, and must drive men at once from the intermediary degrees of moral sentiment and action either to the utmost of devotion or to the extreme of revolt. But, foolish and slow of heart, man does not so learn the meekness and gentleness of the Christ. The human dulness and inertia are not forgotten by him to whom the ages belong, and "who willeth that all men should be saved, and come to the knowledge of the truth." Our weakness of apprehension, our immaturity of judgment, our lack of spiritual susceptibility, our preoccupation with earthly things, our blindness to heavenly realities, — all these have to do not only with the duration of our trial, but also with the thoroughness of our moral discipline. Our spiritual transformation is not held up as the miracle of an instant, but as the continuous experience in which we are of our own choice workers together with God.

The principles of the animal and worldly life are ever in our mortal nature. The long-suffering of God, which we are taught to count as our salvation, takes into partnership with itself the patient working, waiting, and suffering of man. The Scriptural conception of the world-history holds out no prospect of peace on earth except in the maintenance of the Christian warfare; calls to no sitting together in heavenly places but through the riches of a victorious yet still militant grace; predicts no Christian civilization that shall be proof against the inroads of barbaric rudeness and sensuality; announces no holy church that is not liable to degenerate into a practical denial of the Christ; and foreshadows no period of triumphant virtue that shall render impossible the outbreak of bold wickedness. In the process of development the forms of good and evil are modified, but the relation of good and evil does not disappear. The historic world has many ages, but is of one kind.

The reconciliation of all things in Christ is for the spiritual ages of divine revelation. Enough for those who bear the image of the earthly humanity, if with the Lord from heaven they can contribute their personal efforts and sacrifices to the consummation and bliss of the eternal society, according to the divine Law of Atonement.

PART FIFTH.

THE LAW OF ATONEMENT.

"Neither pray I for these alone, but for them also which shall believe on me through their word: that they all may be one, as thou, Father, art in me, and I in thee, that they also may be one in us: that the world may believe that thou hast sent me."
John xvii. 20, 21.

"Now I rejoice in my sufferings for your sake, and fill up on my part that which is lacking of the afflictions of Christ in my flesh for his body's sake, which is the church."
Colossians i. 24.

"Quod homo est, esse Christus voluit, ut homo possit esse quod Christus est."
Cyprian, quoted by Hagenbach, History of Doctrines, vol. i. p. 177.

"As there is one end to many things, so there spring from one beginning many differences and varieties, which again, through the goodness of God, and by subjection to Christ, and through the unity of the Holy Spirit, are recalled to one end, which is like unto the beginning."
Origen, De Principiis, lib. i. c. vi.

PART FIFTH.

THE LAW OF ATONEMENT.

CHAPTER I.

RECAPITULATION AND TRANSITION.

THE Scripture teaching, so far as we have been able to verify it, contemplates nature as one whole, and as partly known to us in conscious experience, while with our common knowledge is joined a movement of rational faith; namely, the faith in one God, — the Cause of nature and the Source of man's moral discipline in the world.

Without this faith, the suggestions, demands, and prophetic assurances of nature cannot be combined in a rational system of thought. But with this faith, not only can the teachings of nature be systematized, but the infinite Reason working through nature is brought more and more into finite apprehension and action; and in this way there can be a practical revelation of God in man.

God's revelation of himself in man is found to be not only through primitive suggestions of divine agency and authority, but through continually renewed examples of personal faith and service, such as mark the progress of a spiritual creation in the history of our race, and point to one personal Revelation, the Object and End of Scripture testimony.

Though the Scriptures have to do with the world's history as one whole, under one eternal direction, yet their representations are accommodated to the conscious moment and limited apprehension of the human mind. Indeed, that divine teaching is grounded in universal reality is proved by its finding expression in special facts; for particular facts cannot be disengaged or dissected away from the organic whole to which they belong, nor can they be understood in an isolated or abstract conception of them.

For example, the world's schooling is fact and experience of the instant, and so is fact and experience of the ages. The error attributed to primitive humanity is recognized as real and natural, because it is the error of mankind under all phases of tutelage. The righteousness of faith is ratified, reasonable, and acceptable for the moment, because it goes on to fulfil itself without limits of time. The sin of unbelief, on the other hand, is pardonable, curable, and temporal, as springing from the imperfect knowledge, partial judgment, and sensual appetite of the moment, which the order of nature is constituted to overrule according to the creative intention.

The elements of thought thus briefly recapitulated are elements of life. It is impossible to consider them with any degree of attention and not come to an awakening of the spirit with respect to some divine purpose and rational consummation towards which man is working his way. As the spontaneous development of nature is evermore asserting differences and antagonisms, so the universal government of nature is evermore composing these differences and antagonisms in a higher order. It is in this way that the process of personal development on the part of man is made the medium of a personal revelation on the part of God, and that in the practical progress of revelation there appear tokens of a purpose, not only to overrule, but to rule out whatever obstructs man's communion with his Maker, and to make man perfect in faith, love, and practical loyalty. It is the working out of this reconciling purpose in history which gives expression to what we may call the law of atonement.

A hard fate has befallen the word "atonement." It has fared worse, if possible, than "justification." It has been not only warped in the struggles of opinion, but colored according to vagaries of imagination; while the more it has been bandied by parties, the more it has incurred the odium of a *shibboleth* with thinkers who prided themselves upon either their indifference or their catholicity. In the Revised New Testament the word does not appear; but it cannot be made to disappear from the records of religious thought. It deserves, therefore, to be redeemed from unnatural bondage and brought back to its original service.

Reconciliation, as between the Creator and his rational creatures, may signify a moral relation to be preserved, or a moral relation to be attained. In either case it can demand nothing more than perfect faith and obedience, and can be realized by nothing less. Milton's seraph Abdiel, "faithful found among the faithless,"[1] is represented as preserving his loyalty, and his peace with God, by continually renewed acts of duty in a career of unbroken communion. The Christ of the New Testament stands forth as the Apostle and High Priest of

[1] Paradise Lost, b. v. 1. 896 *et seq.*

universal reconciliation, by preserving his own spiritual oneness with the Father, in that unswerving devotion which is the proper obedience of the Son. There can be no expiatory suffering incident to creaturely devotion that does not find its place in the infinitude of divine requirement; as there can be no divine requirement of sacrifice, which is not first of all proof of the Father's long-suffering in the creation and government of the worlds. It is He, who, through all the ritual of sacrifice in nature is reconciling his worlds unto himself, — lifting the struggles of life under low and transitory conditions up into the higher service of spiritual emancipation.

The word *atonement* contemplates the condition not of perfect beings, but of beings to be perfected. Not only in systematic teaching but in ordinary speech it refers, if I am not mistaken, to motive, means, efforts, for the attainment of an end; and this end, whether conceived as attained or to be attained, is reconciliation with God, the Supreme Father, in a possible perfection and universal harmony. In the applications of detail, atonement refers especially to pains and sacrifices in the way of duty; reconciliation, to joy and triumph in the approval and success of service done: atonement stands for the economy of the divine Goodness in subordinating universal nature to the motive and service of love; reconciliation is the harmony of spiritual beings in whom love is the fulfilling of law: atonement implies the necessary discipline of finite agents, in bringing them to be, intelligently and voluntarily, at one with God in his universal aim; reconciliation implies the result of discipline which the Father aims to achieve in his whole family. In fine, atonement declares that the world is constituted for the development and trial of personal virtue, not for the exhibition of constitutional impeccability;[1] while reconciliation holds out the promise that even material nature shall share in, and show forth, the glory of humanity redeemed from the bondage of error, and made free in the service of the Father.

The law of atonement involves of necessity the relation of moral agents to all law; and is grounded in the eternal rectitude which forbids that one jot or tittle should in anywise pass from law until all be fulfilled. But there is the mark or sign of atonement, which brings to our rational recognition a universal method of the divine working; and it is this which must determine and guide the inquiry before us.

---

[1] Turretin, following St. Augustine, says: "*Libertas Adami fuit posse non peccare.*" [Institutio Theologiæ Elencticæ, vol. i. p. 515.] Relatively to some limits of action unmistakably defined this may be admitted; but beyond such limits, and according to the notion that takes law to be nothing less than the divine intention for the entire moral contents and spiritual development of human nature, *posse non peccare* is not predicable of man's immature agency any more than is *non posse peccare*. The case admits of brief discussion with respect to its rational elements. *Non posse peccare* is properly predicated of the mere animal basis of human life, before the beginning of moral agency; and then it is practically identical with *posse non peccare*. Either of the two phrases can stand for no more and no less than the other. Again, personal development under divine direction may be conceived as going on until the human spirit is brought into perfect communion with the divine Spirit; and then *posse non peccare* is morally identical with *non posse peccare*. But between these two extremes there is logically an "excluded middle." From the point where the merely physical *non posse peccare* ceases to the point where the perfect spiritual *posse non peccare* begins, neither phrase, in any other than a relative sense, is a verifiable predicate of human agency. What is verifiable of man in this middle region, on the score both of his moral energy and of his spiritual imperfection, is given in the clear confession of St. Paul: "To will is present with me; but to work out the good is not" (Rom. vii. 18).

What redemptive and reconciling process is realized in nature? What is the law of thought and teaching concerning the same in Scripture?

We have not to seek any detail of analogies, such as might show the teaching of Scripture to be open only to objections that could be urged with equal force against the system of nature. What our inquiry seeks is evidence of a universal intention and process of reconciliation revealed in nature and witnessed to in Scripture — a point of view from which things seemingly objectionable in detail should much rather appear to be indispensable upon the whole. All finite quantities are mathematically zero in comparison with infinity. How then should anything be anything by itself, when actually the thing has no existence as it is separately conceived, and is real only as merging in the infinite reality to which it belongs? Indeed it is only as we learn to know what addresses itself pointedly to our confined observation and momentary judgment as belonging to the unity of things, without limits of space or time, that we win our way in the faith of one eternal Word — God, with one qualitative equivalent — Love.

Nor, again, have we anything to do with those governmental schemes which represent to us a reign of God under the image and superscription of Cæsar. Our movement is not in a sphere of limited legal judgments and compensatory legal fictions. "Imputation," "substitution," "satisfaction," in the sphere of law, are signs which are liable to import what is essentially false, though intended to signify what is relatively true. For the present we will drop the pontifical phrases, leaving to Cæsar the things that are Cæsar's, in order that we may apprehend in their simplicity and sincerity the things that are God's. Is not thought constituted to move in that universal realm, which is physical creation and moral government in one? Is it not in the unity of revelation that we are to find the wisdom of God, which can rebuke partial criticism and silence petty apology? Is it for us to take care that the divine government receive no detriment, in case the sins and sufferings of human beings are made subservient to the development of personal virtue, which is. itself the surcease at length of sin and sorrow? And what puerility of logical pleading is so depressingly trivial, as the familiar one of pointing out that the difficulty as regards a government of absolute perfection is one and the same, whether evil be the disciplinary bitterness of a day, or the war and wail of endless duration? It must be distinctly premised, therefore, that, for the purpose of the present study, punishment is the expression of divine displeasure against the guilty, — not legal satisfaction for guilt. On the other hand, suffering in the divine economy, far from having any necessarily punitive character, may be the unavoidable incident of an effort that is to achieve an infinitely preponderating good.

CHAPTER II.

THE LAW OF ATONEMENT IN ITS PHYSICAL TYPE.

OUR first effort shall be to get a clear conception of the law of atonement in its physical type.

The whole order of material nature is one whose harmony is in the reconciliation of differences and the adjournment of conflicts. We are often told of an obtrusive contrast between the physical economy and the spiritual economy, as regards the reconciliation of discords. Material nature is held up as the realm of unrelenting law, equally remote from any thought of pity or hint of hope to the transgressor, whether his offence be wilful or accidental. In the pulpit and through religious publications, how often have high authorities used all their eloquence to impress upon the popular imagination and judgment the idea that physical nature is the antithesis rather than the type of redeeming effort, such as is revealed in the gospel of our spiritual salvation. It is amply set forth that if we suffer shipwreck we shall be drowned; if we are caught asleep in a burning house or amidst the fumes of charcoal, we shall suffer the natural consequences; if we take poison, we can count upon the poison to work on in its ordinary way; if we fall from a height, or if something falls from a height upon us, we cannot escape our exact due of injury. For the sake of a special argument, all-reviving and all-restoring nature, which the sentient creation loves, is ungraciously construed in a sense exactly contrary to the general tendency of things. Nature is charged with being as merciless to transgressors, irrespective of their intentions, as she is propitious to those who obey her laws, irrespective of their intentions; and it is not always added that the seeming cruelty is in order to the greater kindness.

But because nature rebukes lawlessness, are we unreconciled to nature? Because nature taxes life in detail for the salvation of life in general, do we put ourselves in permanent conflict with nature? On the contrary, we try to be reconciled to nature in active obedience; and so far as this is found to be impossible we submit to be reconciled in suffering. As a rule, we do not suffer shipwreck, or perish in burning houses, or come to our death by the sudden action of poison; or, if we do, our suffering is for the safety of all who know how to take warning from our fate. The faith in which we are rationally reconciled to nature is that the infinite firmness of law in the constitution of things is one with the infinite fervor of love in the administration of things. If the service which matter and motion fulfil in the physical order are too important to yield to the momentary comfort and convenience of individuals, and so injuries take place which, with all her pains, nature is not constituted to heal except by the panacea of death; is it according to the higher nature of man to grudge the sacrifice and rebel against necessity? Or, rather, seeing the body quietly reassimilated to the congenial earth, does not the spirit of man tend to the persuasion that it shall prolong its days in higher recognition and enjoyment of the divine economy that can so graciously use and distribute the sufferings inseparable from the attainment of infinite good?

At any rate, the simple fact is that we are members one of another. We live and die, not unto ourselves alone, but unto our kind and unto our Creator. Nature is constituted to exact the sacrifice of atonement in the temporary efforts and sufferings of the few, that the life of reconciliation and harmony may be more abundantly enjoyed by the many. In the persistency of this sacrificial law we find the security and conservation of all life here below. Because the laws of nature are too sure of their meaning to remit their appropriate exactions, the pupils of nature become studiously obedient. They not only work out their salvation from natural evils, but, what is much more important, they do this in a way to develop just such habits of attention and loyalty as will avail them in working out their welfare under the spiritual economy.

Nor in this subjection to the law of sacrifice is life to be looked upon as for the most part servile and passive. If the creative hand reaches through nature in order to mould men to their proper obedience, the same power reaches equally through men in order to mould material nature into closer conformity with man's developed thought and desire. Nature endows man with the liberty of her laws; and so the laws of nature become the charter under which man rules and redeems those parts of nature over which he presides. Docility and intelligence on our part win nature to our will, so that nature yields herself to our service in regenerate forms and richer products.

Knowing that we are to try conclusions with the

storm, we learn how to build our ships. Aware that we must be ruled by compass and chart, or else ruled by rocks and shoals, we master the laws and catch the auguries of navigation. The conquest of vast and resistless elements is grand and stimulating in proportion to the risks taken in seemingly blind paroxysms of fury into which the elements are sometimes thrown. And when physically conquered, there is a certain inspiration of his Maker in man, by which he looks beyond nature as if the supernatural were ever his real home. He seems to be overcome indeed, but only by the restlessness of matter under the divine energy, through which all nature exists, — and exists for the sake of man as heir and ruler of the realm.

Is it the decree of nature that the unsightly and unhealthy marsh shall forever resist the progress of husbandry, and mar the beauty of its neighborhood? On the contrary, nature shall yield the offending part to the service and to the taste of man, as soon as man shall make the sacrifice necessary for its redemption. To drain, grub, burn, plough, and fertilize, — this is the toil and sacrifice of atonement. By this means the displeasing locality is reconciled. The intractable becomes the genial; the foul is turned into the beautiful; the injurious and obstructive is changed to the harmonious and useful.

Whenever the experience of man opens his mind to those respects in which he can mould nature into harmony with himself, and man takes up the instruments of intelligent toil to subdue the earth, the earth's reaction is in the way of reconciliation. Resistance is overcome. The wilderness and the solitary place are glad. Deserts rejoice and blossom as the rose. Pastures are clothed with flocks, and valleys are covered over with corn. The mountains and hills break forth into singing, and the trees of the field clap their hands.

Inaccessible heights, everlasting snows, and the most dangerous seas are gradually brought into the unity and harmony of thought. It is ascertained in what way they are necessary and serviceable, as well as sublime or beautiful. They are found to exist according to a constitution of the globe in mysterious harmony with the constitution of its inhabitants. The more deeply the elements of nature are penetrated, the more thorough and comprehensive is the reconciliation of thought and things. The jury of finite intelligences to which the Creator has entrusted a certain trial of his works is ever rendering a spontaneous verdict of faith in their goodness, though ever remote from the comprehension of their infinite design.

In what concerns the economy of life in the physical sense, the law of sacrifice in a process of reconciliation and redemption is at once striking and universal. There is no preservation of life but at the cost of life. In earth, air, and water, the redemption of all living things from cunning and violence in quest of blood is at the price of blood. Life pays for life. The destruction of a few, comparatively, in every species secures for the moment immunity from death to the many; at the same time enforcing the instinctive caution and activity that make up the enjoyment of existence during its natural term. One species preys upon another; but there is the enormous vegetable growth offered from year to year for the support of animal life, and so the hostile tribes abide in a comparatively peaceful society. Always animal life is immensely in excess of the consumption of animal life.

The ever-recurring pursuit and flight does not threaten the survival of kinds, in a vast preponderance of living specimens as compared with the slain; while only by a continual sacrifice is the equilibrium preserved between different orders of living things and their natural resources of nourishment. Instincts of parents and offspring, natural economies of protection, all efforts that make us recognize the patterns of intellectual and moral action in the brute creation, are due to the struggle as well as to the constitution of life. To enjoy life is to expend life. Throughout the innumerable ranks of sentient creatures, the truth holds that to save existence in sluggish or cowardly retirement is to lose life. One moment of awakening terror is ecstasy of life, compared with lingering decay. If life be good, then is death also good, which, by limiting individual existence, secures collective persistence. Be it active destruction or natural decay that works out the beneficent result, the orders of living things are made to be at one with each other, — to be at one with inanimate nature, in a common possession of life, only through death.

The same law is most strongly marked in the relation of man to the lower animals. To distinguish, to name, to subjugate, the creatures of brute intelligence, is a work of danger and sacrifice proportioned to its interest and importance. The triumph and rule of man is not without cost both to himself and the subject races. To live and let live is a law of reconciliation which is never administered except with the incidental offering up of life. Peace is at the price of war. Offence and defence afford the temporary exercise which will ensure the succeeding repose. For men to combine against wild beasts is to enter upon the labors of peace and civil order with respect to each other. Take away resistance, and progress is no more.

And then, in domestication, animals become the willing servants and companions of man. They profit by their dependence, as man profits by his control. They are slain for food; they are sacrificed in witness of a spiritual faith, and thus denote the homage paid to the Creator of all; yet, upon the whole, their life is made better by being subjected to higher life. The choice victim predestined to secure by its own death the exemption of others of its race from the claim of sacrifice, is for its day the most cherished of the flock. So, too, the kinds that furnish man not only nourishment for the body, but means of expressing his spiritual desire to honor and propitiate the Lord of all, are most highly prized. It is remarkable that the law of eating and drinking among men has held a permanent relation to the law of sacrifice in the offices of worship, exactly as the law of physical nourishment holds a constant relation to the law of spiritual duty. What is necessary and most agreeable in the economy of man's life seems most fit to determine his offerings to the Author of life, — on whom all depend, but whom man alone of creatures, on behalf of all, is moved to thank and to supplicate.

Indeed, we cannot forget the extreme to which humanity has been carried in the sacrifice of human victims on behalf of the collective life. It required the recoil from mistaken immolation to teach that obedience, involving its necessary sacrifices, — not sacrifice irrespective of obedience, — is the way of spiritual reconciliation to supreme authority. But what wonder, if, in the midst of a universal economy of sacrifice, no creature, living or dying in its own interest merely, man should think it a not unpromising service to worship the Source of life in an exemplary surrender of life? How could it be certain that a more satisfactory career for survivors might not be purchased at a vicarious cost, and the rights of the victim be safe with the Divinity to whom the victim was devoted? At any rate, the law of atonement in its physical type is clear, terribly as man may have erred in attempting to interpret the divine requirement of which it is the expression. Nature is right in what God intends her to teach; but it is a long work for man, through nature, to be taught of God.

One thing appears indisputable, namely, that throughout the course of nature there rules a law of atonement, in the continual reconciliation of differences by means of appropriate sacrifices. The inanimate earth is redeemed to the service of living beings at a sacrifice. Living beings are adjusted to their natural term of life by spontaneous efforts that have by and by exhausted the vital energy. Life in lower species pays tribute to life in higher species. In fine, all creatures, up to man himself, live and die in unconscious but necessary homage to one creative Power, — who is in all, through all, over all. The reconciliation of all beings with each other is their common subjection to creation's law. The bringing of things into harmony and oneness by service and sacrifice, voluntary or involuntary, is the rule of nature, — not the exception. It is not a mystery of detail to be referred to a system; it is the note of a universal system accounting for all difficulties of detail, — the law by which all things consist.

CHAPTER III.

THE LAW OF ATONEMENT IN GENERAL HISTORY.

THE physical law of atonement is the type of a spiritual procedure.

How shall man, as the rational representative of subject nature, conceive and express the subjection of his own mind and will to the Author of being? The difference between God, the absolute Truth and Love, and man, ignorant and self-seeking, — by what sacrifice can it give place to an assured communion and oneness of man with God? The Example and Legislator of man's spiritual reconciliation with the infinite Spirit, — has he appeared? What is his word?

Material nature is outward, of the senses. Revelation is inward, of the spirit. But the outward and the inward exist as one; and the revelation of God makes use of material nature in order to have its way in the human spirit. We may say, generally, that in creation the Revealer determines organic laws and sensible limits of outward phenomena, in order to furnish the medium and symbols of an interior communication. God, the Prime-mover, is thus the Supernatural by relation with the natural, the divine by relation with the human, — the Revealer, the Redeemer, the Saviour, in virtue of a spiritual effort and causation in man's history, such as these appellations indicate. The postulate of revelation is that the Creator subjects spirits to their outward conditions in order to complete his work by making outward conditions the means of teaching, strengthening, and perfecting spirits in the communion of divine truth and life. No kingdoms of this world but for the sake of the spiritual reign of God. No ages of vanity and dissolution, but that they may furnish some elements of immortality to powers whom their Creator will not leave to decay. No antithesis of God and the adversary of God, of God and the world, or of God and man, which does not signify a synthesis — a reconciliation; as appears from the fact that divine revelation is effectively carried on only by causing the reason and will of God to prevail over the limitations and misdoings of ignorant men.

Therefore, whatever the revelation of God may by and by have done with nature, we know the revelation now only as having to do with nature. The divine Spirit is working in human history, and passing into ever-new expression through the decay and regeneration of society. It is only because God is working through nature that he can be apprehended in nature. No particle of the outward universe can be taken away from the divine Spirit, whose living temple is man. The divine testimony is not confined to any cycle of miracles; it is in the whole course of nature. But the distinguishing mark of revelation is in the spiritual law which governs its special organs, through which they become guides and judges of their fellow-men.

It is evident that there is no sacred history, so called, which is not part and parcel of a larger reality, — universal history. There is no holy nation which does not emerge from, hold commerce with, work for, and pass into, the common humanity. There is no elect agent or typical epoch of divine teaching but appears in natural relation both with the common order and the universal aim of God's creation. If the human family, needing a man chosen and called of God, be naturally employed in bringing such a man into bounds of time and conditions of being, the man of God shall not fail to make his calling and election sure, by impressing his own spiritual motive and character upon the men of his day for a testimony to those who shall come after them. If the man of the divine idea and spirit be conceived as the first-begotten of the Father, the mediatorial Prince, the personal type of human perfection, and as such the organ and prophecy of universal regeneration; then it follows, from the very postulate of his pre-eminence, that other men are but imperfectly prepared to understand him or to believe in him. The difficulties he shall surmount are one measure of the triumph he shall achieve. The fulfilment of his office, — the reconciliation of all to the truth, mediation ending in universal communion, — this implies not merely the service of the Teacher, but the discipline of every learner in the school of personal responsibility.

Looking at the history of mankind with reference to its spiritual facts, as distinguished from its physical phenomena, we find that the law of reconciliation by means of sacrifice pervades the whole domain; while the Scripture testimony is concerned with that advancing light, culminating in a fulness of personal revelation, in which the same law is pre-eminently magnified and made honorable. Hence, the whole spiritual progress of our race, quite irrespective of any specially inspired interpretation of the same, is the proper field of inquiry as to the law of our redemption from error, and our sanctification in the truth. One would willingly know if there is any canon of reason or of art that can give a human being the nimbus of the saint, except in consideration of his having personally borne, in his own degree, the cross of the martyr.

The unity of history depends upon the development of differences for the sake of reconciliation upon a higher basis of mutual service and general harmony. Physical law, as we have already seen, is a law of atonement, not without sacrifice. But the cosmical rule deals very gently with our sensibilities. The tree absorbs its own elements from earth and air; and not until leaves and fruit fall to the ground are we reminded of what the tree has to pay back. Inorganic matter and the grower's art must have their dues. But when we contemplate all the units of personal intelligence, conscience, and will, that are summed up in the world's moral movement, we are instantly impressed with a sense of cost and pains in the composition and reconciliation of numberless individual energies, every one being constitutionally determined to take its own line.

To reconcile growing spirits to the vast intention of their Creator would seem to involve no slight outlay on their part, were each one treated with reference to himself alone. As we are made, the least part of the cost of personal progress is the exhaustion of physical resources, — the whole organism through which sensation is brought in for the training of judgment being destined to expend its resources in due proportion whether to their use or their abuse. This would simply enforce the costly spiritual endeavor to apprehend the genuine object for which all sacrifices should properly avail. It is not an easy and spontaneous action so to use the things that are passing out of hand as to secure the qualities most worthy of continued being, in merely a personal experience. But we are creatures of a complex society. There is a vaster if not superior life, — a collective, pre-existent, and surviving humanity, which is constituted not only to produce, but also to control and dispose of, individual existence. Our Creator has determined our dependence upon our kind, and required our service to the race. A man is an effect with reference to his becoming a cause.

Inasmuch, therefore, as the individual man is of society, and through society, and to society, he becomes a possession and, if need be, a sacrifice to the family, the tribe, the nation, the race, and finally to the Creator of all, in working out the universal glory and joy. His faculties are made up with due regard to his relations. Personal duty, no matter how costly, is of infinite promise to the personal agent, with respect both to his own possible survival of all sufferings, and to the unending efficiency of his conduct in the being of others. The personal career and interest of every one enters into the idea of any one's moral accountability and retributive experience. Let a man live or die for his kind, let a patriot fight or perish for king and country, let a martyr sacrifice himself for his testimony, — is the loss on the part of the sufferer alone, and not on the part of the humanity and Divinity for whom he suffers? And the gain, — is that for those who inherit the immediate or remote effects of sacrifice under the government of God, to the exclusion of the vicarious sufferers, through whose good offices the gain ensues? Break the vital connection of men with one another and with the Father of all, and the bond of human obligation is broken. But grant us to be members in particular of a universal family, and the inevitable effect is that, if one member suffer, all the members suffer with it; or if one member be honored, all the members rejoice with it. Not that this effect is of necessity a matter of immediate consciousness; it ensues in the administration of eternal law.

Is there wonder, then, at the abounding expenditure of life, and not much more wonder at the superabounding development and improvement of life, in which the cost is accounted for? Is there scandal and complaint on the score of savage violence, desolating wars, barbarous civil and military punishments, and fiendish persecutions of religious faith; and may we not rationally ask if that system of sacrifice can be denounced as upon the whole practically excessive, which comes to a necessary mitigation of its horrors exactly in proportion as man is brought on to better principles and nobler habits of living? Is the cost too great of redeeming society from its primitive rudeness to its better soul? Not to redeem it is the greater cost; and the price of wellbeing must needs have been paid, or how should we appreciate the good to which we have attained?

Not by beautiful reasons and fine phrases, but through the actual struggles out of which speech is struck, must the ignorant get their schooling from the better instructed. A pains-taking master must lift up to the level of his own efforts a pains-taking pupil. The strong can help the weak, not chiefly by an eloquent and pleasing address, but by bearing the burdens and feeling the resistance of the weak; till the weak are made strong with much trouble to themselves, and the strong are made stronger, not only by trial of their own powers, but by the strength they have treasured up in those who before were unable to help themselves. With what infinite patience, then, must God bear the burdens of all finite beings, while educating them to be workers together with him!

Is there any exchange of services, however small, but implies an overcoming of obstacles and a reconciling of differences in effecting the exchange? The commerce of neighbors and friends, — is it carried on without a certain degree of cautious self-interest, a little conflict of personal judgments? But how shall strange or hostile peoples become neighbors and friends, when each is holding out a temptation to the ambition or cupidity of the other, and neither likes the difficulty and delay of negotiation when an affair can be more neatly accomplished by force? The intellectual and moral assimilation of masses is apt to be preceded by violent collisions. External conditions and prejudices of habit have to be shaken by wasteful warfare, that the combatants may rise to higher things through a preliminary trial — short, sharp, and decisive. Tribes that own a certain affinity of blood do not come to their sense of spiritual oneness so long as they are fighting out their natural differences. But when the opinionated and predetermined fight of seeming good has been fought, it remains to fight the good fight of faith according to the actual situation. Material weapons are laid aside, that the spiritual struggle may have freer play and reach a more satisfactory result.

The great chapters of history, which we learn to read by their titles, — do they give us any ages of culture and refinement that were not proud to own their indebtedness to times of heroism and suffering? And how long is poetic art or philosophic reflection allowed to hold its own against invaders ready to disperse the treasures accumulated, if society be unready for new sacrifices in their defence? Alexander cannot master the world without Aristotle; nor Aristotle without Alexander. But when Greek thought marches in the might of conquering armies, enters the gates of captured cities, founds new seats of empire and of learning, dictates the language of enlightened policy and superior culture, then the wisdom of the West combines with the faith of the East. The Hebrew Scriptures in the Greek language become the riches of the world. Moses and the prophets had to take gifts from the Greeks in preparing the way of the living Word; while Roman aggression and domination made the way into a highway with incalculable expenditure of life, before the supreme Pontiff and Prince of Peace could proceed upon his career of sacrifice and triumph.

Human experience is a ritual of sacrifice, voluntary and involuntary, through which conflicting interests and powers are brought into accord under one divine control. The ritual is determined, sustained, directed, by the creative governance. Nothing can be offered to the Author of being which is not already his. All victims are provided by him, whether for the nourishment of bodies or the redemption of souls; and his are the sufferings through which his children pass from blind conflicts of error to the reign of righteousness, peace, and joy. The kingdom of common intelligence, commerce, and law is a kingdom that suffereth violence; and the violent take it by force. Conflict is before order. The more important the interests at stake in the apprehension of contending parties, the more fierce the struggle, the more bloody the sacrifice by which the final composition will be bought; and, presumably, the last ruling will be upon the whole beneficent in proportion to the cost of arriving at it. Men force their way from anarchy to liberty by contending stoutly for what they hold to be right; and any custom or statute long held in respect will be unsettled at much risk, even for the purpose of fulfilling its original spirit. The literal law is most nervously exacting, whether as regards observance or penalty, just before it is to pass away; and then the prophet of fulfilment has his great hour, if he be ready to sacrifice himself for the real law, against erroneous constructions. All ages are to him who is wanting to no claim, whether of the future or of the past.

Besides, the fulfilling of law does not avoid the conflict of laws. The motives of duty are complex. There are claims, each seemingly authoritative in itself, that are not easily reconciled with each other. The conscientious judgment oscillates sensitively, and cannot settle itself to one direction except by a determination, possibly very painful, to sacrifice the lower to the higher requirement. The claims of family, of country, of humanity, of Divinity, — who is sufficient for such a hierarchy of obligations, if the lower appear to be not in practical coincidence with the higher? The supreme Love is indeed the whole law; but the sacrifice of faith in God, obedience to divine inspiration as the fulfilment of all devotion, is not easy, when the self-surrender implies the denial of all that common affection holds dear. Yet God's perfect revelation in man is possible *a priori* only in conjunction with man's perfect faith in God. Given a man perfectly receptive, and God, by the perfection of his being, is perfectly communicative. In such a man the divine and human are not in antithesis, but in synthesis, — the divine possessing the human, the human possessed of the divine. In such a man there could be no distraction of duties; since the supreme Love would be in him the reconciliation and satisfaction of all claims. Heir of the eternal Rectitude he could submit to no limitation of his moral authority, as he could know no decay of spiritual life. Temporary obstruction could import to him no permanent failure, premature and formal submission no genuine success. As the example of righteousness calling all to his standard, yet declining to be hailed as chief by men as yet alien to his rule, it would be for him to move in the majesty of his moral testimony and in the energy of his spiritual influence, till all men should be his willing disciples and subjects. Meanwhile how could he achieve this progress and triumph among men, but by bearing their ignorance and perversity, and so revealing, as teacher, priest, ruler, the perfection of truth and power in the perfection of patience and mercy? How, in a word, should not the perfect service offer the perfect sacrifice?

Now, apart from the Scriptures, in which the gospel is specifically proclaimed, we have a testimony to Jesus in the natural progress of human society. The sign of the Christ in history, his attribute in art, his ideal in thought, his appeal to emotion, — these belong to him naturally, because he came into the course of nature. No special testimony could avail without this natural corroboration. The man Jesus has an eminence and authority in the world not scrupulously configured to the testimony of his apostles, or to the teaching of his church, — an attention and veneration freely accorded to him, through whatever medium he may present himself to men's minds. That he was a man unhesitating in his persuasion and utterance of the truth; that he evinced his faith in God through the power of an obedient and submissive piety, speaking and doing the things of the Father; that he shed upon the world a light too pure for selfish policy or conventional success; that still he atoned for the transcendent character of his ministry by freely subjecting his claims to laws and judgments of the world's routine, thus sanctioning temporary condescensions and just sacrifices as an indispensable feature in the method of reconciling the lower to the higher purpose; that he became the Exemplar and Founder of a faith through which alone the personal communion and consummation of mankind was held by him to be possible; and that this faith contemplated nothing less than the regeneration of humanity, and incidentally the regeneration of outward nature, through a spiritual ministration mediated by its Author from age to age, — all this has entered into the disinterested thought and sentiment of many generations, and become matter of recognition and representation on the part of thousands upon thousands, who were not careful to call themselves Christians, or whose discipleship was an affair of ordinary discipline rather than of high spiritual aspiration. Literature, art, philanthropy, civil government, military enterprise and administration, professional ethics, habits of society and personal conscience, have been so quietly penetrated and colored by the influence of Jesus, that vast multitudes are by no means ready in referring his qualities and conceptions to their source; or, possibly, the remote example is disowned out of an overweening regard for self-development. The force that, according to the New Testament, invades and overcomes the world in "the incarnate Word," is resolved into a general potency of creative thought moving in the direction of fine ideals, without reference to any authentic image of the Father as the pattern of our ultimate glory and virtue.

This spiritual infiltration of Christianity, which, passing beyond those who have owned their allegiance to Jesus as King of men, penetrates the whole movement of society, is important as showing the intellectual and moral vicinage of his more effective supremacy. It instructs us as to what elements and proportions of the Christ's teaching are suited to take possession of society, without much force of outward authority or special propagandism. Nay, it even intimates to us what law of faith prevails by the very constitution of the human mind, in spite of the often injudicious and injurious zeal of those who profess and call themselves Christians. The constitutional sway of Jesus among men not his declared adherents is indicated in a general uplifting of thought, effort, and hope, above the necessities and gratifications of the moment; in a changed conception and treatment of the present existence, growing out of a belief or doubt inseparable from the very idea of a future life. We are here to work out what we justly desire, not to receive it otherwise, not to attain it at once. We are here, not to be always saving our individual lives, but to accept and encourage the bestowment of life that cannot be saved in the interest of life that ought not to be lost. It is ours, not to grudge the sacrifices we are called upon to make, but to rejoice in the good our offerings may win; not to despair of those no longer seen, but to await the manifestation of the sons of God; not to be forever chanting a tedious threnody over human mortality and sorrow, but rather to cheer the march and fight of transitory existence with songs of hope, in anticipation of life that shall turn the sufferings of a day into permanent peace and joy. This elevation of life, belonging to the whole world of mankind, as the tidal wave belongs to the ocean, is the natural response of human society to ideas and motives that find their highest expression in the Christ.

In passing, the thought suggests itself that it is partly because the spiritual Revelation is through nature, and according to the law of nature, that many have supposed it to be of nature. They have their apology. They prefer to construe nature as including the unknowable energy, rather than to believe that a personal Creator is, or can be, accredited in nature. This is one mode of the antithesis of partial knowledge and universal reason. It represents the attitude of an unsatisfied agnosticism, as against the rational conception of faith. Faith takes in a range of life from the infinite Father to the flowers of the field, and insists that a universal moral order cannot be physically developed from below, unless it be rationally determined and constituted from above. The testimony of the historic church, despite the conflicts of detail, is that creation is of God, through the divine Word, the Christ of the Scriptures, unto all men, to the end that all men joined together in the faith of the Christ, and living unto God in love, may be turned betimes from unreasonable absorption in lower objects of desire, to find their eternal satisfaction in Him from whom they came. Here is the circle, not of a vicious logic, but of a real creation, wherein nature is evermore proceeding from and returning to its Author; only in such a way that physical necessities and social obligations are made to serve the ends of personal education. The church in all ages is properly against the rest of the world only in order that all men may be brought into peaceful communion with their Maker; and the Scriptures of the church are distinguished from other honest records of human experience, not by the intrusion of any power or principle foreign to nature, but by the clearer and mightier expression, through all stages of divine communication, till we come to the divine Man, of what is the meaning and law of universal being.

The method of divine teaching is practical. The Scriptures have the ground of their coherency in a real history, their complete significance in a real man. They are the revised, re-edited, and strikingly illustrated teachings wherein nature is set forth as universally moved by the divine Spirit; they culminate in a human enshrinement of the divine character; they record a unique and perfect crisis of personal condescension, devotion, and self-sacrifice; they testify to the consummate filial obedience of One who is Son of God and Son of man, to the service which is all-satisfying and all-availing, to righteousness without fiction and without flaw, to a human perfection which cannot be more and cannot be less, — a qualitative completeness in the love of the Father. If the Scriptures bear witness in such sort to the love of God, we look to find them true to the inmost and utmost reality of nature.

CHAPTER IV.

THE LAW OF ATONEMENT IN SCRIPTURE HISTORY. PRIMITIVE AND PATRIARCHAL SACRIFICE.

THE Scriptures do not advise us that we have great need of collateral testimonies in our efforts to understand them. On the contrary, they set up a peremptory claim to speak for themselves. Happily, we can hardly mistake their general drift, however great may be our lack of particular knowledge.

Especially as regards the law of atonement we have to do, not with any clever handling of symbols or lucky coincidences of phraseology, but with successive examples from life, whether the type of experience represented to us belong to the antediluvian, patriarchal, or national period. Our appeal is "to the law and to the testimony." [1]

Again, happily, the Scriptures represent, not an inspiration holding itself aloof from the feeble initiative and restricted action of primitive faith, but an inspiration working through the efforts of faith from the very beginning. Even the great prophetic burdens are not made up chiefly of apocalyptic foreshadowings, but are brought home to men's business and bosoms in realistic and historic expression. The canon of Scripture has not

[1] Is. viii. 20.

provided for its own verification by outward criteria, — and for the very good reason that the practical discipline of reconciliation with God through the sacrifices of faith and obedience is the canon of the canon; the organic law of revelation brings its own elements into vital unity, and disowns what is foreign to its purpose. Higher than the heights, deeper than the depths, the divine Reason, like the air we breathe, finds us in the very centre of conscious life, and is never needing to be brought from far. The note of revelation is this: "The word is very nigh unto thee, in thy mouth, and in thy heart, that thou mayest do it."[1]

The offering of gifts and sacrifices to an unseen Power, as represented either in the holy Scriptures or in general history, is the worship of primitive culture. Tentative at first, this worship is expanded and systematized with the progress of thought and experience, until the original faith and motive are analyzed into various elements, and these elements are noted by variations of ritual in accordance with an essential unity of purpose. But the germinal idea of all sacrifice is worship; and since this idea, even as a germ, involves man's whole moral constitution, we are sure that in its fullest growth it cannot surpass the essential quality of its vital beginning. Hence the original simplicity of motive and thought in sacrifice is the clue to guide us through any labyrinth of ceremonies in a sacrificial economy. An action, speaking more plainly than words, gives a simple, solid sense; while words and phrases may divide and diffuse the same sense in a lore of details, that have their oneness and life in the original action. To go back to the earliest and simplest rite of worship is to gain a starting-

[1] Deut. xxx. 11–13. Rom. x. 6–9.

point for appreciating the whole order and movement of spiritual facts.

Let us turn to the fourth chapter of Genesis, and beginning at the third verse read on through the seventh. We are held to read simply what is there stated, the body and pressure of the time, not the constructions and inferences of subsequent ages and systems of thought. Two men of one family, heirs of a fresh world that has rewarded their several industries, each bringing an offering of such things as he has to the unseen Power, Life of all life and Ruler of all being, — what does it mean? There is only one sphere of thought in which the different parts of their action can be combined. It is worship. The language is: "Thou, Source of life, art sovereign and sufficient; I am tributary and dependent. Thou hast ordained the lower orders of living things for the service of the higher, and through us dost summon all things to the acknowledgment and service of thyself, who art the Highest. I offer thee of what is thine, as I am thine. Let me be at one with thee in the way of homage and obedience." Could the act of sacrifice properly signify less than this, however darkly understood? And, with whatever distinctions and developments of the conception, could it possibly mean more? Nay, the day of righteousness is signified in the dawn of faith, and the first true devotion is fulfilled in the final reconciliation.

But insincerity in the expression of homage is not worship. It is the contradiction of worship. The spirit must give validity to the form, if the form is not to belie the spirit. No harmony with divine truth, but only consciousness of rebuke and remorse, while the sin of hypocrisy is lying at the door. By the steadfast faith of the doer, is the character and significance of the thing done; and so "by faith," not otherwise, "Abel offered unto God a more excellent sacrifice than Cain."[1] And by the same faith Abel had in himself the testimony of his righteousness, while Cain had the conviction of sin and the sense of divine displeasure, as inseparable from his unbelief and formality.

Could any rational being suppose that the Maker of all things would respect an offering for what it was in itself, and not for what it was in the intention of him who brought it? The offering was an instrument of communication, a bond of attention, a testimony of desire and trustful expectation, a pledge of loyalty, that might be interpreted as the sign and seal of a mutual covenant, by the divine response in the faithful soul supported by the divine goodness in the ordering of the world. Thus, while recognizing faith as the one principle of man's communion with his Creator, the story of this primitive sacrifice conveys the correlative truth of the Creator's disciplinary judgment declared in the conscience of man.

Life devoted to the service of life, life passing by death into higher life, — this, as we have seen, is the law by which all orders of living things are adjusted to each other and to their common end in the physical domain. And now, as the spiritual manhood rises above its physical necessities, it is held under the same law. We see man tributary to the divine government, called to a spiritual homage in the very fact of being open to suggestions from above, and moved to express that homage in the consecration and sacrifice of physical life, animal or vegetable, in accordance with its demands. The

[1] Heb. xi. 4.

sacrifice is practically a recognition of physical death as entering into the divine economy of life, not, indeed, for the sake of death, but for the sake of more and better life to come. The worship of sacrifice is of a nature to combine ideally with all experience and history, to absorb meaning from the divine dealings, and to sustain the faltering steps of man as he follows his invisible Guide in a way of ever-new life, whose end he cannot make out.

Accordingly, when the flood had swept away a violent and intractable race, and in the silence that ensued there was the hushed submission of one redeemed family, the head of that family was not without a deep conviction of what the judgment signified. As the sacrifice of faith was burning upon Noah's altar,[1] a covenant of new life and hope was defining its great promise in his soul. The race was saved. Creation was risen out of the deluge. In a world of waters and of clouds there was to be henceforth the all-ruling sun, and the bow in the cloud; instead of the present devastation, seasons and harvests, unfailing proof of the divine bounty and forbearance, though the imagination of man's heart be evil from his youth.

Here is sacrifice of identical yet developed significance. The expression of personal homage and devotion is made the vehicle of a divine interpretation of history. A signal advance is announced in the reconciling process, as a mighty impact of divine thought and energy has taken effect upon the course of nature. Henceforth worship shall have such meaning, and law such sanction for mankind, that the exceptional piety of one family shall not be vindicated in a general destruction. Rather the

---

[1] Gen. viii. 20.

sacrifices of personal righteousness shall avail for the salvation of successive generations. The persistency of human society, being compatible with the progressive revelation of the divine character, becomes subservient to the propagation of a rational faith.

The simple and majestic personality of Abraham [1] appropriately sums up the trials and successes of patriarchal faith. His is a character not merely dutiful as respects the daily intimations of a higher Will; he is a man of far-reaching forecast, of watchful and prophetic devotion, — a man to enter, by such sacrificial offices as the wisdom of the time and his own inspiration pointed out, into a covenanted co-operation with God for bringing to pass the future of mankind. A man of God, for the reason among others that he was a man to command his children and his household after him, Abraham was not unfit to receive circumcision as the sign and seal of a family consecration to the divine service. Still he was by no means shut up to personal and family considerations, but gladly paid the homage of tithes to Melchizedeck, regarding simply the priest's eternal function, no matter from whom inherited or to whom transmitted. He was more than the father of a faithful progeny in the ordinary sense — a father of the faithful in a transcendent sense. From him in the order of nature was to come the consummate Example of faith, in whom all families of the earth should be blessed.[2]

Sacrificial worship, that makes its appearance with no explanatory reference to how it originated, that becomes the note of a sharp moral distinction between Abel and Cain, that, after the Deluge, serves Noah as a sign of the Creator's reconciliation with man, in view of his future

---

[1] Gen. xv.   [2] Gen. xii. 3 and xxviii. 14.

trial, — this same worship not only served in the experience of Abraham as the medium through which he made and received the ratification of his covenant with God, much as men were accustomed to ratify covenants with each other, but gave its outward form to the severest test of the patriarch's faith.[1]

The spirit of Abraham was too active and aspiring for religious routine; nor could he yield his judgment to the fiction that by any outward measure of sacrifices his due to God could be definitively paid. The choice tribute from herd and flock, or from the products of the ground, what was this but the pledge of endless personal devotion, of unlimited practical surrender? Whatever God could ask, that it should be his joy to yield. And what could God ask? Might he not — did he not — demand a return of his best gifts? Could any offering bespeak more confidence than the Creator of all things deserved? Could even the child of promise be withheld? Might not this lamb also have been provided for a sacrifice? Impossible, did it seem? For that very reason why might it not be true? Shall faith confine itself to what is possible with men, and do no honor to what is possible only with God?

Whatever example, suggestion, or argument may have wrought in the patriarch's mind, all is summed up in his persuasion that the strange and terrible thought was not his own but his Maker's; while at the same time he was strong in the belief that no part of the divine promise as to him and his seed should fail. "In the mount of the Lord it shall be seen."[2] Supported by his trust the father of the faithful took his journey to the mount of the Lord, and made ready for the sacrifice. Then,

---

[1] Gen. xxii.   [2] Gen. xxii. 14.

indeed, and there, it was seen — seen in the light of a conclusive experience — that obedience, unconditional confidence and devotion of spirit, the very essence of acceptable service, was the reality desired by God. But the literal offering up of a child upon the altar was by no means permitted, could not have been the divine intention, as it was not when human sacrifices were forbidden under the Law. Abraham offered a living sacrifice, a reasonable service. He surrendered himself to God as a willing organ of the divine thought; and so was made to understand, not how far the sacrifice of self could go, but how far the sacrifice of another could not go.

But, though the high priest of self-sacrifice was yet to come; though the way, the truth, and the life, of personal consecration to the Father on behalf of the brethren, was not fully revealed; yet, was not all sacrifice properly self-sacrifice ? Was it the victim and not himself, — the victim instead of himself, — the offering, of whatever kind, as a commutation for self-surrender, that was the meaning of sacrificial worship? If tribute however small signifies subjection and loyalty to human authorities, must not tribute to the Supreme mean unconditional submission on man's part, — even in the very fact of making appeal for protection or forgiveness ? When the patriarch's loyalty is well proved, a sacrifice is provided to express it, not to oppress it; and Isaac is reserved to offer himself a living sacrifice, as the way shall be opened to his devotion and service.

It is thus, through tentative and typical stages, that the law of sacrifice moves on to its fulfilment in the Christ; when it becomes universal, not as the offering up of victims at all, but as the consecration of personal life.

The gospel preached before unto Abraham [1] was the same in effect which became afterwards the Word of God to all the world: "He that taketh not his cross and followeth after me, is not worthy of me." [2]

But, though the ritual of sacrifice, — the form of worship in which man pays his voluntary tribute of submission to the divine ordering of life, — may begin and change, and as to some of its features pass away, the real sacrifice, the actual submission of life to the divine disposal, in the course of nature and in the administration of moral government, dates from the foundation of the world, and cannot pass away till all the law of it be fulfilled. All that a man hath as a creature of the cosmos shall he give for that life which is his as heir of God and of eternity. The sweat of his brow, the products of his toil, the fruit of his body, yea, his very flesh and blood, shall denote simply his tribute to a spiritual creation and an immortal life. The first offering is fulfilled in the final offering. The gifts of God are duly acknowledged only as they all pass, in dutiful submission to his law, through all forms of sacrifice by which the consummation of being can be subserved.

This is what people before the flood are conceived as slow to learn. The preponderance of a lusty animal force was the relative suppression of spiritual virtue. Yet the divine law of atonement did not leave them out. If they were not ready then to come to terms with their Maker, by presenting their bodies a living sacrifice in a reasonable service, their Maker had the alternative of asserting his claim in a judgment which could not be resisted. The divine administration simply adjusted its procedure to the eternal righteousness, — and made the

[1] Gal. iii. 8.   [2] Matt. x. 38.

disobedient generation an involuntary sacrifice for the redemption of human society, in anticipation of that just One, who, having freely tasted death for every man, is represented by his Apostle as bearing the good news of spiritual refuge and reconciliation to those very antediluvians, who sought no escape from impending ruin, when the typical ark was preparing.[1] Thus the long-suffering of God is salvation in universal history. The sacrifice of a day may seem exorbitant to the children of a day; but the economy of sacrifice, in its infinite range, can mean neither less nor more than the greatest good at the least expense.

Good, not evil, is the vital energy and rational suggestion of history at every period. The process of reconciling mankind to the Father involves the proof of divine sympathy with suffering, — even suffering incurred by sin, — and of divine satisfaction in view of all evil giving way, through the struggle of faith, to the peace of obedience; a divine sympathy and satisfaction least understood when a world is given over to physical destruction for the moral rescue of mankind in a single family, — most persuasively revealed when One like the Son of man endures the last physical agony, for the spiritual redemption of all the families of the earth.

[1] 1 Peter iii. 18-20.

CHAPTER V.

SACRIFICE UNDER THE LAW.

THE movement of patriarchal life is toward national life. There is a corresponding advance in sacrificial worship.

So long as the household lives the life of its head, the patriarch fulfils all mediatorial offices on behalf of his family. He is prophet, priest, and king. He presents a striking type of the one Mediator, through whom the universal Father deals with the whole household of faith through all generations. But when patriarchal pre-eminence gives way to the national spirit and authority, then a redeemed and consecrated society becomes in Scripture the comprehensive unity, type of universal humanity, conceived as under the moral discipline of the Father and object of his redeeming love, while the function of mediating the divine teaching and direction for the government of all is specialized in different official persons, — the prophet, the priest, the king.

The patriarchal experience was clearly to the effect that exemplary sacrifices could be a source of no satisfaction to the Eternal, except as the genuine token of submission and duty on the part of man. It was by his faith, not by sacrifice as an outward ceremonial, that Abraham came into his communion with divine truth and goodness, and to his consequent separation from the sensuality and superstition of the time. This faith, coming down by spiritual descent, was illustrated anew when the children of Abraham and of Israel were brought out of Egypt to be planted, as a holy nation and heir of God, in their promised inheritance.

The story needs to be recalled only in its moral features, by way of keeping up the connection of our argument. The ruler of Egypt, usurping the prerogatives of God, had enslaved the people of God, and so was alienating them from the divine service. Israel, the real prince in the earthly household, was to be rehabilitated. The spirit of religion was to call into action the feeling of nationality, and patriotic zeal was to be enlisted in working out the divine intention on behalf of all mankind. In the name of Jehovah the Israelites asked permission to leave their burdens for three days, that they might worship in the wilderness. But Egypt did not recognize the God of Israel, and paid him no willing tribute of obedience. Therefore Israel was redeemed from bondage at greater cost, and especially at greater cost to Egypt. Israel was called the chosen son of Jehovah, his first-born. Should not the Egyptians be made to feel Jehovah's displeasure at their offence, even at the sacrifice of their own first-born sons if other chastisements should fail?[1]

With Israel, also, the crisis was one of life and death. They saw themselves in an evil case. For not only had they roused the tyranny and violence of the Egyptians, but their God, so they thought, might bring pestilence upon them, if they failed of paying due honor to his call. Their faith and obedience were appealed to as the ground

[1] Exodus iv. 22, 23.

of a difference to be put between them and their oppressors. In the emergency the Passover celebration was instituted, as a token of their fellowship in the divine counsels, and as a pledge of their exemption from the signal infliction which Egypt's obstinacy had at last made necessary. The Passover was thereafter a perpetual memorial, not only of a popular redemption and national birth, but of a divine ministration of life, strength, and joy.

Here, again, the ruling idea of sacrifice is not wanton waste or uncalled-for surrender; it is much rather the levying of a wise and discriminating tax upon physical life for the correction and conservation of spiritual humanity as a whole. The flesh prepared and eaten in strenuous haste, as the nourishment of sudden resolve and urgent enterprise, becomes a sacramental element, — the sign and pledge of seasonable succor evermore ministered by unchangeable Goodness; though the blood upon the lintel told of unoffending human victims prematurely taken out of a genial existence in the cause of Israel's emancipation. How could Israel's debt to such victims be paid, unless for them also Israel, the Son of God, was was to offer himself freely in working out a universal redemption?

The transition from patriarchal to national religion, marked by the Passover institution,[1] involved no change of principle, great as was the change of political and social economy which it contemplated. Under the leadership of Moses, the man of God, the national organization is set forth as distinctively that of the people of God. In the Hebrew political economy not only educational interests, but the moral and sanitary regulation of

[1] Exodus xii.

society was inseparably linked with the public service of God in the national worship. The worship of the nation claimed the devoted and exclusive attention of a tribe, while the priestly functions were still further specialized in a family, and came to their consummation in a single man. Thus not only the rights and privileges of citizenship, but the national charters and hopes were guaranteed under an elaborate system of religious observances, wherein all personal obligations were determined with a scrupulous regard to the unities of time, place, and action.

Oneness of national worship required not only that the priests be separated from other pursuits and consecrated to one service, but also that all objects belonging to the holy place, or utensils employed in the sacred ceremonies, should likewise be separated from common uses, and devoted to their peculiar purpose. To make holy, to set apart any object from common relations to a sacred function or to a religious use, implied the two correlative ideas of separation and atonement, — separation from all common applications, atonement to one spiritual aim. Thus on behalf of the whole nation was to be presented one unadulterated worship, one grateful tribute of the best to the Giver of all, the homage in which every loyal soul should have his personal offering more worthily presented.

To the same purpose, also, the blood[1] taken as the unity of physical life was made the sacrificial symbol of a higher unity, the oneness of spiritual reconciliation. It was evident then as now that there could be no unity of spiritual devotion unless all physical life were in

---

[1] Lev. viii., xvi., xvii. 11-14; Deut. xii. 23; Heb. ix. 22-28; xiii. 12.

effect laid upon the altar. To live physically might mean to die spiritually, while to live spiritually would assuredly demand, sooner or later, the giving up to death of the flesh. And so, living or dying, it was for the people of Jehovah to be his. They were to find in him their inheritance and their home for the time present and forever. The blood of the sacrifice was the token of sanctification, not only for all inanimate things, but also for the priests, and through them for the people. They were a peculiar people, set apart from foreign entanglements, united in the same spiritual motive and obedience. Their sacrifice meant, not that they were asking to be exempted from physical death and moral correction, but that they were held to surrender their animal and worldly existence, with its warring lusts, to the law and Spirit of Jehovah — One in All.

As has been already intimated, distinctions of form in sacrificial worship, while they may set in clearer light interior relations of thought, cannot add to what is essentially involved in the primitive burnt-offering. Growth develops only what the germ contains. But what seems at first concrete and simple, may push its substance out into many branches. To make an offering by fire, to pay the tribute of life to the Giver of life, is to express worship in its complete or undivided sense, — submission with respect to whatever may be feared, dependence as to all that can be desired or hoped for. Such worship has its natural reaction in the loyal spirit. There ensues the peace of faith, the persuasion that what was well-meant on the worshipper's part must be "blessed, approved, ratified, reasonable, and acceptable," on the part of the Being adored. The peace of submission passes into the joy of communion; and this, again, suggests a new phase of the same worship. A peace-offering may be brought, a festive, eucharistic worship, part of the victim going up by fire to the Source of being, part eaten by the worshippers in thankful assurance of harmony with their God and with one another. Yet the original worship includes all, both the act of surrender and the peace of submission. To trust in Goodness is to enter into the inheritance of joy. The thank-offering may be allowed a place and order of its own. This is only to enrich the language of worship, not to transcend its necessary sense.

In this way the spiritual oneness of worship determines a significant variation of forms. The vague sense of ignorance, error, and possible offence, if not the clear conviction of wrong-doing, is essential to worship of the rudest type, as it is original in man. But with law comes the clear knowledge of sin, which finds a specific expression in the sin-offering. The duller and darker appeal, of a stranger in the earth seeking direction from above, grows to the quickened moral perception and penitential desire expressed in the expiatory sacrifice, — a form of worship which requires confession, and perhaps restitution, in consequence of actual disobedience, after the divine command has been distinctly given.

The law points out the practical conditions on which the divine favor is pledged. It sets forth the terms on which it is sought to bring the chosen people more and more into spiritual accord with their Protector and Prince. How can one share in a common worship under the law when one is not careful to cherish an habitual reverence for the law? A citizen must hold to the compact if he is not to be cut off from the covenant-keeping people. But if he has violated the covenant, however ignorantly, then in penitence, absolution, and reconciliation is his hope. The moral discipline and the visible symbols by means of which the atoning process is practically administered, so as to legitimate and fortify the sense of reconciliation, are essential to the effectiveness and perpetuity of the theocratic idea. If a loyal spirit can be begotten and sustained, then the law of the Lord, which is perfect, converting the soul, can work in accordance with its infinite intention; then the King of Israel can teach and guide his people, opening their way out of errors and sufferings into virtue and peace.

But a law that is to impress its spirit upon unschooled subjects must make provision for a becoming patience and considerateness of discipline. It must avoid the extremes both of penalty and of indulgence; or else, instead of reconciling and governing the transgressor, it may precipitate a fatal event. Hence, while the theocratic economy is ever intent upon reconciling transgressors, the atonement is not without sacrifice. If the way of transgressors is hard, the grace of reconciliation, though free, is not allowed to be held cheap. Something must set forth the offence, and mark the repentance; that the offender may be treated without untruth or illusion. But once the offender is reconciled to law he is in no equivocal position. He belongs to the loyal society without protest or suspicion. To him, as to all the true Israel, pertain "the adoption, and the glory, and the covenants, and the giving of the law, and the service of God, and the promises."[1] He has only to be willing and obedient; he shall be taken gradually into the fellowship and service of the supreme Ruler.

In the atonement here contemplated a vital process is

[1] Rom. ix. 4.

carried on by means of specific acts. The specific acts of atonement have to be repeated, in order that the spiritual work of atonement may be completed. The law sustains an economy of practical discipline in the interest of spiritual reconciliation; but does not bring to pass the final oneness of God and his children. That all change may have reference to one end, all effort to one motive, all conduct to one principle, all possessions to one purpose, all words to one thought, all notes to one harmony, — just as all life, circulating in the veins of all flesh, is referred to one living and immortal Creator, — such is the atonement in its larger import, of which the blood of the consecrated victim is made a sign. Physical solidarity is laid under tribute in the cause of spiritual unification. Life is poured forth from its physical channels, that it may return to God in testimony of loyal spirits, who have been taught betimes that all provisional organization is to be offered up in the divine service.

The worship of Israel under the law is therefore identical with the patriarchal and primitive sacrifice, — only it is accommodated in details of ritual to new conditions. To be at one with the Eternal is what the popular worship seeks in the daily sacrifice. That transgressors may not fatally break away from the law, so as to forfeit their personal interest in the constant offices and spiritual comforts of the national worship, but be kept in wholesome allegiance and perpetual peace, — such is the atonement which the sin-offering and the kindred trespass-offering are designed to signify and secure. Take away from the altar service the idea of national and personal consecration, — the idea of bringing human spirits to harmony and oneness according to the divine thought, —

and what is left is not worship, but the contradiction of worship. To confess, to repudiate and to forsake sin, and so to find the promised mercy and relief; to submit one's life to the divine disposal, to accept the will of God both in action and suffering at whatever cost, and so to be at one with him; what else can all the symbols of purgation and devotion signify? Communion with the Wisdom that makes for righteousness, through truth as at present ministered, in hope of higher communion with the same Wisdom, through truth yet to be disclosed, is the only guaranty, as it is the universal law, of man's spiritual development and moral harmony.

The law was not to be satisfied with perfunctory ritual. It demanded that men should really live and learn. No regulation diligence, no prescriptive decencies, could avail without sincerity of soul. If sacrifices and offerings did not signify worship, they could not but falsify worship. The faculties and forms of religion, set free from the service of rational faith, would be prompt to find a career of worldly profit in a popular and ceremonious superstition. So deep was the concern for spiritual reality, that the calendar of seasonable religious observances was not rounded without a day of positive and painful reflection upon by-gone experiences. To afflict the soul in view of past errors was deemed essential in girding up the loins of the mind for coming trial, — that spirits might rise with new vigor and hope, law be established in new honor and obedience, through a sense of the Goodness that would not allow even the disobedient and unthankful to be without the tokens of continued subjection and reconciliation to the law's control.

Not whenever he might choose, not with ordinary

preparation or any easy presumption of official purity, was even the high-priest to present himself in the presence-chamber of the Eternal.[1] One day in the year, with one series of sacrifices, wherein the sins of the people are not only confessed and repudiated, but borne away in a figure from the habitable earth, so that the abodes of men may become one with the sanctuary of God, — one high-priest, of one consecrated line, on behalf of one holy nation, in one holiest of holy places, presents one universal devotion, the concord of penitential desire and pious resolve, referring all existence to one Creator, and all law to one Authority.

It cannot be that we are to dissolve and destroy this unity of divine service, by any extreme construction of language that represents the high-priest as acting "for the people."

To be the vicar of any power implies the responsible action of that power, — not its non-recognition or effacement. The vicar is the substitute, only in being the agent, of those for whom he stands. He is not their substitute as distinguished from their organ. He does not act that they may do nothing, but that they may do more worthily. The high-priest passed within the veil, not that the people might be left outside the hallowed precinct, but that they might enter the sacred court with due order and solemnity. He was not serving God in the place of the people because the people were not serving, but because they were serving. He stood for a kingdom of priests and a holy nation in its unity, — for all as at one with the mediating priest; as the priest, in utter submission and devotion, was at one with God.

[1] Lev. xvi.; xxiii. 27; xxv. 9. Heb. x.

The term "atonement," as employed in the law, is neither mystical nor ambiguous. It has its practical applications in a religious economy which contemplates the setting apart of things to the highest and holiest service. If men are to be consecrated to God's service, atonement refers to means and ministries to this end. A subject, alienated in a particular way from his proper obedience to law, may give new proof of personal allegiance, may be reconciled to his permanent obligations and reinstated in forfeited privileges, by means of a particular act of confession and submission for the past, and loyalty for the future; and such an act is called an atonement. The law and the offender are by this means made to be, for a hopeful instant certainly, at one. So in all acts of pious obedience and submission, the divine mind and will are conceived as coming into the motions of humanity, while, reciprocally, the human is drawing towards its consummation in the divine. The real work of reconciliation is nothing less than the eternal revelation of the Father in his children.

In carrying on this revelation the service of the priest cannot dispense with the service of the prophet; and both services must be united and fulfilled in the theocratic King, in order that the reign of God may be apprehended as not the discipline of a peculiar people alone, but of all mankind.

CHAPTER VI.

SACRIFICE ACCORDING TO THE PROPHETS.

AS the priest acts in communion with the people, or else his ministry falls into hopeless neglect, so the sacrifice is recognized as the act of the worshipper who brings it, or else sacrifice sinks into helpless routine. A devoted soul must speak through the devoted thing: the devoted thing cannot make amends for the lack of a devoted soul. Indeed, how should a man alienate himself from the service of God, if not by paying its outward dues as a means of avoiding its inward discipline? Or, how should a man think to escape the consequences of disloyalty, but by shifting his personal liability to the shoulders of a victim? But the fresh, constant, popular inspiration, from which worship originally springs, will look for no escape from punishment, under a just government, but in getting rid of that which deserves and entails punishment. Take joyfully your duty in the service of Truth, Goodness, God; or, expect the prompt and persistent retribution of disaster and sorrow, which God will send as his testimony against your sin, — such is the moral burden of the prophets.

In all crises of the commonwealth, especially, with what vivid and cogent appeals to conscience do they insist that outward ordinances must have their fulfilment in spiritual fidelity, as the condition of their not being profaned by carelessness and hypocrisy. So long as the ritual of the altar was the proof of godliness in the nation, it was also the promise of peace and prosperity; but when piety was discredited, then ceremonial sacrifices became flagrant offences, to be succeeded by condign correction.

"I will go into thy house with burnt-offerings: I will offer unto thee burnt-sacrifices of fatlings with the incense of rams; I will offer bullocks with goats."[1] Such was the resolution of one who had called upon Jehovah in trouble and desired to pay the tribute of pious thankfulness in the day of his deliverance. "Then shall the cities of Judah and the inhabitants of Jerusalem go, and cry unto the gods unto whom they offer incense; but they shall not save them at all in the time of their trouble."[2] "And if ye offer the blind for sacrifice, is it not evil? And if ye offer the lame and sick, is it not evil? Offer it now to thy governor, will he be pleased with thee, or accept thy person?"[3] These are typical passages of prophetic reproof and warning. What are the pictures of national dignity and prosperity, with which prophetic faith fills up the future of a repentant and restored Israel? They are pictures that contemplate the universal prevalence of piety, according to the familiar type of divine service at the Jewish altar. "And they shall come from the cities of Judah and from the places about Jerusalem, and from the land of Benjamin, and from the plain, and from the mountains, and from the South, bringing burnt-offerings, and sacrifices, and meat-offerings, and incense, and bringing sacri-

---

[1] Ps. lxvi. 13, 15.   [2] Jer. xi. 12.   [3] Mal. i. 8.

fices of praise, unto the house of the Lord."[1] "For thus saith the Lord, David shall not want a man to sit upon the throne of the house of Israel; neither shall the priests and the Levites want a man before me to offer burnt-offerings, and to kindle meat-offerings, and to do sacrifice continually."[2] "And the Gentiles shall come to thy light, and kings to the brightness of thy rising. . . . All the flocks of Kedar shall be gathered together unto thee: they shall come up with acceptance upon mine altar, and I will glorify the house of my glory."[3] "And the Lord shall be known to Egypt, and Egypt shall know the Lord in that day, and they shall do sacrifice and oblation; yea, they shall vow a vow unto the Lord, and perform it."[4] Such predictions are looked upon as referring ultimately to the Messianic era, though clothed in the conventional drapery proper to the worship of the day.

But, natural or unavoidable as it may be, that anticipations of the future should be set forth in imagery of the present, too much should not be made of mere imagery. How unnatural, if the prophetic teaching were chargeable with a lack of lively testimony against the weakness and unprofitableness of empty ritual. As a matter of fact, however, when they maintain the validity of the religious spirit irrespective of outward observances, or inveigh against moral decadence dressed in the robes of sanctity, or point out the mean shifts of a time-serving priestcraft to throw off even the ritualistic restraints of a serious worship, it is then that the prophets awaken us to a sense of something greater than moral disgust at hypocrisies and oppressions of the time, —

[1] Jer. xvii. 26.
[2] Jer. xxxiii. 17, 13.
[3] Is. lx. 3–7.
[4] Is. xix. 21.

even an original and eternal conviction possessing them and bearing them on. They speak according to an unchangeable law of divine revelation, — a law from which one jot or one tittle shall in no wise pass, till all be fulfilled. They are as modern as the nineteenth century of our Lord; while the faith of our time is not less ancient than theirs, it being essentially the same yesterday, and to-day, and forever.

The venerable Samuel appears as the typical prophet in his business-like expostulation with King Saul: "Hath the Lord as great delight in burnt-offerings and sacrifices as in obeying the voice of the Lord? Behold, to obey is better than sacrifice, and to hearken than the fat of rams."[1] The same moral inculcation is set forth in a proverb by a wiser king than Saul: "To do justice and judgment is more acceptable to the Lord than sacrifice."[2] The immortal truth becomes the argument of deep personal experience in the Psalms: "Sacrifice and offering thou didst not desire; mine ears hast thou opened; burnt-offering and sin-offering hast thou not required. Then said I, Lo, I come; in the volume of the book it is written of me, I delight to do thy will, O my God: yea, thy law is within my heart."[3] "O Lord, open thou my lips, and my mouth shall show forth thy praise. For thou desirest not sacrifice; else would I give it: thou delightest not in burnt-offering. The sacrifices of God are a broken spirit: a broken and a contrite heart, O God, thou wilt not despise."[4] Isaiah reproves the apostasy of his people in the same strain: "Hear the word of the Lord, ye rulers of Sodom: give ear unto the law of our God, ye people of Gomorrah. To what purpose is

---

[1] 1 Sam. xv. 22.
[2] Prov. xxi. 3.
[3] Ps. xl. 6–8; Heb. x. 5–9.
[4] Ps. li. 15–17.

the multitude of your sacrifices unto me? saith the Lord: I am full of the burnt-offerings of rams, and the fat of fed beasts; and I delight not in the blood of bullocks, or of lambs, or of he-goats. When ye come to appear before me, who hath required this at your hand, to tread my courts? Bring no more vain oblations; incense is an abomination unto me; the new-moons and sabbaths, the calling of assemblies I cannot away with; it is iniquity, even the solemn meeting. Your new-moons and your appointed feasts my soul hateth; they are a trouble unto me; I am weary to bear them. And when ye spread forth your hands, I will hide mine eyes from you; yea, when ye make many prayers, I will not hear; your hands are full of blood."[1]

Is there then no call to repentance, no hope of reconciliation? If the sublime service of the altar has sunk to a sordid ritual of the shambles, is there not a law of atonement, vital and spiritual, such as might restore significance to signs, in giving reality to service? No sacrifices with which God would be well pleased? Hear the response: "Wash you, make you clean; put away the evil of your doings from before mine eyes; cease to do evil; learn to do well; seek judgment, relieve the oppressed, judge the fatherless, plead for the widow."[2] Again: "But to this man will I look, even to him that is poor, and of a contrite spirit, and trembleth at my word. He that killeth an ox is as if he slew a man; he that sacrificeth a lamb, as if he cut off a dog's neck; he that offereth an oblation, as if he offered swine's blood; he that burneth incense, as if he blessed an idol. Yea, they have chosen their own ways, and their soul delighteth in their abominations."[3] All the prophets are moved

---

[1] Is. i. 10–15.　　[2] Is. i. 16, 17.　　[3] Is. lxvi. 2, 3.

by the same moral conviction: "To what purpose cometh there to me incense from Sheba, and the sweet cane from a far country? Your burnt-offerings are not acceptable, nor your sacrifices sweet unto me."[1] "Thus saith the Lord of hosts, the God of Israel; put your burnt-offerings unto your sacrifices, and eat flesh. For I spake not unto your fathers, in the day that I brought them out of Egypt, concerning burnt-offerings or sacrifices; but this thing commanded I them, saying: Obey my voice, and I will be your God, and ye shall be my people: and walk ye in all the ways that I have commanded you, that it may be well unto you."[2] "For I desired mercy and not sacrifice; and the knowledge of God more than burnt-offerings."[3] "I hate, I despise your feast-days, and I will not smell in your solemn assemblies. Though ye offer me burnt-offerings and your meat-offerings, I will not accept them; neither will I regard the peace-offerings of your fat beasts. Take thou away from me the noise of thy songs; for I will not hear the melody of thy viols. But let judgment run down as waters, and righteousness as a mighty stream."[4]

In this characteristic testimony of the prophets there seems to be more than a burning zeal for the restoration of a degraded ritual. The indignant conscience of prophetic souls is outgrowing its respect for the old ceremonies, and is growing into a longing to live in a simple moral rectitude, that should be equal to originating its own practical expression. The sacrificing of beasts as an order of worship was doomed to pass away. It was at best but a grotesque shadow. Hence the spirit of prophecy in its highest flight declined to use the altar language,

[1] Jer. vi. 20. [2] Jer. vii. 21-23.
[3] Hosea vi. 6. [4] Amos v. 21-24.

and rejoiced in anticipations of "a new covenant." "Behold the days come, saith the Lord, that I will make a new covenant with the house of Israel, and with the house of Judah; not according to the covenant that I made with their fathers, in the day that I took them by the hand to bring them out of the land of Egypt, which covenant they break, although I was an husband unto them, saith the Lord; but this shall be the covenant that I will make with the house of Israel: After those days, saith the Lord, I will put my law in their inward parts, and write it in their hearts; and will be their God, and they shall be my people. And they shall teach no more every man his neighbor, and every man his brother, saying, know the Lord; for they shall all know me from the least of them unto the greatest of them, saith the Lord: for I will forgive their iniquity, and I will remember their sin no more."[1] The outward and exemplary teaching can have its meaning only in the inward revelation. There are no atonements that can atone, no humiliations that can move the divine clemency, or satisfactions that can appease the divine displeasure, apart from inward obedience. "The law of the Lord is perfect, converting the soul." Our spiritual progress and our spiritual consummation are in obedience. The maledictions of Mount Ebal are not cancelled by the ministrations of a worldly sanctuary, but are kept in salutary remembrance rather. Eternal oneness with Eternal Righteousness, and this alone, will perfectly supersede their application. The absolute Being must be known as possessing and moving dependent natures.

The law and the prophets and the psalms know only one principle of progressive virtue and ultimate peace,

---

[1] Jer. xxxi. 31-34; Heb. x. 15-18.

namely, faith moving in obedience to the revelation of God. No canonized experience gives any principle but faith, or any method but obedience, for superseding the sacrifices of alienation — tears and blood — with the sacrifices of righteousness — joy, praise, thanks. On the contrary, all indulgence of distrust and opposition on the part of moral beings with reference to the Creator is under an unchangeable law of pain and loss, to the end that correction may result in reconciliation. In other words, there is a spiritual regeneration for which nature was originally made, and for which the long-suffering of God is engaged. All messengers and ministers of good-will are workers together with God; and in this holy service the faultless personal consecration consists in perfect obedience to divine inspiration moving on to a perfection of self-sacrifice in benevolent conflict with powers of darkness.

Accordingly, the Scriptures of the New Covenant bring us to one Mediator between God and man, the man Christ Jesus,[1] in whom the Law and the Prophets, all symbols and functions of atonement, are fulfilled for all ages and for all men.

[1] 1 Tim. ii. 5.

CHAPTER VII.

THE LAW OF ATONEMENT FULFILLED IN THE CHRIST.

IT is to be noted that the typical portraiture in which the Scriptures point our regards to the Man of promise and perfection, has reference to his unique personal calling in relation to his fellow-men. All good service is shadow to his substance. He is the Redeemer of his people, saves them from their sins, is the Mediator of a new covenant, — the eternal compact of peace and communion between God and man. His are the days wherein the Son of man is glorified as the Son of God. The First-begotten and Well-beloved of the Father is announced as Teacher and Guide of the human family. In him first God's spiritual adoption of his natural offspring has come to its perfect and authoritative realization. God's reign in humanity is personally revealed. The way of perfection is opened to all. The last times and the best, the times of restitution and consummation, have succeeded to the darker dispensation. The promised Prince of the house of Israel is also the desire of all nations, the universal Reconciler and Ruler. Divine truth in his heart is to move the utterance of human lips till mutual exhortation shall cease in a universal sway of truth, and the remembrance of sins shall pass away in the endless celebration of forgiveness and righteousness.

This divine ideal fills all the moments of our Lord's life, and is owned by him, whether consciously or unconsciously, as the law and inspiration of his career. His ministry is represented by those who could not perfectly appreciate it; and still it is distinctly conceived as that of a man whose spiritual powers were ever at one with the divine thought, in an unshaken constancy of obedience to clear convictions of what the Father would have him to do,—all natural motions and involuntary impulses held in timely check and reasonable subordination. The energies and orbit of personal duty are regarded as continually reaching their practical demonstration and just definition in his conduct, in order, not that the result may be expressed in a scientific formula or poetic delineation, but that the spiritual action may communicate itself through faith, and so pass into the movement of individual life, into the habits of society, into the history of the world.

In fine, the Saviour was to save his people from their sins by bringing them to the life of righteousness; and this, not according to formal prescriptions and rules outworn, but by a renovation of being which should make them ultimately perfect even as the Father in heaven is perfect. God and man, the Father and the Son, in the unity of the same Spirit,—this is the revelation of the Christ; this is the fulfilment of law and prophecy; for the reason that it is the original and eternal conception of the Creator coming through gradual and mysterious processes in nature to its first realization in a perfect man. And this bringing of the First-begotten into the world, this revelation of one man with the unlimited anointing of the divine Spirit, was expressly to the end that all men in like manner might become partakers of the divine nature. To make this reconciliation of the divine and human universal at whatever personal sacrifice determines the Christian law of atonement, the law which the Christ magnified and made honorable through his Cross. This law is one of spiritual causation, and contemplates the necessary cost of overcoming moral inertia and active resistance, so as to vindicate all the outlay of history in a glory of the Father and a consummation of mankind to be ultimately revealed.

But this simple appreciation of the historic reality, — does it truly sum up the Redeemer's most spiritual and solemn conception of his own ministry? Could any words surpass in depth and comprehensiveness those of his supplication to the Father on the eve of his crucifixion? "Neither pray I for these alone, but for them also which shall believe on me through their word, that they all may be one; as thou, Father, art in me, and I in thee, that they also may be one in us: that the world may believe that thou hast sent me."[1] What could he add to this intercession that would enlarge its scope? What could he take away from it without dissolving its completeness? If this prayer be not the assurance of what the Christ sought and hoped on our behalf, of what subordinate desire or less comprehensive travail of soul could he promise us the fulfilment? Again, if this prayer be the worship of his life, and express the spiritual service to which he consecrated himself in death, it must interpret and co-ordinate all details of his ministry.

At any rate, the unique priesthood and worship in which the Christ approaches the consummation of his earthly sacrifice raises humanity above all conventional boundaries of time or space, and presents it as moving

[1] John xvii. 20, 21.

in an eternal order of the universe. Judea and Galilee, Jews and Gentiles, ages of local phenomena and pedantic annals, — how they fade and vanish away in the eternal reign! The kingdom of God the Father includes the whole development of man the Son; it includes man in the thought of the Creator before all worlds, man coming in the order of nature and time, man eternally begotten, the spiritual offspring and immortal heir of the Father, for whose sake the earthly family both lives and dies. The spiritual household of the Father begotten and born from being to being, not of Jews only but of Gentiles also, — is not this the one reality and realm, to which all creatures and all creations, according to our knowledge, are pointing and serving?

This infinite domain of life and power is brought to the consciousness and attention of infantile and wayward members of the universal society, through that spiritual inspiration which determines a physical and moral resistance; and in struggling with resistance men are trained for their high destiny. To animate inertness, to overrule contradiction, to reconcile opposition, to consummate personal loyalty in perfect freedom, in a word, to make God's strength perfect in man's weakness, — such is indeed the type of spiritual causation wherein our present experience is involved; but by faith we see the conflict atoned for in the righteousness, peace, and joy, toward which it tends.

Accordingly, the Christ did not open communication with men from a serene seclusion, as example of an ideal aloofness of divine life from the struggles of humanity; nor did he propose to realize an ordinary peace on earth. He came to inaugurate division, to lead an invading force, to discipline the hosts of faith in practical obedience to the universal Spirit of Love. Triumphal repose was reserved for an ulterior revelation. The miracle of his ministry is that it shows a man of perfect simplicity and intuitive penetration, — one working for God and man, for body and soul, for past and future, yet betrayed by no contrariety of appeals into confusion of thought or vacillation in conduct. Having all counsel and might from within, he acts in perfect faith; and it is the absolute sovereignty of truth in him that wins the confidence and devotion of the faithful, — marking, with an adverse judgment no matter what power or preponderance of unbelief in the present evil world. Emanuel, God with us, — there is no other name for eternal life. Prophet, priest, king, — all are one in the divine Man; and he fulfils all functions of divine service in a daily liturgy of simple action, wherein the supreme dignity is not divorced from the lowliest beneficence, and the immaculate holiness reaches out a hand to bless the penitent, no matter how polluted. His moral impact is so mighty that the world's massive and inveterate habit gives promise, in its resisting shock, of the new movement that shall pervade it. All things are not brought in a moment to their ultimate perfection, but nothing can continue in one stay: no law can abide in its old construction, no prophecy but surpasses its formal limitations, no personal virtue but needs to be born again, no accumulations of ancient wisdom in social order but must dissolve and be reorganized in the age to come. Eternal Reason, in the fulness of an all-loving and all-inspiring zeal, will not allow even a provisional and relative rectitude to limit the law of ultimate perfection; but dutiful Devotion, owning the aptitude for godliness already evinced by man, is calling forward, — saving the very elect from a false appreciation of that whereto they have already attained, and vindicating for the most reprobate the prerogative of entering voluntarily into the calling and election of the divine Love.

If we ask what is the essential element of the glad tidings of God brought by the Christ, the answer meets us everywhere in one word, — Love. The eternal Word of nature becomes the final utterance of Scripture. But the Scriptures give us no conception of Love incarnate, — Love conditioned in human nature and human society for the sake of their regeneration, — without the sign of self-sacrifice. The gospel is a gospel of triumph, under the banner of the cross: "*In hoc signo vinces.*" As the ministry of Jesus was one of love in strenuous conflict with forces of unscrupulous self-will, it was accompanied by a growing sense of the way in which alone it could naturally end.

Was he sent to bring the unchangeable Reason into active contact with mankind? Did he represent the eternal Father as ever rendering the testimony practically due to his own perfections in the treatment of his offspring? Was he the hierophant, also, of the world's proper worship — of what man should render unto God for all his benefits? Then must this man have somewhat to offer.[1] A priest forever, it is for him to offer the human homage, not according to the sentiment and custom of a passing day, but according to the eternal spirit and truth of worship.

Hence, as we study the notices given in the New Testament, of what was said and done by the Christ, we find all rational suggestions and necessary ideas of duty fulfilled in him. He is the organ and expression of uni-

[1] Heb. viii. 4.

versal righteousness, — the absolute righteousness of God as well as the reciprocal duty of man. The well-beloved Son, given from everlasting by the Father for love of his world, consecrating himself to the Father in the unity of the eternal Spirit, for the work that was given him to do, he comes in the fulness of time, as at once the express image of the Father's character and the supreme example of filial devotion. Who could convince him of sin? In what relation did his obedience fail? To what institution of man did he not render due honor for the Father's sake? To what requirement of divine Love was he wanting on behalf of the children? What burden of proof or persuasion was he not ready to assume in his testimony to the truth? What fruit of good living was not to grow, and is not still to grow, from the seed he planted?

Each stage in the proper development of a human being, from the incipient energy of natural existence to spiritual completeness of life in communion with the Father, is marked in the history of Jesus; only, the crises of his career are indicated, not by any reluctance with respect to the new initiative, but by prompt as well as deliberate action. We see one epoch rounding itself to fulness in a new sense of duty that governs the succeeding movement, — in a course of unbroken obedience.

The law of atonement through sacrifice appears in the earliest reconciliation of the inward and the outward life. The submission of childhood to its appointed conditions is not without foretaste of what the higher service will cost. The age of twelve years, the visit to the temple, the exciting contact with grave teachers of the law, the turning of his thought away from customary dependence upon those who had cherished his life as one with theirs, and who now sought him sorrowing, —

what was this but the premonition of a unique Sonship, which, though schooled for about thirty years [1] in subjection to all authorities and institutions that could represent to him the will of the Father, would by and by set him apart from his kindred, in the fact of his being about the Father's business on their behalf?[2] His way was prepared. Crooked places were made straight, and rough places plain. Yet the last and greatest of the servants sent before the advancing Prince could not cause the wilderness to disappear, or make perfect the highway which it was reserved for him alone to open. That lonely trial in the wilderness, wherein the distinction between the divine method of moral influence, and conventional methods of worldly success was brought out in its genuine character, proved the Prince's loyalty to the reign of God, and proved, also, what that loyalty would have to contend with in subduing all things.[3] Then came the strenuous public ministry, brief as strenuous, — vindicating the law and the prophets by the setting forth of their full vigor and reach in word and deed, — the training of apostles, the general yet secret working of truth, popular docility, and consequent opposition of menaced authority, culminating in the crucifixion; and thereafter endless reconciliation and triumph, — the resurrection, the re-animation of the faithful, the great commission, the dispensation of the Holy Spirit, the proclamation of the glad tidings, the exaltation of the Christ, not merely in the glory that was before the foundation of the world, essential and eternal, but in the glory that was ensuing and evermore to follow increasingly, till creation, providence, and redemption should be fulfilled according to one purpose of the Eternal.

---

[1] Luke iii. 23.   [2] Luke ii. 41-52.   [3] Matt. iv. 1-11.

The Evangelists point to the divine Word as uttering itself in syllables and moments, yet so as to signify the absolute truth. The peculiar character of Christ's work is conceived to be in the fact that, as he is addressing himself to men, his teaching reaches its aim with effective precision and authority, and there is no just appeal from faith, nor rational need of argument.

The great Teacher was not a doctrinaire. He did not set himself first of all to correct the intellectual systems or the popular theories of his day. He was the Revealer of spiritual life, not the scribe conventionally instructed in the law. His intuitive faith and devotion recognized the infinite thought and energy in nature, exactly at the point where the grosser medium seems to limit or resist the controlling Will. To teach implies limitation and resistance. To make disciples implies an overcoming influence and constant progress. To be the vital Truth and the quickening Word, to inspire in mankind the assurance that the Father's eternal universe includes and governs the child's passing world, — this implies the regeneration and the world to come. It means, not that the pangs of birth or the dangers of growth are superseded by any magical method, at variance with the law of spiritual creation as already made known, but rather that the same creative process moves on to its highest ends, — in spite of animalism, ignorance, prejudice, — in spite of selfish prepossessions and wilful ambitions, which are permitted to declare themselves without disguise, that the new order may win its way in no illusive success.

It is apparently because ultimate success, in spite of initial resistance, is a necessary mark of divine revelation, that so much is made in Scripture of the opportuneness of the Christ's coming. The Light shining in darkness prevails within a certain range, or it would not shine at all. Its period is not that of impenetrable chaos. When the preparation was fulfilled, then the ruling order began to be manifest. The Saviour appeared in the company of the expectant, the people of alternating hope and fear, who looked for "the acceptable year of the Lord," yet dreaded "the day of vengeance" of their God. Unobtrusively, he entered, not at the massive gates of Jerusalem, but into the lowly tents of the wilderness. His disciples were gathered, not from those whose worldly fortunes perplexed them with fear of change, but from simple people, whose aspirations, if not very intelligent or very high, were at least so genuine as to admit of correction in the progress of their faith. His beatitudes were not for those most flatteringly circumstanced, but for those even under the greatest outward adversities, who were ready for the most devoted co-operation with the reign of God. For, as the kind of work in which Jesus and his disciples were to be engaged implied the kind of suffering their faithfulness would encounter, — so those were the blessed, in comparison with others, who were already disciplined in the common schooling of patience and fortitude. Such, having some preparation for their Christian conflict, would be apt to accept just pains, while shrinking with a true instinct from precipitate and bootless sacrifices.

The few docile spirits whom the Forerunner's words had pointed to the new Teacher, found a ready access to his intimacy, and were very soon made partners of his more general ministry. They became his personal followers, his family and school, chosen and trained that they might duly apprehend the moving principle and ultimate aim of his work, so as to bear a sufficiently ample and undiluted testimony of him to the world. For their sakes he sanctified himself that they also might be sanctified through the truth. As the Father sent him into the world, so he sent them. Meanwhile he took them with him as he went about doing good, that they might know what it would be to follow after him; and taught them to see in his works of power and charity signs of greater works, that should mark the progress of his reign in all the world. There was in him a mystery of personal force to quell opposition and to command observance, and an equal mystery of moderation and meekness in appealing only to the reasonable confidence of men. "If I do not the works of my Father, believe me not. But if I do, though ye believe not me, believe the works: that ye may know and believe that the Father is in me, and I in him."[1] The day's sights and the day's employments were transfigured in his parables. Common things began to glow with a light from heaven, until the very senses, as well as the consciences, of men, were quickened to appreciate the economy of divine Goodness underneath what seemed before the dull routine of existence. But if contemporary processes and aspects of the divine reign were familiarly illustrated in parables, the fulfilment of law and the perfection of life found expression in the Sermon on the Mount. Life was to reach its fulness according to no worldly ideal, but simply in the communion of infinite Love. "Be ye therefore perfect, even as your Father which is in heaven is perfect;"[2] this is real perfection — the eternal life.

The imperfection of the passing existence then, as now, was not shown in a lack of time-honored maxims and

[1] John x. 37, 38.   [2] Matt. v. 48.

wholesome regulations, but rather in false distinctions and inadequate conceptions. Sayings handed down from elder times were perversely employed to limit or to suppress the active moral inspiration of living men. The spirit of law was sacrificed to an arbitrary construction of particular commandments. "Thou shalt not kill;" "thou shalt not commit adultery;" "thou shalt not forswear thyself," — did such requirements signify that the avoidance of crime is the sum total of moral duty, and so make void the fundamental law on which all special prohibitions depend? Is not the law of divine benevolence abrogated when the demand that man should love his neighbor is held to imply the distinction of foreigners or enemies whom it is lawful to hate? Can man be perfect in the love of God, who is not at one with Him in hating nothing that He hath made? But let men apprehend the universal Love as working from the very beginning in all human experience, throwing up betimes certain legal ramparts to guide and restrain the individual action in its progress toward an end; and then they might the more readily apprehend the end contemplated, might see the law fulfilled in the Christ. Could the inspiration of righteousness proceed from any source, or know any end, but the creative Goodness? Could rational worship contemplate anything less than harmony of spirit and action with the divine character; or, aspire to anything more? Was the righteousness of the Father the poor forensic ruling that could know only the literal bond? Was it not the unity of all divine attributes, transcending all temporary judgments, extending tokens of good-will to the evil and the unthankful, that evil might be overcome with good, and disappear in the fulness of life?

At any rate, the Son of God kindled in his disciples a zeal for human beings according to what he declared to be possible with God in their eternal life. He recognized the ideal end of life in life's beginning. To him the Alpha and Omega of human development were indissolubly bound together in one organic whole. He apprehended the consummation sought as involving the progress to be achieved, the instant motive and act as having their integrity in the end to which they were subservient. He sought to mould human efforts by the faith of a divine purpose, which solicited and made use of them. In this way he animated society with a virtue superior to traditions, and called to sacrifices that were more than symbols, — the very actions and proofs of devotion. The so-called administration of justice, which seeks the protection of society by the punishment of offences according to special outward definitions, necessary as it may be, is an administration by which justice is missed even in the fulfilment of law. The divine law has a nobler purpose, if not a costlier method: — "But I say unto you, love your enemies, bless them that curse you, do good to them that hate you, and pray for them which despitefully use you and persecute you, that ye may be the children of your Father which is in heaven; for he maketh his sun to rise on the evil and on the good, and sendeth rain on the just and on the unjust." [1] This is the law which holds eternally to its moral end. It brings the goal of perfection into the method of devotion. It contemplates the triumph of justice as depending upon the sufferings of the faithful more than upon punishment of the disobedient; and supersedes the mere pain even of punitive infliction, by a sense of fatherly

---

[1] Matt. v. 44, 45.

discipline for the sake of complete reconciliation. The Spirit of holiness in possession of a consecrated body, — here at last is the living Temple and the living Sacrifice. To preach righteousness in the great congregation, to find supreme delight in doing the Father's will, to reveal the infinite Love in a service which lays all finite resources upon its altar, to proclaim the glad tidings, — all that God can promise and all that man can enjoy, "not after the law of a carnal commandment, but after the power of indissoluble life,"[1] — such was the Messianic calling. The High Priest of universal nature was to realize the fulness of truth in the fulness of grace, the fulness of peace in the fulness of righteousness.

Of course, in the atoning struggle it was not for the Christ or for his followers to doubt the efficiency of their spiritual testimony because it encountered a natural opposition, nor to be diverted from the fight of faith in order to take up the arms of a worldly warfare. Rather let them welcome afflictions in the flesh, — turning the other cheek to the smiter, outdoing in benevolence the measure even of unjust exactions, communicating in good things with such as are disposed to render only evil things in return; that they may overcome evil with good. It is the glory of the end that demands and sustains the self-devotion of the service. Not political economy, not social equity by standards of common law, not how perfect beings will live together when there is no more knowledge of evil, — the teaching of the Christ is how to redeem the world from the bondage of its own traditions and habits, that men may come to the service which is perfect freedom.

It was the Christ's self-devotion that gave practical

[1] Heb. vii. 16.

embodiment and efficiency to his doctrine, and proved him the perfect Mediator of all needed changes in the convictions and conduct of mankind. The motions of life began to be referred to the true centre and law of spiritual attraction. Attention to matters of everyday existence was both humbled and exalted by being brought into just dependence upon the Father, who in his righteousness was ruling the spiritual orbit of humanity with its unknown times and seasons. Physical suffering and death fell into nothingness by comparison with the glory and triumph of the immortal Man. But as making for this glory and triumph, suffering rose to a significance comporting with the majesty of Truth, and testimony reached its consummation in martyrdom. As the Revelation, most needed on account of its necessary superiority to natural tendencies, would, for the same reason, excite the most violent reaction on the part of the unenlightened; so the chief witness in such a revelation was the predestined victim, that he might become the all-sufficient illuminator of mankind. From the very foundation of the world, there was before him a baptism of suffering. From the very beginning of his earthly ministry, he labored under a sense of how slight was the testimony of word and act, how faint were the successive scintillations of light and heat from within, compared with the final apocalypse of Love, — his dying for the world. If he had not stirred the world to mortal resistance, had he sufficiently vindicated the change which divine Love would work in the world's ways? Must he not suffer as it behooved that the Christ should suffer, that he might enter into his glory?

Hence that very striking representation of the Evangelists, that the Saviour was ever counting upon his cross as the indispensable medium of his revelation in the souls of men. As the faithful of the old dispensation could not fully know what their own lives meant till the promised Messiah had fulfilled his cycle in the flesh, so the most intimate disciple of the Christ had to watch the mystery of his incarnation to its close, in order to apprehend its secret. Whither will he finally lead? This is the question which concerns a faith that shall be loyal to the end. The sovereign Reality must be discovered in order that faith may consciously hold its own. Assurances most simply phrased are realized only in the events to which they refer; and germs of grace lie hid in the comparative sterility of nature, till the chill and darkness are dispersed, and the spiritual atmosphere is pervaded with the regenerating power.

The chosen disciples cannot come to the fulness of their apostleship while the Master is laying restrictions upon their speech, lest by unauthorized outgivings they should hinder the just impression of his own ministry. It requires all their patience and submission to wait for what they are taught to feel they cannot know at present; and no personal sympathy can restrain the words of rebuke and disenchantment which the faithful Teacher addresses to those who are flattering themselves with a mistaken notion of what the way of perfection is. How shall disciples learn that pre-eminence in his kingly court is no prize of vulgar ambition? The serious young ruler, coming in the charm of moral aspiration and prosperous virtue, willing to know what is yet lacking to his destiny, how shall he overcome a natural reluctance at parting with great possessions for the sake of the poor, and at taking up the cross for the sake of his Leader, before that Leader shall by his own example have transfigured the ruggedness of sacrificial experience in the light of eternal life? Or Peter himself, can he follow his Lord in the final trial, before he has been taught by what manner of dying he is to glorify God?

There is one law of self-sacrifice in reconciling the world to the Father, — the law of the Father's love. "It is enough for the disciple that he be as his Master, and the servant as his Lord."[1] But what is enough for the Master? What but that majestic condescension, which is sufficient to make disciples of all nations? If the faithful need to see their perfection in a practical example of goodness upon earth, what shall determine the nature of that example, if not the purpose of penetrating the darkness, and subduing the unbelief, that rejects the just One, repudiates his Sonship and his reign, and owns no king but Cæsar? Is it not in the nature of things that the power of darkness should have its hour? Is it not of temporary necessity that the established unbelief, rather than the infirm faith, should measure the difficulty, and graduate the cost of bringing men to acknowledge the truth? Must there not come the critical conflict, the decisive moment, in the Father's struggle with his erring children? They know neither the Father nor the Son. "They know not what they do." But when their deed is done, its character shall forevermore be recognized. As a general, intent upon victory such as shall be followed by final peace, tries the strength of his antagonist, compelling him to unmask his positions and deploy his forces, that the conclusive action may take place, so the Captain of salvation, with equal prudence and courage, tried the thoughts, dispositions, and tempers of men, conciliating the simple and candid

---

[1] Matt. x. 25.

people, and in that very fact exciting the envy and consolidating the opposition of the hypocritical and designing, until the contradiction of sinners against himself was uttered in the desperate fervor of embattled hostility. Then he said: "Father, the hour is come; glorify thy Son, that thy Son also may glorify thee."

To save the King from his suffering was to save him from his glory. What remained, therefore, but that spiritual power and worldly forces should do their respective works, according to that historic economy of moral freedom and responsibility in which the will of the Father had unchangeably declared itself? It was for the injustice that proved the extremity of man's spiritual need to dictate the suffering that should prove the sufficiency of the Father's love. It is this reconciling condescension of God to man in the person of his Son, which is the motive and assurance of man's reconciliation with God. This is called *the Atonement*, by way of eminence. For until the love of the Father be brought to one focus of revelation; until the world is lighted up with truth and righteousness, with the certainty that every man shall in the long account receive according to what he hath done, yet with an equal assurance of patience, pity, pardon, persuading to what man ought to do, — the universal gospel is not announced. Faith can only linger expectantly about the old altars till the supreme sacrifice is offered. But once it is offered, the offering is once for all: the "right, reasonable, ratified, and acceptable" reality of God's possession of man and man's communion with God, for all ages of redemptive effort, as well as the assurance of immortal felicity in the heavenly reign. The central fact of Christian remembrance embodies the ruling idea of Christian worship, according to a collect in the Roman Missal: "Almighty, everlasting God, who hast ordained thine only-begotten Son to be the Redeemer of the world, and wast pleased to be reconciled unto us in his blood; grant unto us, we beseech thee, so to venerate with solemn rite the price of our redemption, and to be on earth so defended by its power from the evils of the present life, that we may rejoice in its perpetual fruit in heaven."[1]

[1] Collect for Friday after the fourth Sunday in Lent.

CHAPTER VIII.

IMMEDIATE SEQUEL OF THE CHRIST'S INCARNATE MINISTRY.

IT remains to notice briefly what, according to the New Testament, immediately followed the fulfilment of the redeeming ministry which has been sketched.

If the Word of regeneration had been uttered, what proofs of new life disclosed themselves? If with their Master's resurrection his prophetic testimony with respect to his personal pre-eminence and effective mediation came to completeness and coherency in the minds of the disciples, — did the same testimony begin to verify itself in the convictions and experience of society in general?

The apostolic witnesses regard the world from one point of view, — that of its redemption by the Christ. The new faith at once evinced a majesty of moral purpose and a clearness of intellectual outline to awe the world. In spite of infirmities of the flesh and limitations of the letter, in spite of apparent odds against them, the apostles gave a testimony to their Master, which is the very spirit and ideal of prophecy in man.

The oneness of space, the unity of creation, the fact that every house is builded by some man, inferring the transcendent fact that the cosmical dwelling-place is the building of God, — ideas common to both scientific and theological thought, — afforded a natural ground for the moral argument that men should be of one mind in the great house; in fine, that God was reconciling the world unto himself, through a discipline of free personal devotion, whose great Apostle and High Priest had passed into the heavens to appear in the presence of the Father on behalf of mankind. In his light men saw light. Atonement was seen to be the law of life, the cross the banner of redemption, resurrection the type of immortality, sacraments and formulas of faith the symbols of sacrifice ending in triumph. The war-worn hosts of faith, from first to last, were thus at one with their Leader in welcoming the afflictions of a life that cannot endure, as working out for them the incomparable glory of life that cannot decay.[1]

If there were anticipations of an early and sensible reappearance of the risen Christ in power and great glory, there was nevertheless an assurance that the reign of God was deep within, — that it was righteousness, peace, and joy in the Holy Spirit. This interior reign, inspiring the hopes and directing the movements of the faithful servants and soldiers of the Christ, made them at the same time mighty, for the pulling down of strongholds. Things that could be shaken began to disappear, in order that realities which could not be shaken might abide. The phenomenal world was merely the shifting scenery of a spiritual drama, whose successive actions were to illustrate the creative Reason.

Man's sonship, man's filial relation to God, as revealed in the well-beloved Son, and affirmed in the regenerate experience of his disciples, was the reality that overruled

[1] 2 Cor. iv. 17, 18.

all diversities of race, nationality, culture, or condition. With the faithful there was neither Greek nor Jew, circumcision nor uncircumcision, Barbarian, Scythian, bond nor free; but Christ was all and in all. This spiritual indissolubleness of humanity as a whole, in virtue of which the Redeemer had tasted death for every man, demanded the same devotion and vicariousness in suffering on the part of all his followers. If the sinless One had suffered for the unrighteous, that he might reconcile them to God, with what self-abandonment, yea, with what revenge toward themselves, might not those once sinners, but now reconciled, give their testimony of sacrifice to the Prince of Martyrs, who had won them to his devotion? Were they incorporate in the church, the very body of their head, — for what was this growing body intended, but for the long passion, wherein the body that is broken and disappears is given for the life and nourishment of the body that shall be? How otherwise could they know the fellowship of the Christ's sufferings, or come to the fulness of his joy? Yet, as the passion of the Lord, by being the perfect consecration in the fulness of times, reached the most decisive testimony to the truth in the shortest period of suffering, so in the feebler and longer self-sacrifice of his church there was the assurance of faith that the best obedience and devotion was the way of least pain and loss.

The reign of God, as revealed in the Christ and apprehended by the faithful, showed the past and the future of human history under the same prophetic illumination. Every development of good owned its debt to a previous struggle with evil; and every struggle with evil could count with assurance upon an ensuing development of good. Heaven was no longer merely the antithesis of earth; nor was the eternal life exclusive of temporal existence. The finite was pervaded by the Infinite. They sat together in heavenly places and in heavenly seasons, who came into vivid communion of spirit with the glorified Christ. On the other hand, omens of destruction were evermore relaxing the energies of wickedness, and gehennas of fire were quenchlessly active in consuming the elements that deserved to perish. Whatever the Captain of salvation was fighting against with the sword of his mouth, that he would infallibly destroy at last with the brightness of his presence.

Indeed, the process of reconciliation could not but imply a correlative process of judgment. Amnesty, to be sure, was universal through the forbearance of God, that pardon might become personal and particular according to the dispositions of men. But the day was also one of judgment in righteousness. There was a discerning of the thoughts and intents of the heart. There was a discrimination between the ignorant word against the Son of man — the sin against an outward majesty in humility, that might be condoned under a general economy of condescension — and the blasphemy against the Holy Spirit, the sin against the clear inward evidence of truth and goodness, which, unrepented of, is eternally incompatible with forgiveness and reconciliation. Thus the true discipleship was not in word, not in dogmatic or ritualistic profession, but in sincerity of spirit, — inward conviction being the organic law of outward expression; and the unity of the church was the unity of one body and one spirit, one Lord, one faith, one baptism, one God and Father of all, who is above all, through all, in all.[1]

---

[1] Eph. iv. 3–6.

The Christian faith, as it apprehended the way of universal consecration, so it repudiated all trust in merely conventional sanctities. Life's resources, nature, works, days, were not to be divided between God and rival claimants; but were all summed up in the tribute of thankful praise to the giver of all. If "holiness to the Lord" was not written upon the bells of the horses according to the letter of the old prophecy, it had no need to be literally written anywhere. The meaning of the prophecy was fulfilled in the Christian service. The worship of God was ever passing into the service of man; the service of man into the worship of God. The highest spiritual function was not alien to the lowliest of household offices; and the humblest Christian was joined with his Lord in the universal priesthood of humanity. The service of God on earth was one with the service of God in heaven. The veil before the face of all peoples, hiding from them the inner sanctuary which they desired to enter, was withdrawn, and through the Christ the way into the holiest of all was made manifest.

The Epistle to the Hebrews is the account of how Judaism was transfigured in Christianity: Jesus, the High Priest, not of a nation or of an age, but of humanity forever; the cross his altar; his own body the victim of his perfect devotion; his flesh the veil, withdrawn when he passed once for all from the holy tabernacle of his earthly ministry to the most holy sanctuary of his invisible service; his blood the redemption from the bondage of the old dispensation; his intercession the assurance of eternal life and peace under the new covenant; his complete revelation the antitype and fulfilment of all that had been foreshadowed in the law, or in the prophets.

With Jesus the altar-language rose from the dead. It too, was henceforth spirit and life.

And now the faithful of the Gentiles were fellow-citizens and fellow-heirs with the believing Jews in one household of God. All religions had given token of certain common elements of faith and hope; and all had made their sign in a sacrificial cipher which they could not adequately interpret. For all the cross of the Redeemer was the key to the cipher, and his religion its final interpretation. The apostle to the Gentiles was determined to know nothing among them but the Christ — crucified and risen from the dead.

Finally, as the era of consummation had set in, and the reign of God in man was without assignable limits of duration, whether in the past or in the future, it was natural for faith to prefigure the glory to be revealed. The prophetic promise of consummation was that the Redeemer should "see of the travail of his soul," and should "be satisfied." [1] The unity and universality of the Father's law — what but that could be the satisfaction of the Son? Accordingly, St. Paul sums up his ultimate anticipation in these words: "Then cometh the end, when he shall have delivered up the kingdom to God, even the Father, when he shall have put down all rule, and all authority and power. For he must reign until he hath put all enemies under his feet. The last enemy that shall be destroyed is death. And when all things shall be subdued unto him, then shall the Son also himself be subject unto him that put all things under him, that God may be all in all." [2]

[1] Isa. liii. 11. [2] 1 Cor. xv. 24-28.

PART SIXTH.

CRISES IN THE PROCESS OF REDEMPTION.

"Now is the judgment [*crisis*] of this world."

JOHN xii. 31.

"THE times of ignorance, therefore, God overlooked; but now he commandeth men that they should all everywhere repent: inasmuch as he hath appointed a day, in the which he will judge the world (τὴν οἰκουμένην) in righteousness, by the man whom he hath ordained, whereof he hath given assurance unto all men, in that he hath raised him from the dead."

THE ACTS, xvii. 30, 31.

"That but this blow
Might be the be-all and the end-all here,
But here, upon this bank and shoal of time, —
We'd jump the life to come. But, in these cases,
We still have judgment here."

SHAKSPEARE: Macbeth, Act i. Scene 7.

PART SIXTH.

CRISES IN THE PROCESS OF REDEMPTION.

CHAPTER I.

OF JUSTICE AND JUDGMENT.

THE justice of God towards mankind is very commonly contemplated in its relation to the punishment of sin. The revelation of divine justice in nature, on the other hand, evinces a primary and persistent reference to the development of virtue.

Whatever the uneasy conscience may at any time forebode, — the fact is that the Creator is apprehended as a just God, because he reveals himself as Redeemer and Saviour. Moreover, he reveals himself as Redeemer and Saviour in the judicial determinations, as well as in the reconciling efforts of his government. By his judgments he enforces the just appeals of self-sacrificing condescension in favor of righteousness; while condescension, patience, pardon, inasmuch as they are notes of a redemptive process, give unmistakable assurance of judgments that are to ensue with reference to the practical workings of a dispensation of grace. Grant that all man's faculties shall move, without fret or friction, in obedience to divine inspiration as soon as man is made perfect in love; such a spiritual consummation does not depend alone upon the law of atonement, but just as really upon crises of individual and collective experience. These crises are judgments of God, evermore abroad in the creation, by which the people learn what is right. The official effort and legal apparatus of advanced society for the protection of rights and the punishment of crimes is simply proof of the deeper administration of justice pervading our world-ages, by the law of nature, for man's moral development.

Parts of divine revelation require the whole. The depths of self-sacrifice in the crisis of atonement cannot dispense with the heights of dignity and authority in the crisis of judgment. The former may be spoken of as the depths of mercy, the latter as the heights of justice; but mercy is not mercy apart from justice, and justice is not justice apart from mercy. The quality of the part cannot be grounded or constituted except in the character of the whole.

Atonement and judgment are actions contemplating the same end. Therefore, if the consummate effort of atonement fail of its proper effect in any upon whose attention it is pressed, what follows for them? Not a greater sacrifice for sin; not another incarnation and passion of the Christ, but "a certain, fearful expectation of judgment."[1] The fatherly grace, that keeps the door of reconciliation and righteousness eternally open to the repentant offender, does not shrink from the use of wholesome severity; but awakens to repentance by making betimes a judicial distinction between opposing moral dispositions.

Hence it is that the judicial aspects of the world's redemption — the crises wherein the judgments of God

[1] Heb. x. 26, 27.

disclose themselves in nature, so as to find a record and interpretation in Scripture, — demand a distinct consideration.

To believe that the judgments of God ensue eternally upon things done according to their innermost spirit and total quality is to renounce our own interested partialities and illusive forecastings in favor of those larger and better conceptions, that are gauged for us by words which stand for the most devout human insight put to service in the administration of revered law. The word *judgment* stands for a sacred function in which man becomes the sworn and consecrated minister of God. But the word *judgment*, as the expression for a personal function, is affiliated with the word *crisis*, which contemplates a judicial decision, to be sure, but with special reference, in our language, not to personal function, but to general and immanent law. Thus, when it is said of a sick man that he must certainly die, or that he is very likely to recover, the saying may have special reference to the *judgment* of the physician, or to the *crisis* of the disease. But the professional judgment is held to depend upon the immanent law in the case; and the two combine in one conviction of truth. A catastrophe in nature, or revolution in history, is possibly pointed out as a *crisis* with respect to the laws according to which interior forces have acted together in producing a sudden result; but when referred to the divine thought and governance conceived as laying up the possibility or certainty of such a result in the constitution of things, the same fact is called a *judgment*. It depends simply upon the relation of thought designed to be made prominent, whether we speak of our late civil war as a *crisis* in the national history or as a *judgment* of the universal Ruler.

Similarly in the New Testament Greek, the word *crisis* is so penetrated with the faith of God's personal intention as to be generally rendered *judgment* in the New Testament English: and this though the reference be expressly to transactions, not as belonging in any peculiar sense to the high court of heaven, but as taking place in the natural order of events here below.

The judgment of God is conceived as determining the crisis of events, the crisis of events as expressing the judgment of God. We do not disengage the elements of thought, or dissolve the reality of things, by the different terms we employ. We have simply a rational freedom in the use of terms, that the various phases of one ever-unfolding Providence may be represented with more accurate shading.

CHAPTER II.

CRISES UNDER LAWS OF PHYSICAL CHANGE.

THE two words, *crisis* and *judgment*, with their substantial oneness of meaning, suggest what experience confirms, namely, that vicissitudes, even the most sudden and unlooked-for, are due to imperceptible processes of change, in which all finite and arbitrary intention is merged and overruled. Personal existence is embarked upon the stream of general being. The individual life, that seems to have a current of its own, is shooting through the larger current of society. The general tendencies or sudden checks of a nation's career affect each citizen; and still the citizens go their several ways, occupy themselves with their own affairs, anticipating, it may be, in a passive and helpless way, the crises that are coming to impress a new movement and character, as upon the mass so upon every atom composing the mass.

Men trust themselves to general tendencies, though aware that tendency means vicissitude also. Nature shows us many movements that run a certain round; but the round is a round of changes. Gradual preparation is often turning to precipitate conclusion. Quiet evaporation from a world of waters, and clouds that float in air make their report in drops or crystals that of a sudden begin to fall upon the earth. And, again, a silent change of temperature makes its sign in the sudden turning of water into ice. Strange that, by change of temperature or possibly by mere evaporation, an apparently homogeneous fluid should by and by undergo a sudden reconstitution according to mysterious affinities and mathematical definitions; as if the creative spirit were moving in the turbid waters of the chemist's laboratory, exactly as the Spirit of God is said to have moved upon the face of the weltering world in the beginning! The laws of crystallization are mysterious; but the crisis of crystallization is unmistakable. At the end of the process the fiat is pronounced.

The crust of our globe gives distinct chapters of its own history, written out in successive geological formations. Each chapter records the progress to its completion of a definite cosmical movement. The story becomes peculiarly impressive, we are told, when it reaches the period of organic remains. As the earth is moulded and tempered to fitness for living things, a vast populace of plants and animals swarms into possession. But the work of creation, complete as to certain ends, had still other ends in view; and, moving on toward those ends, nature is found by and by to have passed the fatal bourn for the primitive orders of animated existence. They had had their day, and were doomed to disappear. It only remained to give them a worthy burial while compassing their gradual but necessary extinction.

Yet the change was not so gradual as to fail of indicating a crisis. We are even assured of a marked distinction between the earlier and the later stone age. The palæolithic man was a very different creature from the neolithic man; and the two inhabited different worlds.

It is asserted that the palæolithic inhabitant made his mark in art; that carved representations distinguish his career, such as are entirely wanting among all discovered relics of his neolithic successors. The art of that early race was buried with it; and the next human effort was put forth with reference to new conditions of life. Thus a crisis — something to be called the end or consummation of an age, a last judgment of the world as respects a clearly distinguishable phase of its history — is recognized as a recurring fact, and has passed into a scientific conception, from dateless depositions that have been only recently deciphered.

We judge of what shall be from what has been. Inductions shape and color anticipations. The human mind is constituted to discredit prophesyings that are alien to the logic of history. There is nothing, however, in which men believe more easily, in a theoretical way, than in judgments to come. The sun is still rejoicing "as a giant to run his course;" but it is easy to believe that his strength is not infinite. The winds and waters that carry on the distribution of our shifting soil are never still. The volcanic energy that has buttressed the globe may be counted upon for new activities. Atlantis may rise again from the bosom of the deep, and continents be invaded by the ocean.

> "There rolls the deep where grew the tree.
> O earth, what changes hast thou seen!
> There where the long street roars hath been
> The stillness of the central sea."

The crisis of a measureless prehistoric period is a matter of rational inference from subsequent observations. The same slow movement of material nature goes on through all historic ages, and only gives vague hints of change to the watchers of a passing day. The solar system might pass from original star-dust to star-dust again, and the agitations be so tempered and distributed that the human race should come forth to life, fulfil its physsical cycle, and be consummated in personal immortality, with a prevailing experience of order and quietness in nature. As human annals do not reach back to the beginning of geological history, so, it may be presumed, they cannot reach forward to the end. Earth's mortal pangs, the denouement and dissolution of matter, are likely to outlast the drama of man's mortal history. In the mean time occasional floods and fiery storms, a few formidable earthquakes, exceptional instances of brusque fatality, readily compose themselves to the common course of things, and exert but a moderate influence upon the thoughts of men. Yet the immovable fact remains, that the law of change is deeply interfused and all-pervading, and that living things must go as well as come in subordination to vast economies of existence, throughout a duration that has no assignable limits. The great globe itself, so generously submitted for their time to the ruling of its temporary occupants, is reserved and remade for other generations, who will take it in their turn; and this consideration is one of moment in the intellectual and moral discipline of those who are stewards of their children's estates. That a natural crisis is rationally anticipated as likely to come upon descendants is evidence that the distributive justice of the universe will not fail to bring home a moral judgment to the fathers.

Tell men, as some prophets do, that they are spoiling streams, filling up harbors, making their sea-coasts and river-valleys malarious, — by foul débris lazily washed away, which ought to be prudently disinfected, and restored as a fertilizing substance to the ground, — and how do they act? Possibly they smile at impracticable idealism; more probably they deprecate the evil tendency in a calm persuasion of their personal inability to withstand it; certainly they make themselves welcome to any solace derivable from "after us the deluge." How should the prophetic soul not take some hope from intermediate stages of trial, if a fatal conclusion cannot be reached to-day? But rational forecast is not without assurance that the crisis which announces chaos come again, as well as the crisis of a new creation, will appear when due, and sum up all the elements of the case, whether for past or future, according to law.

But man's effective discipline with respect to remote liabilities depends very much upon recurring experiences wherein the crisis of natural retribution follows close upon a crisis of personal effort. Seed-time and harvest are correlative crises separated by no inappreciable duration. The duty of the first cannot be distributed over many days; and the retribution of the second is not so far off that men can forget their accounts, or presume that the fruitful earth will not render to every man according to his works. When the harvest reckoning is complete the judgment of the year is declared. The crisis may be one of joy or distress; but either way it is the ruling fact. Be it great Rome herself that is anxiously awaiting the corn-ships from Alexandria, the ships can bring only so much corn as the year's production allows.

Who shall tell what man's prudence, promptitude, and co-operation owe to the order of material nature? The assurance that mother Earth will pay her debts to human endeavor, as well as exact her penalties for negligence and misdoing, with peremptory and critical exactness, what does it signify — or, rather, what does it not signify — in relation to that credit accorded to promises of payment by which men facilitate the exchange of services with one another? All promises to pay are distinguished from promises to pay nothing, by contemplating a crisis of maturity, — a day of decisive judgment as to how much the promise is worth.

CHAPTER III.

CRISES UNDER LAWS OF SPIRITUAL DEVELOPMENT.

AS in the material world ultimate atoms and occult energies are making continual contributions, to be summed up in ulterior consummations, so the secret and momentary actions of the human spirit become appreciable in successive crises of personal and social experience. The most sudden and radical change in history, — what is it but the summing up under creative superintendence of instantaneous personal impulses and efforts, whose result is at length registered so — and not otherwise.

Grant that matter and spirit are as different in kind as fixed fate and free-will; yet the world of spiritual powers is like the world of physical forces in this: there is no possible escape of particular elements from the sway of universal law. Hence it is that personal will, though constituted to be the very type of freedom as of power, is practically checked and restrained, until by means of intelligent judgment and loyalty to moral convictions it makes its way to the liberty of law. Ultimate freedom of will is in that orbit of movement which never violates the harmony of the spiritual universe. Only in the lowest phase of spiritual development do we find those capricious oscillations of conduct that are made up from the two extremes of wilfulness and constraint, which always accompany each other. Not that we are to charge the fits and starts of an unschooled nature to the account of the will alone. Why blame the executive power especially for capricious and tentative movements that accuse the immaturity of the legislative and judicial faculties?

Childhood's inadequacy to self-government is general. A similar inadequacy belongs to the childhood of peoples. The less endowed and less disciplined races meet the crisis of their fate in the touch of a potent civilization. Populations that can neither resist successfully the force brought to bear upon them, nor accommodate themselves kindly to novel situations that arise under the control of their superiors, are judged accordingly. There must be an irresistible logic in history, if history is to be the vehicle of a teaching not to be mistaken. The trial and decision of to-day must lead on to the trial and decision of to-morrow. Some ruling motive that is simple and universal must prove that political and military combinations are not fortuitous, and teach us to refer provisional arrangements to a permanent principle of human action.

The crises of nations are in general too limited in spiritual scope to exhibit, in the broadest light, the reality of a universal judgment in the history of mankind. For proof of this we need to look at the general progress of society, and to see the course of the common life as irrespective of national boundaries, in a history well understood and easily sketched; and yet, a history wherein a common faith in divine government, the deep religious tendency of the race is recognized as determining the plans of statesmen and the struggle of armies.

What grand movement of the modern world gives a clearer account of itself than "the Reformation of the sixteenth century"? Define the movement as we may in space or time, we know that it surpasses our definitions; while, on the other hand, the infinite complexity of personal aims and party interests cannot hide the simple issue in law that was on trial, nor nullify our sense of a judicial direction that governed the procedure as a whole.

The church of Luther's day was universal, in distinction from national, — not universal as being adequate to the spiritual guidance of all men. Yet the church, according to her charter, contemplated a spiritual empire absolutely universal; and was proudly conscious of the recognition accorded to her claims by the leading secular powers. But the real potency of the faith was held in check by a lifeless crust of ecclesiastical tradition and routine. In spite of all restraints, however, there was a stirring of thought, an awakening of inquiry, a musing about what were the realities the church had so long been undertaking to represent; and this mental motion was not without heat. The fire burned in the heart of Luther while he was musing. Then he spake with his lips — with his pen; and the secret was out. There was a remarkable response to his testimony. That fresh plant of righteousness named "justification by faith," — faith implying the certainty of sincere obedience to the truth embraced, — found a spiritual climate in which it could live and bear fruit. The old stalk of justification by pious works, on the contrary, as such works were understood and practised in the Roman routine, was seen to be dried up and dying down to the ground.

To the poor novice, in his convent of the Augustines, there came a crisis hardly less marked and decisive than that which overtook Saul of Tarsus on the road to Damascus. Luther knew the letter of his New Testament better than almost anybody else; for he had found its solid contents in the university, while clergy and laity as a rule were familiar with only fragments delivered in church. He had become a monk under the impulse of superstitious terror, and in defiance of his father's authority. Set to menial services, suffering insolence from the brotherhood, confessing every day, persecuted with penances, the submissive disciple treated the rough monastic tyranny as a kind of counter-irritant to the more tormenting trouble of his spirit about his relations with God. Naturally, he fell sick in body also. In the repose of weakness, soothed by the wise counsels of the good Staupitz, he beheld the dawn. The sun arose with healing. Martin Luther found himself the elect of a fresh revelation. He became a man of God, with a mission to the world. With God he was in the majority against any power that needed to be called in question.

The monk's new initiative was as bold as his previous temper had been diffident. Ordained priest, he appealed to the Scriptures for the correction of the church; made professor at Wittenberg, he threw off the shackles of scholastic philosophy; sent to Rome on business for his order, he brought the judgment of an unsophisticated conscience to bear upon that holy city, and gave warning of the wrath to come; unable to get redress for manifold abuses connected with the sale of indulgences, he nailed his ninety-five propositions to the Wittenberg church-door; his writings burnt and himself excommunicated, he burned the bull of excommunication with retorted scorn; summoned to the Diet of Worms, he stood unquailing before princes and emperor, and answered with such conscientious and uncompromising fidelity to his faith, that the muse of history delights to depict him in lowly garb before that tinselled and magnificent assembly, — the incomparable spiritual magnate of the hour.

From the crisis in the monk's cell at Erfurth, we date the orderly and dramatic evolution of the reforming energy. That was a crisis of individual initiative, with respect to the characteristic spiritual movement of the time.

As Luther's personal experience was not unconnected with a general awakening of thought and revival of learning, — for there were reformers before the Reformation, — so, when the Reformation was fairly inaugurated, it was to combine of necessity with all the thought and tendency of the age. Especially, the reformation in religion was to quicken the national spirit that in various countries was feeling its way towards the emancipation of secular authority from ecclesiastical domination. Richelieu, for example, as prince of the church, should have been a leading power in the Catholic league; but, as statesman and prime minister of France, he actually became an important ally of the Protestant cause.

So it came to pass, exactly one hundred years after the nailing of Luther's theses to the church-door, that the Reformation was on the eve of a general crisis, — the great military trial of its history. For thirty years (1618 – 1648) there raged a desultory but destructive warfare, that left Germany devastated through its whole extent. The question at issue was, not which league should win a permanent ascendency over the other; but rather, whether both Catholics and Protestants should agree to live and let live. The decision was upon the whole in favor of the modern spirit, — in favor of the right to think, to speak, and so to seek the reformation of the church, in its head or in its members, as well as the reformation of political institutions, in a sense favorable to populations in distinction from princes.

This tedious struggle was far enough from exhibiting a dramatic unity of action, as has been intimated. But, on the other hand, it was not so incoherent that we may not reasonably point to the battle of Lützen as the crisis of the war; and certainly the death of Gustavus Adolphus marked the crisis of Lützen when, in the words of Schiller, "the battle already half lost was won over the king's corpse."

Thus, without going beyond the proper range of the word, we find that one crisis in human experience is related to another. The crisis of personal conviction, of individual initiative, when the world's teaching is brought to a focus in the judgment of a single epoch-making man, looks forward to the crisis of a general movement, in which extensive combinations and persistent struggles submit to a decision that is for the time without appeal. We have only to generalize this distinction, to remember that the epoch-making man, so called, is like every other human being; that the world's teaching is brought to a focus, and determines an initiative, in every soul, according to the nature of the teaching and the nature of the soul; and we rationally conclude, what we actually find to be the case, that the general judgment, the overruling determination in human affairs, is the opening of a new trial, with further opportunities for men in detail. The government of the universal Ruler is made to subserve, with perfect discrimination, the discipline of the universal Father toward each one of his children in particular; that every child may become in turn a loyal subject to the Sovereign and Judge of all.

Nor, as human society improves, does the work of regeneration cease. Personal determinations may grow more rational and less heated; general judgments may become less frequent and more significant. Yet even the apocalyptic millennium is not proof against the recrudescence of evil. Peace on earth degenerating into careless security is the opportunity of adventurous wrongdoing. But when the strange challenge of evil awakens peaceful virtue to martial ardor, the struggle is brief and victory decisive. The judgment is most conclusive which has the greatest disciplinary effect. The infinite law works its way eternally in the limited powers of rational creatures, — cancelling errors and compensating pains.

CHAPTER IV.

CRISES ACCORDING TO THE OLD TESTAMENT TEACHING.

HISTORY may be figured as the outer court, and worship as the inner sanctuary, of universal reality. It is much that Anaxagoras or Hegel should ground philosophy on the assurance that the reason which we bring to the study of creation is a reflex of the Reason according to which creation is carried on. But is it not much more that the same truth should live in the devout faith of mankind in general, a worshipful, though indefinable persuasion of one God, Author of all things? It must be remembered, however, that religious conviction, as well as speculative assurance is realized through discipline; only the discipline of faith is in a much sterner school than that of philosophy.

The Old Testament sets before us the career of a people raised to an express and incontestable primacy in the knowledge of God and the service of faith. In their history the oneness of God stood for the unity of nature. If there was one only Creator of things visible and invisible, then from Him was the supernatural governance of nature as well as the original constitution of nature. Hence the gods of the heathen — the nature gods — fell down into the order of nature, and became no gods, — rather vanity and a lie. Jehovah, who made the heavens, was Ruler and Judge of all the earth; and the faith of his chosen people was to be ultimately the faith of mankind.

But the unique service to which Israel was called of God, though a service of great dignity, involving the spiritual welfare of men in all ages, was no easy service. On the contrary, it seemed easy for the servants of Jehovah to be drawn aside into unprincipled complications with their idolatrous neighbors; and their seducing neighbors became in turn the rod of Jehovah, when he awoke to judgment, and punished his people's unfaithfulness to the covenant between him and them. Still, though often cast down, Israel was not destroyed. Though triumphant for a season, the hostile nations were by and by judged. The banner of hope was held up before the wayward and afflicted servants of Jehovah in the name of "Emanuel, God with us." When the lesson taught by the execution of judgment had been learned, then humiliating captivity gave way before a new fervor of faith, in the remnant that lived to see the day of deliverance. And so was made good the word of promise, that evermore pointed the moral and tempered the severity of prophetic denunciation: "Although I have cast them far off among the heathen, and although I have scattered them among the countries, yet will I be to them a little sanctuary in the countries where they shall come." "I will even gather you from the people, and assemble you out of the countries where ye have been scattered, and I will give you the land of Israel. And they shall come thither, and they shall take away all the detestable things thereof, and all the abominations thereof, from thence. And I will give them one heart, and I will put a new spirit within you; and I will take the stony heart out of their flesh, and give them an heart of flesh: that they may walk in my statutes, and keep mine ordinances, and do them: and they shall be my people, and I will be their God." [1]

[1] Ez. xi. 16–20

CHAPTER V.

CRISES INTERPRETED BY THE CHRIST.

THE New Testament opens to us the new era. It announces the dispensation of the last times, the period of personal faith made free from external bonds, — the ultimate type of worship in the whole family of the Father.

The doctrine of one God cannot, according to its own idea, be the permanent peculiarity of a single people, still less the mark of an intellectual class, — the contemplative and philosophic few. It is set forth in the New Testament as passing into the possession of all nations and all men, without respect of national or personal distinctions, through the revelation of one Mediator between God and man, namely, the Christ. The rude and magisterial ways of messengers and ministers that went before are held to have been judged and superseded by the condescension and brotherliness of the well-beloved Son. His function is unique. He can have no rival and no vicar. "One is your master, even the Christ," — this is the note of universal discipleship, — "and all ye are brethren." Principalities and powers, visible or invisible, are held to do homage of right to the redeeming Word of God.

Here was announced a crisis of the world. Now was opening a new opportunity and a new trial of faith, —

not for the Jews only. The personal initiative of the great Teacher was to be followed by personal determinations of men in all nations; and general judgments were to declare themselves, that should herald the consummation, not of that age only, but of all world-ages. What, then, is the Christ's conception of crises in history? What is his doctrine and administration of judgment, as set forth by evangelists and apostles from his own lips?

The crises and judgments of this world are contemplated in the New Testament as belonging to an eternal reign of righteousness. They have their appointed days, times, and seasons, — not to be known of men, because they are in the power of the Father. But they come in the process of divine revelation. God's ways are everlasting. The living Word, summing up all truth that has been or shall be in human experience, comes into contact with individual minds through a spiritual operation. Judgment begins in human consciousness at the house of God, in convictions of sin and righteousness that take possession of believers in the Christ; but the absolute spiritual Authority moving the responsible action of enlightened men, at length brings to pass a change, — a re-arrangement of human society, which points to what the relative end must be of those who obey not the gospel.

As faith draws men into fellowship with the Christ's voluntary sufferings, so judgment, the vindication of faith, dooms the men of unbelief, who repudiate the law of self-sacrifice, to the punitive consequences of their voluntary doings. To Israel of old the faith of one God involved a life-long national discipline. So the faith of one Lord Jesus Christ involves a life-long personal, as well as social, discipline, to the spiritual Israel of God.

The work of redeeming mankind from original earthly tendencies to the best spiritual possibilities, is one in which children in experience are taught to know the Father's patience and forgiveness, in the fact of his setting before them "an open door." None who desire it are ever excluded from the work and discipline of faith on account of past misdoings. But faith signifies work and discipline, — by no means a far-off felicity, having no respect to conduct. First and last, here and hereafter, the judgment of God is "to every man according to his works."

Yet in what utterance or action of the great Teacher does it appear that he ever looked for any change of personal determination, or for any new cast of the world's moral drama, except under the law of universal reality; that is, the will of the Father expressed in the constitution of things? Did redemption mean, in his thought, that established institutions and authorities would of a sudden lose all their original energy, and quietly abdicate their time-honored pretensions, as soon as a prophetic judgment should find them wanting, and doom them to pass away? On the contrary, he counted upon their very falsities and oppressions to call into action the new spirit of righteousness, that should shatter the legality of the letter, when its measure of absurdity and iniquity should be full. He proposed to train his disciples in a struggle wherein the ideal energy would find both strength and correction from resistance of actual powers, that also had in them rudiments of divine wisdom, the guarantees of their provisional authority. The advancing spiritual reign contemplated a method of change that, from age to age, was turning to practical account the dispositions and habits already contracted among men.

Man's original constitution is recognized as including the subjective law of his transformation. Hence Jesus Christ, as the prophet of regeneration for all mankind, points out, according to strictly natural principles, the persons in whom the new life must come to conscious action earliest; and through whom, consequently, it must make its initial effort on behalf of other men. Even the divine disclosure of personal perfection and universal hope does not abruptly overpower the natural motives in possession of human beings; does not initiate the most far-reaching renovations of society, through men whose natural instincts as to what concerns their immediate interests render them distrustful of any change.

The Sermon on the Mount is very explicit in this regard. The reign of God belongs effectively to those to whom it comes, in its higher aims, as a greater relief and refreshment than to others, — to those, in a word, who naturally feel the need of it, in consequence of the discipline through which they have already passed in their training for it. The candidates for immediate discipleship are not the rich, the self-satisfied, the men of the world, whose portion in this life has intoxicated them with ambitions and pleasures of a day, and dulled them to spiritual needs and immortal hopes. To such the reign of God announces no immediate blessedness. Prosperous selfishness has for its correction the judicial menace of woe, — the threat of loss and unwilling sacrifice, in those judgments that shall dissolve the world that is, for the sake of the world that is to come. Meanwhile, the meek, the merciful, the peace-making men, those hungering and thirsting after righteousness, those who have already realized what righteousness means, enough to be persecuted on account of it, — are the characters to whom the reign of God, with its voluntary sacrifices and eternal rewards, appropriately appeals.

Yet, though as a rule the wise, mighty, or noble of the world were not at first effectually appealed to, but rather rebuked and repelled ; though the particular people for whom the great supper was prepared began with one consent to make excuse ; though a young man, as candid and lovable as he was rich, must needs go sorrowfully away from the good Teacher, before he could learn that eternal life is not in exclusive possession, but in communicating love and redeeming service ; though it is natural for the poor to rejoice in that he is exalted, and not so natural for the rich to rejoice in that he is made low ; nevertheless, what is impossible with men is not impossible with God, and what seems unnatural with men may simply indicate the quality to be developed in human nature, — as men become spiritually inspired and practically taught of God.

If natural motives were recognized as of critical significance in the Sermon on the Mount, with respect to that initial discipleship, which waited upon the humble teaching of the Christ, — the same motives do not lose their importance, as the truth moves on towards universal supremacy, while the Son of man sits upon the throne of his glory, and all nations are gathered before him. Accordingly, the judgment scene in the twenty-fifth chapter of Matthew sets before us, in grand classifications of character, and appropriate retributive distinctions, how the original struggles of the faith are to be regarded among men in the crises of its triumph.

The history of redemption is an ideal assize. Spontaneous choices, personal decisions that took form in acts when the actors knew not what they did, claims of divine justice and compassion listened to or rejected in the appeals of a common humanity, — all come up together for adjudication, according to the sum total of responsible activity with respect to the divine revelation. "I was an hungered," says the exalted Christ, in the judicial majesty of human sympathy, "I was thirsty," "I was a stranger," "I was naked," "I was sick, and in prison;" and such, or so different, was the treatment accorded to me. What but the judgment of times and ages can declare the essential quality and limitless reach of personal conduct? What but the æonian retributions can bring home to the conscious experience of men the spiritual reign, which they dimly recognize or carelessly deny, but which it behooves them at any cost to appreciate and own?

To work with the Christ as one of his disciples and messengers, to share in the gracious efforts and glorious results of redemption; or to array one's self with the adverse power, and partake of what is prepared for, as it is prepared by, the adversary and his angels, — such is the alternative before which the spiritual development of every man comes to its real significance. Human conduct not only moves outward, to take effect upon the existing world of space, and to be affected in its turn; it moves onward, also, to affect the successive ages of history, and to be affected by them. The actions of men make or mar the æons; but cannot defeat the æonian judgments, through which the works of men, in general and in particular, become their own inheritance. Personal conviction carries within it the certainty of general judgment. Truth spoken in the ear and in closets is proof that the mighty secret shall come to light and publicity. The day when the universal church is born in the person of her Head, is the day when the ancient world is judged; albeit the world is unconscious of the divine determination, and will pass away not without a great noise.

The spiritual crises contemplated in the New Testament impart their moral and coloring to outward conceptions, and help themselves to physical symbols. Apocalyptic visions are given for the encouragement and warning of the persecuted church. The pangs of earth draw attention and service from the armies of heaven. What seems a forlorn hope to the eye of sense becomes an assurance of victory to the eye of faith. The seer of Patmos apparently intended that it should be impossible to verify in detail the significance of his imposing and mysterious symbolism, and equally impossible to mistake its general purport. The awe-inspiring crises that successively present themselves have one unmistakable meaning, — the vindication of righteousness in the painful coercion of hostile forces, until all the perverse moral energy that enters into the power and state of the arch-adversary is defeated, and destructions come to a perpetual end, according to the universal justice of the great white throne, and Him that sat upon it.[1] No martial imagery, no colors of blood and flame can blind the prophet to the inner reality of history, that men are judged, collectively and severally, "according to their works."

St. Peter has his apocalypse, as well as St. John. He foresaw the day of judgment and destruction of ungodly men, as coming like a thief, in a fiery deluge, for which the heavens and the earth were kept in store, in anticipation of new heavens and a new earth, — the abode of righteousness. This is his appeal to the faithful: "See-

[1] Rev. xx. 11-15.

ing that these things are thus all to be dissolved, what manner of persons ought ye to be in all holy living and godliness, looking for and earnestly desiring the coming of the day of God, by reason of which the heavens being on fire shall be dissolved, and the elements shall melt with fervent heat? But, according to his promise, we look for new heavens and a new earth, wherein dwelleth righteousness." [1]

This deluge of destruction to the ungodly, and of deliverance to the faithful, however, like its prototype in the days of Noah, is a judgment "according to men in the flesh," — a judgment not of necessity to destroy, but possibly to emancipate and purify the life, "according to God in the spirit." [2]

Whether it be the spiritual reign within or the natural government without that chiefly fastens attention, each is inseparable from the other. Material nature has ever its highest significance as the theatre and property of moral agents. But outward representations of coming crises are pictures upon a flat surface. They are so foreshortened that the prompt imagination cannot at all appreciate the historical perspective, and takes the whole as being at hand. It is St. Paul who sets himself to correct the habit, apparently too prevalent in the early church, of looking for a speedy consummation of the Christ's militant reign in a final triumph. Especially the Epistles to the Thessalonians are addressed, in part, to a certain disquieting pre-occupation about times and seasons; and the faithful are exhorted to the watchfulness and sobriety appropriate to children of the light, — forewarned and forearmed.[3] Again, they are told not to

---

[1] 2 Peter iii. 1–13. [2] 1 Peter iv. 6; and iii. 19, 20.
[3] 1 Thess. v. 1–11.

be quickly shaken or troubled in mind, as that the day of the Lord is present.[1] The prophetic soul of the Apostle to the Gentiles is expanding to the spiritual proportions of the Christian conflict: such mighty powers of opposition are holding in restraint the ultimate revelation, — when the last enemy shall be destroyed, and through the complete subjection of all things to the mediatorial King, God shall be all in all.[2] Still, St. Paul draws his picture of the day of the Lord rather from circumstances of triumph than from incidents of destruction. That presence (*parousia*), which sustains the disciples in their personal conflicts, will change to a triumphal revelation of the Leader's person, when the war shall end. Meanwhile no one is to wait idly for the Lord's appearance. No one is to fancy that those who are remaining in the body at the final day will have any advantage or precedence as compared with those who have fallen asleep in death. For, says the apostle, "the Lord himself shall descend from heaven with a shout, with the voice of the archangel, and with the trump of God: and the dead in Christ shall rise first: then we that are alive, that are left, shall, together with them, be caught up in the clouds, to meet the Lord in the air; and so shall we ever be with the Lord." [3]

Diverging rays of thought in the writings of apostles lead back to their source in the Lord's teaching. It was the Christ who, knowing the import of his own initiative, appreciated the crisis in history which would soon declare itself as an inevitable sequel. The more men's characters and tendencies were made manifest through his ministry, the more the hour drew on, to the apprehension of Jesus, when his own crucifixion would be

[1] 2 Thess. ii. 1–12. [2] 1 Cor. xv. 25–28. [3] 1 Thess. iv. 16, 17.

reached. But it was not his crucifixion, so much as the portentous judgment that would ensue upon it, that weighed upon his spirit. A judgment of such awful finality, of such condemnatory severity, — a crisis involving such destruction and dispersion of his own people, when as their spiritual Prince he would have led them in the way of peace, — how could he endure the anticipation of it, — especially the thought that they would bring it upon themselves by a tumultuary and defiant overruling of Cæsar's representative, upon the hypocritical pretence of loyalty to Cæsar, and in blind rejection of the reign of God? But if the Jews neither rendered to Cæsar the things that were Cæsar's nor to God the things that were God's, surely Rome's stern reckoning with provincial tempers of this sort was neither doubtful nor distant; and it was in effect the reckoning, not of Cæsar alone, but of the universal Judge.

The cities of Galilee were warned. Their day of judgment would overwhelm them in a catastrophe less tolerable than even the most exemplary calamities of other cities, — so much more flagrantly had they offended, against far mightier persuasions of truth and goodness. The repentance of the men of Nineveh, the docility of the queen of the South, — these were examples to rise up in the judgment and condemn the men of that generation. Upon Jerusalem woe, as unparalleled as her wickedness! "O Jerusalem, Jerusalem, which killest the prophets, and stonest them which are sent unto thee, how often would I have gathered thy children together, even as a hen gathereth her chickens under her wings, and ye would not. Behold, your house is left unto you desolate."[1]

[1] Matt. xxiii. 37, 38.

"And when he drew nigh he saw the city, and wept over it, saying, If thou hadst known in this day, even thou, the things that belong unto peace! But now they are hid from thine eyes. For the days shall come upon thee, when thine enemies shall cast up a bank about thee, and compass thee round, and keep thee in on every side, and shall dash thee to the ground, and thy children within thee; and they shall not leave in thee one stone upon another, because thou knewest not the time of thy visitation." [1]

The disciples, far from exhibiting any anxiety at first about their personal fortunes, seem to have taken the part of advocates, — making appeal to their Master on behalf of the city unconscious of her doom, pointing as they passed, with affectionate pride, to the well-laid stones of the temple-buildings, — so worthy to be spared, if not likely to resist assault. But when the unwelcome prediction was repeated, and Jesus, with his group of followers, had reached the Mount of Olives, there were some that sought private instruction, as if for their personal guidance in the trials before them. The interview is given by three evangelists, with remarkable harmony of coloring and distinctness of detail.[2] It opens with the request: "Tell us when shall these things be? and what shall be the sign of thy coming, and of the end of the world?" — the end of the world being, as we have seen, the consummation of the *æon*, or world-period.

Far from rebuking them for an unavailing curiosity about what was beyond their range, our Lord ministers to their practical prudence out of his own prophetic intuition; and though the prophetic imagery, as usual, is of a kind to suggest the infinite dominion to which our

---

[1] Luke xix. 41-44.   [2] Matt. xxiv.; Mark xiii.; Luke xxi.

earthly existence belongs, the immediate application of his words is governed by the emphatic declaration: "Verily I say unto you, this generation shall not pass away, till all these things be accomplished." The Leader sets before his followers the trials they will encounter, — the earlier premonitions, which need give them no immediate trouble; the later warnings, pointing to instant flight; the supreme tribulation, "such as hath not been from the beginning of the world until now; no, nor ever shall be." The acme of judicial terror and destruction in the world's history was near; and the parable of the fig-tree was added, that they might be on the watch; because the day and hour could not be noted in the calendar, but were in the power of God, according to the law of things.

If the crisis of the ante-Christian world was to be one of unexampled tribulation, what did the faith of the Christ hold forth as to the character and consummation of the new world-movement? The new dispensation was conceived as that of the "last days" and the "last times." It contemplated seasons of refreshing from the presence of the Lord; "whom the heaven must receive until the times of restitution of all things, whereof God spake by the mouth of his holy prophets which have been since the world began."[1] It was to have a consummation in direct contrast with that of the old world, — not the destruction of a desecrated Jerusalem, but "the new Jerusalem coming down out of heaven from God;" not even the dissolution of the physical order, as anything more than an incident of spiritual history, which would demand "new heavens and a new earth," — fit scene for "the revelation of the sons of God."

[1] Acts iii. 19-21.

Yet the two world-movements, represented by such contrasted consummations, are one. The latter grows out of the former. No quality in either is wholly wanting to the other. If the first is stronger in corporate constraint, it is not because there is no individual initiative, — rather because personal caprices have special need of being reduced to general order. If the last movement is stronger in individual initiative, it is not because corporate inertia does not offer a resisting medium to personal endeavor, but that, under the highest example and inspiration, the social body becomes sympathetic and apt in the appreciation of prophets of the day. Similarly, if the first world-period was one of waste and destruction, it was not without its creative processes; and if the last is a period of production and conservation, there are nevertheless destructions which it cannot dispense with. If the crisis of divine forbearance and condescension was when Jesus said, "Father, forgive them, for they know not what they do;"[1] then the crisis of triumph and glory shall be when, all things having been subjected unto him, "the Son also himself shall be subjected to him that did subject all things unto him, that God may be all in all."[2] This is the crisis of resurrection, when destruction itself is destroyed; for, "the last enemy that shall be abolished is death."[3]

But, meanwhile, how many an appointed day, in which God will judge the inhabitants of earth in righteousness, by the man whom he hath ordained; whereof he hath given assurance unto all men, in that he hath raised him from the dead.[4] How many nations shall pass before his judgment-seat; and he shall discern between

[1] Luke xxiii. 34.   [2] 1 Cor. xv. 28.
[3] 1 Cor. xv. 26.   [4] Acts xvii. 31.

the righteous and the wicked, — setting them apart from one another spiritually, as a shepherd divideth his sheep from the goats, — in order that each character may enter upon an æonian retribution, according to the disposition declared and the discipline required. The government of mankind is not physical at first in order to be moral by and by; it is a moral government from the beginning, that it may by and by bring men to spiritual maturity beyond the present order of nature.

One germ, one principle of growth, one end and aim of being, one solid society, whether in the body or out of the body, one age of ages pervading things visible and things invisible, — such is the Scriptural conception of history. It is a conception unspeakably majestic, — so essentially simple as to reconcile all diversities of experience. The physical and moral transformations which æonian life contemplates cannot be carried on without the reciprocal service of society and individuals, of ages and ages. The spiritual creation of God is subjected to earthly conditions and temporary struggles, till the time of change, the crisis of victory and freedom is reached. Nothing is for itself alone. If the experience of the past has been of service as to the experience of the future, shall not the men of the future pay their debt to the men of the past? Had the ages of the prophets nothing to hope from the ages of the Christ? But, according to St. Peter, the prophets had the assurance of ministering to other times than theirs, and of ministering to the knowledge of things which were to be preached in the Gospel of Christ, "by the Holy Ghost sent down from heaven, — which things angels desire to look into."[1]

[1] 1 Pet. i. 10-12.

"But I say unto you, love your enemies, and pray for them that persecute you; that ye may be the sons of your Father which is in heaven: for he maketh his sun to rise on the evil and the good, and sendeth rain on the just and the unjust." On whom, then, does the Sun of righteousness rise? The spiritual light of the world, — how long shall it shine? Certainly upon all who are judged in righteousness; and so long as they shall be so judged. Judgment is teaching, — the application of law, which is perfect, converting the soul. There is no revelation without it. The reign of God and righteousness is for none but free spirits; and to free spirits the privilege of obedience is implied in the demand of law. The great Teacher appears as the considerate apologist and just advocate of those who err through natural inability or ignorance, the uncompromising antagonist and stern censor of such as knowingly resist the call of duty, having ample resources for fulfilling it. Men are warned of catastrophes, which their inertness, egoism, and obstinacy may precipitate, of consequences that propagate themselves from age to age; yet never are they warned that the law of rational responsibility, according to which every recorded judgment becomes a basis for the reconsideration and rearrangement of moral relations, can be abrogated. While, therefore, the divine Father is revealed as ever favorable to those who follow after righteousness, he is equally gracious and faithful in his judgments upon those who choose the ways of transgression. A creature of God cannot come to the latest judgment upon practical disobedience without reaching the latest degree of voluntary alienation from duty; while in all, — those who are reconciled to the Father through the revelation of the Christ or those who are not, — the reign of universal love is eternally determining the awards of distributive justice, — "to every man according to his works."

In fine, whatever intimations we have in Scripture touching a "last judgment" and a "last day," — chiefly that pregnant saying of the great Teacher, "He that rejecteth me, and receiveth not my sayings, hath one that judgeth him: the word that I spake, the same shall judge him in the last day,"[1] — must not be made to contradict the majesty of divine government by a petty literalism in the construction of words and figures. How can a transcendent idea be accommodated to our thoughts but in the language of common life? Are not all judgments of God last judgments in the sense of being ultimate — without appeal and without revision? But Christian faith has pictured a "last judgment" for a "last day," — the closing up of a governmental economy in the consummation of a world-history. Here, of course, as elsewhere, "last" is last in a given order of things. According to St. Augustine the last judgment is not only *judicium ultimum*, but *judicium novissimum*,[2] the *latest* judgment in a known order of divine revelation. But this known order of divine revelation in the Scripture rendering of it is vital in every part with the teaching that justice and judgment do not begin or end with world-ages. They are enthroned with the Eternal.

[1] John xii. 48.   [2] De Civitate Dei, lib. xx. c. 1.

CONCLUSION.

"LET your moderation be known unto all men."
                                        PHILIPPIANS iv. 5.

"THAT you o'erstep not the modesty of nature."
                        SHAKSPEARE: Hamlet, Act iii. Scene 2.

CONCLUSION.

IF the study now brought to an end could convey even to a few minds a sober impression of what is the difference between searching the Scriptures with a conscientious reference to the real life and movement of which they speak, and searching the Scriptures with an equally conscientious regard to a system of abstract doctrines, deduced, or to be deduced, from a careful dissection and microscopic examination of their literal tissue, — it would not be a trivial result. But this result is not to be gained without some apprehension of divine revelation in its organic unity and boundless scope; and with this apprehension all interest begins to be turned to the reality and spirit of revelation, as distinguished from the record and letter of the same. We begin to see that it is not about otherwise unknowable or secret things that we are invited to consult the "lively oracles." Our inquiry is about things of the common and familiar creation, things of nature, "these things," — whether they are so or otherwise. Within this range we can form some judgment as to what responses are true to reality, and what are marked with the ambiguity and incoherency of conventional or perfunctory divination.

We have been contemplating one reality under various relations of thought, intending that each succeeding aspect or movement of inquiry should take up and carry on the truth of all that preceded it toward one general impression. But in such a progress something is of necessity left behind. Special impressions and arguments of detail are lost to recollection. Hence, when the matter under consideration is the most important in kind, it is well perhaps not to take abrupt leave of one's work, but to sum up briefly what has appeared to be true, in a way to indicate the logical connection and practical bearings of the argument as a whole.

Nature in Scripture is not only nature according to common sense, but universal nature, — the sum total of dependent existence, without assignable limits in space or time.

Man, as part of nature, is represented in Scripture as having his discipline in space and time, under conditions that are determined for him, rather than by him, — conditions, however, which he is constituted to interpret rationally and to treat responsibly, as bringing into personal experience more and more the divine ruling.

The divine ruling becomes effective in the movement of human society through the faith and conduct of the better inspired of men; and is represented in the New Testament as reaching a rounded and complete revelation in one Man, announced in the fulness of time as the first-begotten Son of the divine Father, — Teacher, and Ruler, in a unique sense, — in fine, the personal Wisdom and practical Word of God for universal humanity.

The revelation of God is conceived in Scripture as not incidental to the course of nature, but the ground of it; and, similarly, the revelation of God in man is regarded, not as contingent upon any particular action of any individual, but as that for which generic man was originally constituted in the order of nature. In other words, the divine revelation is inclusive of nature, and nature is penetrated with the purpose of God; while man in particular is taught to apprehend himself not only as the creature of the Creator, but as the ward and pupil, so to speak, of the divine Reason in the process of revelation; and thus the divine Word is the expression of patient Love "from the foundation of the world," that it may be the utterance of regenerating Goodness in "the consummation of the age."

Accordingly, the Scriptures set before us certain inseparable parts or aspects of the divine procedure, provided for in the constitution of things and verifiable in the common experience of men. In these we are presented with a series of moral, not to say mathematical, equations, namely, —

First, a personal manhood, animal and spiritual, started, in ignorance and dependence, upon a career involved in an infinite creative purpose, is equal only to a manhood whose moral development will be one involving difficulty and danger, wherein personal righteousness will depend of necessity upon faith in a direction afforded, and not, in the beginning at any rate, upon recognized perfection in things done.

Secondly, the same manhood developed in a race, whose complex constitution is ever determining a distinction of better and worse in the aims and examples of society, yet ever sustaining a personal freedom of choice respecting the objects to be immediately pursued, is equal only to a moral discipline, wherein the effort to realize a positive good will determine the knowledge of relative evil, and spiritual law will exact free personal sacrifices as a method of reconciling provisional efforts with the demands of ideal and ulterior life.

Thirdly, the moral government which exacts free sacrifices of personal loyalty for spiritual ends, while not forcibly arresting the wilful pursuit of selfish satisfactions, is identical with the moral government which determines crises, — wherein the communion of self-sacrifice for the universal good is to be recognized by all as "the cup of blessing," in contrast with the "poisoned chalice" of selfish enjoyment at the common cost.

Thus, the fact that "the law of the Eternal is perfect, converting the soul," implies the fact that the soul of man is in a process of growth and discipline, passing through its conversions. But human progress is recognized in Scripture as not one of pure physical determinism, and not one of unembarrassed spiritual freedom. Consequently, man is treated, not as a being whose behavior on earth can be justly appreciated in the order of purely scientific thought, or in the order of purely moral judgments, but as a being who must reach his maturity of character, find the just significance of his actions, and give account of himself to God, in an order of spiritual relations beyond the range of a transitory physical economy.

As, however, the consummation of mankind is held to depend upon the revelation of the Father, so spiritual changes are set forth in Scripture as having their intellectual preparations and their voluntary crises in the development of human nature. Hence there is conceived a turning-point to be called *the* conversion: in the individual, it is when spirit and truth are definitively affirmed as the dominant and enduring reality; in the race, it is when the Christ supersedes the religious ruling of the tribe, the worship of places and of forms, by the loyal faith of the personal child of the Father, the worship "in spirit and in truth."

Accordingly, in personal experience as well as in prophetic teaching, the efficiency of the Christ, as Messenger of the Father, is properly apprehended in relation to universal history. His service is not summed up in spiritual phenomena of detail, not confined to the church as distinguished from the world, not for men of faith to the exclusion of unbelievers; but embraces the whole movement of human history as related to the whole revelation of God. The saying of Pascal, "without Jesus Christ we know neither what life is, nor what death is, nor what God is, nor what we ourselves are,"[1] is the negative expression of what is stated positively by St. John, that Jesus Christ was the true light "which lighteth every man."

That communication of truth and life called regeneration, and conceived in the teaching of the Christ as identical with the spiritual reign of God, is for man as man; while the normal and clear manifestation of it is in man as receptive of the truth and faithful to conscientious conviction, in order that, working together with the divine Spirit, he may be led on from his birth as the offspring of the Creator to his birth as the spiritual child and heir of the Father. Regeneration reaches its perfect type and revelation in the Christ, Son of man and Son of God; and the note or exemplary affirmation of this, according to the Scripture testimony, is the baptism of water and of the spirit, which signalizes the Son's deliberate devotion to the Father and the Father's reciprocal recognition of the Son.[2]

---

[1] Pensées, vol. ii. p. 317.
[2] Matt. iii. 13–17; Mark i. 9–11; Luke iii. 21, 22.

The reign of God in man, by virtue of its being "regeneration," is set forth as "salvation" also. Not only those who allow the Word of God to have free course and to be glorified in their spirits are saved from sins and sufferings into which they might otherwise fall; but those also who, through disloyalty and disobedience to salutary teaching from above have fallen into error and blindness wherein they are lost to the rational faith and peaceful enjoyment of the divine goodness, — even they can be saved from their sins by the efficiency of the Father's love in the Son's condescension. Man's unbelief cannot make the faith of God of none effect.

Jesus Christ, as Minister of the regeneration, is also Master, as respects the method of man's discipleship. His address to the Father in prayer for his disciples is: "I have given unto them the words which thou gavest me."[1] So his disciples are required to learn of him that they may teach others; while none are permitted to be masters in the Christian school, as having authority to check or limit teaching and learning by a personal judgment still liable to error. Thus the effort of thought in Christian disciples is clearly recognized as relative, not only to the powers of the thinker, but to nature environing the thinker. Its praise is sincerity, not infallibility.

Progress in truth depends upon one's not pretending to know, when one only believes; and progress in faith depends upon one's not pretending to believe, when one only assents. The expression of common Christian integrity, whether in teaching or learning, is: "We having the same spirit of faith according as it is written, I believed, and therefore have I spoken: we also believe and therefore speak."[2]

---

[1] John xvii. 8. [2] 2 Cor. iv. 13.

As, however, there is a constitution of material nature which holds through all physical changes, and a constitution of the human mind the same through all spiritual transformations, this constitution of things material and spiritual becomes the basis and law of scientific, philosophic, and moral verification; or, what is the same thing, it ensures to man the possibility of making progress in truth, notwithstanding his liability of falling into error.

By one constitution of nature men are ever drawn towards unity of thought and knowledge, through endless contradictions of scientific opinion. By one Lord and Master of the spiritual life men are likewise drawn towards unity of faith and obedience, through the more passionate contradictions of metaphysical speculation and dogmatic dicta. No wonder, therefore, that our Lord took care to teach that men might have to seize upon the comfortable hopes of the Father's reign by faith in the Father, — and not without what might be called "violence" with respect to established authorities and conventional constructions of holy texts.

But in Scripture as elsewhere "the truth itself"[1] of St. Augustine, — that is, reality, the law of nature unmistakably verifying itself in common experience, — assumes a predominance in the domain of faith on the ground of its unimpeachable quality of certitude. And this is as much as to say that testimonies and representations naturally unverifiable, though accepted as standing for what is true, cannot rule in human conviction with the authority of self-evidence. Such elements in the Bible, as in other literature, are open to doubt and discussion by the very law of our human faculties, — on the ground,

---

[1] "Sed loquitur [Deus] ipsa veritate."

at least, that the lack of known example or rational proof of what exactly was meant by the sacred writer is equivalent to the liability of misunderstanding on the part of even the most believing reader. While, however, things imperfectly understood, and carrying, possibly, no proof of historic exactness in detail, have often great importance and effectiveness in the general picture of reality, they cannot properly derogate at all, even in minds that assent to no pretension of canonicity, from the rational claim of the Scriptures to stand for the teaching of God, in so far as they are true to the nature of things.

But, again, if sacred books have become such by a real relation to the process of God's teaching, then the persistency of God's teaching may be relied upon to sustain their authority. Therefore, over-anxious restriction of thought, certainly not less than over-confident freedom of inquiry, is a sign of dulness and decay in religious faith. Faith requires that in the free play of conflicting ideas, men should devoutly own a common allegiance to the truth as one. But the oneness of truth is the unity of nature. It is nature that saves Scriptures of whatever class from private judgments and one-sided interpretations. It is the law of nature in Scripture which forbids us to press opposite representations of detail to their logical extremes, till they contradict, not only each other, but the postulates of universal reason. It is taught that God is with the faithful as he is not with the unfaithful; that the disciples of Christ are "not of the world," inasmuch as their leader has "chosen them out of the world;" that the idolatrous nations were "dead in trespasses and sins" relatively to that peculiar quickening contemplated in the Christian life; that "having no hope and without God [atheists] in the world" expresses a genuine contrast between the degradation of popular paganism and the faith in God, the "reasonable, religious, and holy hope," of sincere Christians; that sacraments become a channel of grace to the faithful, above and beyond the ministrations of divine Goodness to men as children of nature. But if all this is to be affirmed, something else must not be denied. There is grace in nature; there is light and hope from life's Source for every man; there is faith in the East and the West, in the North and in the South, to shame the unbelief of an ecclesiastical elect; there is a gospel of quickening and resurrection for the unrighteous as well as for the just; God is not far from every one of us, " for in him we live, and move, and have our being;" the divine effort to regenerate society demands recognition and co-operation from all men without exception and according to reason.

As Christian faith passes into practical endeavor, the transformation of moral activity through the renewing of the mind becomes the ruling idea of life. To realize by faithful trials " the good, the acceptable, the perfect, the will of God," — not to accommodate one's ways to the fashion of a passing world, — is the effort proper to man. For so the perishable body becomes a living sacrifice to the Father through the constant devotion of the spirit.[1] The tribute of the instant, required "according to that a man hath and not according to that he hath not," becomes the type of an eternal service, wherein "to him that hath shall more be given," that he may have and give abundantly.

Similarly, when the Christian calling is conceived as the working out of salvation from evil habits and the

[1] Rom. xii. 1, 2.

bondage of error, albeit "with fear and trembling," it is still a reasonable service; because "it is God who worketh in us both to will and to do of his good pleasure." Man's co-operation with God is nowhere set forth in Scripture, according to the type of that more or less fantastic theurgy, which construes the divine Spirit as making no sign, the divine operations as inadequate or behind their time, appropriate results as not realized, the kingdom of God as here or there rather than within,— and the universal Presence as "in a journey," to be summoned, to be stayed, to be entreated not to pass by.

Especially does the great Teacher guard childhood against any such phrasing of religious experience as would discredit what the unsophisticated "little one" has done, or discourage the undertaking of what remains to do. The expectation of a special and conspicuous interposition of God for bringing to pass such a crisis and change as shall stand a monumental boundary between an assumed predominance of adverse instincts and the voluntary acknowledgment of spiritual authority, is corrected by the Saviour's habit of referring moral conduct, at every period of life, to its proper principle, and by his never treating it as a foregone conclusion, or matter of course. No temporary resolution or emotion was treated by him as proof of determined character, apart from the practical trial of every-day duty. He laid his hands on little children and blessed them, warned his disciples to take heed and not cause them to stumble, recognized the relation of infantile simplicity to permanent discipleship as well as to present dangers, declared that it was not the will of the Father that one of these little ones should come to the ruin of life, — and all this without any express reference to a critical standard of experience which at some particular time, sooner or later, they might be expected to exhibit.

So, finally, in regard to the remote issues of human conduct, — men conceived as reaching a clear determination of mind and will, either for or against whatsoever things are true, venerable, just, pure, lovely, and of good report, not without the discipline and tests of experience, are necessarily conceived as reaching also the general types of destiny appropriate to opposing courses of conduct, not abruptly, but by a gradual effort, and through a thorough trial of personal preferences. No forebodings of terror are commissioned to disturb the sane and trustful souls, whose is "the peace of God that passeth all understanding;" and no promises of felicity can bring solace to the remorseful spirit, till Nemesis shall have wrought well in her moral teaching. Conscious guilt cannot "pronounce amen" to any benediction. Conscious virtue need not "fear the might of any adversary." "The speech of mortals is pliant," says Homer, "the range of words wide, this way and that way."[1] Neither the sacred writers nor their interpreters constitute an exception to the rule. St. Augustine finds the reign of God figured in Scripture as a militant state, and takes the highest exhibition of Roman majesty — "to spare the vanquished and to coerce the proud"[2] — as the changeless type of the heavenly empire. But Greek philosophy is as significant as Roman imperialism in the interpretation of the divine Word. Origen will have it that a result which might indeed be "impossible to those who are still in the body," is "not so to those who are released from it." "Our belief is," he

---

[1] Iliad, b. xx. l. 248, 249.
[2] "Parcere subjectis, et debellare superbos."

writes, "that the Word shall prevail over the entire rational creation, and change every soul into his own perfection." "For," he adds, "stronger than all the evils in the soul is the Word, and the healing power that dwells in Him; and this healing He applies, according to the will of God, to every man."[1] Origen and Augustine stand for alternations of thought in the prophetic soul of humanity; and these alternations, like the swinging of the pendulum, are both sustained and checked by one universal law. Under this law the future of mankind is something to be wrought out; and we are called upon to win our modest successes in the moral struggle of life on the plain assurance that every actual contribution to individual and collective history shall take due effect, without limits of time, upon subsequent experience; while the consummation of æons will record only decisions of the creative Reason, that rules from age to age as the fundamental law of the human spirit.

[1] Against Celsus, b. viii. ch. 72. Ante-Nicene Christian Library, T. & T. Clark.

INDEX.

INDEX.

Abraham, example of faith, 247–249.
Act, man's first, of disobedience, 117–119.
Action, of the instant, judged from the series to which it belongs, 103.
Æon, in distinction from cosmos, 10, 11; not abstract, but concrete, 12, 13.
Æonian, New Testament use of, 14–17.
Afflictions, a trial of faith, 170; not in any peculiar sense mysterious, 170.
Ages, of faith or of unbelief, 194.
Alternative, giving life its moral significance, 324.
Apostles, continuing the testimony of their Master, 201, 202; now regarding the world, 202.
Assurance, on three points, 51, 52.
Atonement, hard fate of the word, 215; comparison of it with reconciliation, 216; law of, involving all law, 217; as a spiritual procedure, 228; as providentially administered, 250, 251; use of term in the Mosaic law, 262; law of, in successive epochs of Christ's ministry, 277, 278; the, by way of eminence, 288; implies judgment, 300.
Augustine, St., process of moral defection, 72; how God speaks and man is to hear, 73; creation of angels, 79; interpretation of primitive apostasy, 83; spiritual death, 96, 97; man's desert, God's justice and mercy, 172, note; *judicium ultimum, judicium novissimum*, 334; "the truth itself," 343, note; conception of God's reign compared with Origen's, 347, 348.

Bacon, on words, 6.
Bible, studied in different ways, iii.
Butler, Bishop, life a state of probation, 24.

Calling, of the first human pair, 122, 123; discussed on different hypotheses, 124–126.
Childhood, guarded by Christ's teaching, 346.
Christ, in all things pre-eminent, 48, 49; Interpreter of history, 49–51; to whom revealed, 50, 51; Example of faith, 137–141; manifested in the flesh, 138; justified in the spirit, 139; justified by the Father, 139–141; interprets death as related to life, 180; how claiming faith, 194; divisive effect of his coming, 194, 195; arraignment of men provisional and disciplinary, 195, 196; appreciation of infancy, 199, 200; in relation to human responsibility, 201; end of law for righteousness, 206, 207; as a personal standard, 207, 208; in history, 237; typical portraiture of, 271; ideal of his own career, 272; Saviour, 272, 273; unique priesthood, 273, 274; awakening resistance, 274; how opening communications, 274; ministry, 275;

the glad tidings, 276; self-sacrifice proving moral perfection, 276, 277; exemplified the law of atonement, 277, 278; not a doctrinaire, 279; opportuneness of his coming, 279, 280; beatitudes, for whom, 280; disciples, and their training, 281-287; correction of time-honored maxims, 281, 282; taught love of man with reference to eternal life, 283; distinguished between justice as divine, and human administrations of it, 283, 284; counted on the efficiency of spiritual testimony, 284; referred the motions of life to their true centre, 285; raised suffering and death to their highest moral significance, 285; anticipated and counted upon the cross, 285, 286; aware that the Master must be glorified before the disciples could become apostles, 286; fulfilling the Father's law, 287; Captain of salvation, 287, 288; anticipations of his reappearance, 291; revealed man's sonship, 291, 292; source and unity of divergent tendencies in apostolic thought, 327, 328; judgment to follow his death, 328-330; warnings of a coming day, 328, 329; special instructions to the disciples, 329, 330; minister of the regeneration, 342.

Christianity, spiritual infiltration of, 239.

Church, unable to compose conflicts and consecrate society, 37; at variance with the state, 37, 38; of Luther's day, 311.

Conscience, developed by trials of good and evil, 69.

Consequences, a source of instruction, 84.

Conversion, conditioned upon divine revelation and human progress, 340, 341.

Conviction, religious, realized through discipline, 316.

Cosmos, primitive and ultimate significance of, 8, 9.

Council of Trent, justification, 145.

Creator, superior to partisanship, 157.

Crises, of personal and social experience, 309-315; spiritual, take physical symbols, 325.

Crisis, in nature, foreshadowing a moral judgment, 306, 307; of natural retribution following personal trial, 307, 308; of the thirty years' war, Lützen, 313, 314; of individual initiative, and of general movement, 314.

Danger, of life, in transgressing the law of life, 61.

Death, as affecting ideas of good and evil, 169; set forth in two phrases, 175, 176; making for better life, 178; cannot efface the idea of personal survival, 178; as belonging to an economy of universal goodwill, 179; as affecting man's choice of alternatives presented to him, 182; power of, wielded by man, 184, 185; made serviceable to life and proving the moral rank of a people, 185; bearing upon man's spiritual discipline, 185, 186; use of, illustrated by antediluvian experience, 186, 187.

Destiny, the individual as a factor in his own, 57; of mankind on earth, as betokening the divine dealings, 171-174; how wrought out, 347.

Development, man's normal, its direction and ruling purpose, 27; its relation to cosmical environment, 28; its teaching as to human ability, 29; its suggestion as to the source of created things, 30; its dependence upon social environment, 31-38.

Discipleship, under Christ's teaching, its progressive character, 198, 199.

Discipline, of the child, dependent on progress of the race, 32; provisional, its purpose, 43.

INDEX. 353

Disobedience, the first, palliations of, 67, 68; relation to moral progress, 68.

Drama, of the Fall, type of universal experience, 87; verifiable in the natural sense, 88-96.

Duke of Argyle, man an exception to the unity of nature, 146, 147.

Duties, waiting upon one another, 33.

Duty, conception of, grows with discipline, 42.

Economy, physical in distinction from moral, 176; alleged contrast of the physical and the spiritual, 220, 221.

Eden, conceived according to historic experience, 58; law of life in, 89; naturally construed, 90-94.

Elements, cosmical, their relation to life, 84, 85.

Epictetus, on personality, 177.

Equations, moral series of, 339, 340.

Era, Christian, its sign not sudden revolution, 196, 197; of consummation, 295.

Error, primitive, in the light of long experience, 57; inherited and organized, lays claim to pity, 149, 150.

Evangelists, how conceiving Christ's work, 279.

Evil, moral, common aspect of, 155; in different periods, 156; exciting animosity in prophetic spirits, 156, 157; range of, 168; as error and misconduct incident to moral development, 188.

Experience, determines the growth and play of ideas, 42, 43; human, a ritual of sacrifice, 235.

Failure, primitive liability to, 64, 65.

Faith, growing by experience, 102; the essential element of righteousness, 102; what it lays hold of, 104; law of, respecting duty, 105;
respecting judgment, 105, 106; as indicated in man's spiritual history, 107, 108; not an affair of formal logic, 108, 109; essential to perfect life, 135, 136; principle of obedience, 136, 137; not consummated in one critical act, 141; antithesis of, 141; vital element in divine revelation, 142; with respect to the lower tendencies of human nature, 146; its necessary correlation with unbelief, 161, 162; faults and discipline of, 163, 164; careless of conventional sanctities, 294.

Fall, of man, due to the quality of his nature, 71, 72; its consequences naturally conceived, 81; different conceptions of it, 97.

Flood, spiritual lesson of, 256.

Fruit, forbidden, beyond the just measure of its use, 85.

Functions, of society, distinguished and specialized, 33, 34.

Genesis, two accounts, and a distinction between them, 74, 75; of the cosmos, 75, 76; of the æon, 76, 77; cosmical, scenery and prelude of an æonian revelation, 79; conception of God and man, 127.

Gentiles, fellow-heirs with the Jews, 295.

Gifts, and sacrifices, the worship of primitive culture, 243; example of, in the fourth chapter of Genesis, 244; why Abel's sacrifice was more excellent than Cain's, 244, 245.

Globe, crust of, keeping record of its own changes, 304; indicating crises, 304, 305.

God, thought of, how coming to man, 32; reign of, revealed in Christ, 292, 293; to whom first making appeal, 322, 323; attaching importance to natural motives, 323.

Good, absolute in the Creator, what this implies, 158; and evil, uncertain apprehension of, 169, 170;

distinction of, according to human nature, 193.
Goodness, creative, proof of, 43.
Gospel, to whom given, 112, 113.
Government, divine, different interpretations of, 171–174.

HIGH PRIEST, of Israel, in what sense acting for the people, 261.
History, sacred, universal, 229, 230; pervaded by a law of reconciliation through sacrifice, 230; unity of, on what depending, 231; great chapters of, 234, 235; scriptural conception of, 332.
Homer, on speech and words, 347.

IDOLS, referred to by Bacon, 110; of Schopenhauer and others, 111.
Inductions, shape anticipations, 305.
Initiation, man's moral, pictured from life, and so verifiable, 58.
Irenæus, holds that God made man free from the beginning, 133.
Israel, called out of Egypt, 253, 254; called to high service and hard discipline, 317.

JUDAISM, transfigured, 294.
Judge, the divine, corrects error in all and for all, 157.
Judgment, crisis, how the two words are related, 301, 302; has regard to disciplinary effects, 315; contrasted crises in one spiritual movement, 331; day of, one but recurring, 331, 332; application of law, 333; last, and "last day," 334.
Justice, of God, how commonly contemplated, how actually revealed, 299, 300.
Justification, of man, starting-point and reach of the idea, 101; in what respects it is of faith, 106, 107; of our first parents, as related to knowledge, 121, 122; increase of, Council of Trent, 145.

KNOWLEDGE, of primitive man concerning God, 128.

LANGUAGE, organic structure of, 6.
Law, vital and progressive, 69; of life, forbids what is negative to life in any degree, 84; of physical deterioration as related to the lifetime, 90, 91; of correlative proportions, maxima and minima, 119; outward, not the test or measure of righteousness, 135; as related to conflict of laws, 236; of Israel, as setting forth conditions on which the divine favor is pledged, 257, 258; as providing for patience and considerateness in its administration, 258; specific acts of atonement conducive to a vital process, 259; governing man's moral struggle, 348.
Leader, the perfect, an object of desire, 47; his forerunners, how chosen, 47.
Leadership, creative, shown in any genuine leader, 46.
Liberty, keeping pace with law, 41; under the banner of religion, 41, 42; instinct of, in earliest life, 44; transformation and mature type of, 44; consummation of, impossible to the mortal existence, 45.
Life, a schooling, 23; personal, its mystery, 104; physical, demanding care first in the order of time, 120; of individuals and of the race, 177; why so precious, 178; expenditure of, 233; devoted to the service of life, 245, 246.
Luther, crisis in his experience, 311, 312; his new initiative, 312; his movement not independent of a general one, 313.

MAN, how conceived by the author of Genesis, 127; natural and spiritual, 132, 133; as respects the unity of nature, 146; his original constitution as including a law of trans-

formation, 322; as a part of nature, 338.
Manhood, in a process of transformation, 103.
Miracle, of universal nature, 194.
Mortality, universal, its practical teaching, 177.
Motives, reaching their predominance in an order of time, 33.
Mystery, in relation to faith, 170, 171.

NAME, how suggested and enlarged, 4, 5; its relation to mind and object, 5.
Nature, as set forth in Scripture, iv; and Scripture, witnesses for each other, 19; creation in distinction from the Creator, 81, 82; of man, to be divinely guided through nature, 82; human, its complexity, 151; bodily development as related to spiritual discipline, 151, 152; vindicating the intention of its author, 179; determining the construction of Scriptures, 344, 345.

NEWMAN, Cardinal, argument as to original sin, 147, 148.
New Testament, opens a new era, 319; doctrine of one God and one Mediator, 319; announced a new opportunity and trial, 319, 320; how contemplating the world's crises, 320, 321; how setting forth Christ's method of redemption, 321.
Noah, meaning of his sacrifice, 246, 247.

OLD TESTAMENT, Israel in relation to mankind, 316, 317.
Organization, physical, its relation to conscious personality, 180, 181.
Origen, on the "days" in Genesis i., 76; relation of earthly experience to an illimitable age, 174; and Augustine, stand for alternations of thought, 348.

PAIN, discipline of, 162, 163.
Passover, its ruling idea, 254; note of transition from patriarchal to national religion, 254, 255.
Patriarch, as forerunner of the nation, 252, 253.
Paul, St., judgment of sin depending on the revelation of righteousness, 203-208; defensive and offensive teaching, 204, 205; consummation of Christ's militant reign, 295; Christ's constant presence, and triumphal appearing, 327.
Penalty, ensuing upon the first transgression, 94-96.
Perfection, law of man's, not in himself, 102.
Peter, St., his apocalypse, 325, 326.
Phrases, for different aspects of death, 175, 176.
Poles, of thought, in the sphere of morals, 70.
Priest, and sacrifice, in popular worship, 263.
Principle, of progressive virtue and final peace, 269, 270.
Probation, source and limits of the idea, 24-26; inclusive of retribution — not excluded from retribution, 25, 26; common experience, 27.
Progress, human, evils incident to, 36, 37; in truth, on what depending, 342.
Prophets, charged with fresh moral inspiration, 263, 264; how predicting the general prevalence of piety, 264, 265; possessed of an original conviction, 265, 266; Samuel, 266; Isaiah, 266, 267; Jeremiah, and others, 268; characteristic testimony of, 268, 269.

RECONCILIATION, of all things in Christ, 210; its complete significance, 215; and atonement, mutual relation of the words, 216; and redemption, scope of inquiry, 218, 219; of spirits to the intention of their Creator, 231, 232;

and to society, 232, 233; of differences between individuals and masses, 234; process of, implying a correlative process of judgment, 293.

Redemption, history of, an ideal assize, 323, 324.

Reformation, of the sixteenth century, 311-314.

Regeneration, for man as man, 341; its perfect type, 341; vital element of salvation, 342.

Religion, first in dignity, latest in reaching its perfect reality, 35; abuse of its authority, 35; natural history of, 109-111.

Responsibility, as related to the sense of failure or fault, 67; degrees of, 119; reached in the exercise of free choice, 160.

Revelation, in the Scriptures, vi, vii; response to man's seeking after God, 109, 110; in the divine man, 112, 113; through nature, 193; spiritual, 228; postulate of, as to spirits and their conditions, 229; moves in the whole course of nature, 229; how possible to man, 236, 237; through nature, but not of nature, 240, 241; its parts require the whole, 300; how conceived in Scripture, 338.

Righteousness, as realized in human nature and represented in Scripture, 145.

Ruling, the divine, how becoming effective in human society, 338.

SACRIFICE, exacted by nature, 222; accepted by man, 222, 223; indispensable in enterprise and improvements, 222-224; a law of physical life, 224, 225; in the progress of civilization and religion, 225, 226; of human victims, 226, 227; law by which all things consist, 227; of self, type of all true obedience and worship, 249; ritual changing, law abiding, 250.

Salvation, working out of, 345, 346.

Schooling, in the world, its grand aspects, 33; through mistakes, 61-63; legal, whereto it serves, 114.

Scripture or Scriptures, as related to nature and defined in history, iv; grand distinction of, 46; their fulfilment in Christ, 48, 49; truth to nature, 73; silence of, 96; true to the struggle of the hour and the consummation of the age, 112; why appealed to, 115; to be construed with reason and reverence, 116; meet us on the ground of common sense and common faith, 117; their claim to credence, 193; testimony to Christ's estimate of human behavior, 197, 198; teaching grounded in universal reality, yet accommodated to particular facts, 214; claim to speak for themselves, 242; proof of their inspiration, 242, 243; searching and verification of, 337; set forth a series of moral equations, 339, 340; their unverifiable elements, 343, 344; authority, how acquired and sustained, 344.

Sin, Adam's, sequel of, 129, 130; inquiry and judgment upon, 130, 131; ensuing discipline, 131.

Speech, genesis of, 3, 4.

Suffering, in the voluntary discipline of life, 165, 166.

TEACHERS, compared with those taught, 24.

Teaching, divine, its necessary condescension, 59, 60; its practical method, 241.

Temptation, the first, naturally conceived, 79, 80.

Tendency, of man's development, 183, 184.

Terms, that suggest governmental schemes, 218.

Time, image of eternity, Plato, 12; in the concrete, life-time, 78.

Training, should not exaggerate childish errors, 114, 115; moral, its period, 152; for the manifestation and maturing of character, 153–155.

Transformation, of moral activity, 345.

Trees, of Eden, 91–93.

Trial, human, nature of, 52; reaching back to original man, 53; its social character, 60; primitive, its peculiar liability, 64.

Turretin, *Libertas Adami*, 217, note.

UNBELIEF, error of immature intelligence, 158, 159; against man's best thought or persuasion, 188, 189; its spiritual character, 188–190; related to personal responsibility, 190, 191; negative to truth, positive in personal energy, 191, 192; stimulus of resistance to the argument of faith, 192.

Unity, of thought, how men are drawn toward it, 343.

VERIFICATION, two kinds of, v; of any writing according to its own order of thought, 79.

Vicissitudes, sudden, from imperceptible processes of change, 303, 304.

Victims, by whom provided, why offered, 235, 236.

Virtue, not perfected in its ascetic type, 166.

WAR, for subsistence, 175.

Wisdom, "a tree of life," 86; how imparted to mortals, 86, 87.

Witnesses, apostolic, how they regarded the world, 290, 291.

Words, what like, 6.

World, import of the word, growth of its meaning, 7; conceived as continuing, 9; cosmical and æonian, 18; necessity and cost of its transformation, 167, 168.

World-history, how affected by the coming of Christ, 194, 195; Scriptural conception of, 209, 210.

Worship, of Israel, its oneness, 255, 256; use of blood as a sacrificial symbol, 255, 256; distinctions of form, 256, 257; identical in substance however accommodated in ritual, 259, 260; concern for spiritual reality, 260, 261.

www.ingramcontent.com/pod-product-compliance
Lightning Source LLC
Chambersburg PA
CBHW020223240426
43672CB00006B/398